hotels • safari lodges • resorts • vineyards • restaurants • spas

southafricachic

hotels • safari lodges • resorts • vineyards • restaurants • spas

southafricachic

text simon farrell • yu-mei balasingamchow • melanie lee • james leong

RICHMARK
HOLDINGS (PTY) LTD GROUP OF COMPANIES

thechiccollection

publisher'sacknowledgements

It's been three years since the first edition of *South Africa Chic* and much has happened in South Africa since then. It's tough keeping pace with progress in this fascinating country. Visitor numbers are rising—and will undoubtedly continue to do so, with the 2010 FIFA World Cup poised to draw record crowds—whilst the choice of fabulous places to stay just grows and grows. Whether its a chic Cape Town boutique hotel, a Winelands guesthouse, a private bush home or stunning beachfront location that you require, South Africa has the pick of them—and some of the world's finest food and wine at some of the world's finest prices, for good measure! Having been to the far-flung corners of the world in pursuit of the best travel destinations, I can say with utmost conviction that nothing matches the thrill of entering the animals' environment whilst ensconced in the luxury that only a South African bush experience can offer.

I would like to thank all of the featured properties for their support during the production of this book. This book would not have happened without Gavin Varejes, who supports his country in quite a remarkable fashion, in a variety of ways which space constraints will not permit me to list here—Gavin: thank you. To my colleague James McLeod for bringing your indefatigable commitment to the project. To Melisa, Suzanne, Bobby and the dedicated team at Editions Didier Millet for once more producing a great publication that South Africa and her people can be proud of.

Thank you, reader, for taking the time to peruse *South Africa Chic*—I trust you will find something and somewhere for all tastes here. Forget what you may have heard, take a look at the following pages, and head to South Africa as soon as you can!

Nigel Bolding

executive editor
melisa teo

editor
suzanne wong

designer
chan hui yee

production manager
sin kam cheong

first published 2005 • second edition 2008
bolding books
the studio, 27 high street
godalming gu7 1au, united kingdom
enquiries : nigel.bolding@thechiccollection.com
website : www.thechiccollection.com

designed and produced by
editions didier millet pte ltd
121 telok ayer street, #03-01
singapore 068590
telephone : +65.6324 9260
facsimile : +65.6324 9261
enquiries : edm@edmbooks.com.sg
website : www.edmbooks.com

©2005, 2008 bolding books
design and layout © editions didier millet pte ltd

Printed in Singapore.

isbn: 978-981-4217-14-9

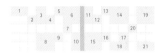

COVER CAPTIONS:

1: A luxurious suite at Madikwe Hills Private Game Lodge.
2 AND 4: Gorah Elephant Camp wildlife.
3: Fine dining at Tintswalo Safari Lodge.
5: Jembisa has a child-friendly policy.
6: Table Mountain and Cape Town.
7: Outdoor bath at Morukuru Lodge.
8: A guest bedroom at Fordoun.
9: Fresh oysters and champagne at Winchester Mansions Hotel.
10: A passing elephant takes a quick sip from a pool at Etali Safari Lodge.
11: A thatched sala at Thanda.
12: The mouthwatering chocolate dessert at The Cellars-Hohenort.
13: Relax and take in the evening view while enjoying a bath at Londolozi.
14: A magnificent herd of elephants silhouetted against the sunset.
15 AND PAGE 2: The open-air verandah at Kwandwe Private Game Reserve.
16: A room at Makweti Safari Lodge.
17: Ancient South African rock art.
18: Johannesburg glows at night.
19 AND 21: Sabi Sabi Private Game Reserve offers opulent accommodation.
20: A family of lions at Chitwa Chitwa.
THIS PAGE: *Street lights of Johannesburg.*
OPPOSITE: *A bird's eye view of Cape Town.*
PAGES 8 AND 9: *Deep in Marakele National Park in Limpopo, Marataba Safari Company commands excellent vistas.*

contents

gauteng+freestate 18

mpumalanga 48

limpopo 74

southafrica**by**provinces

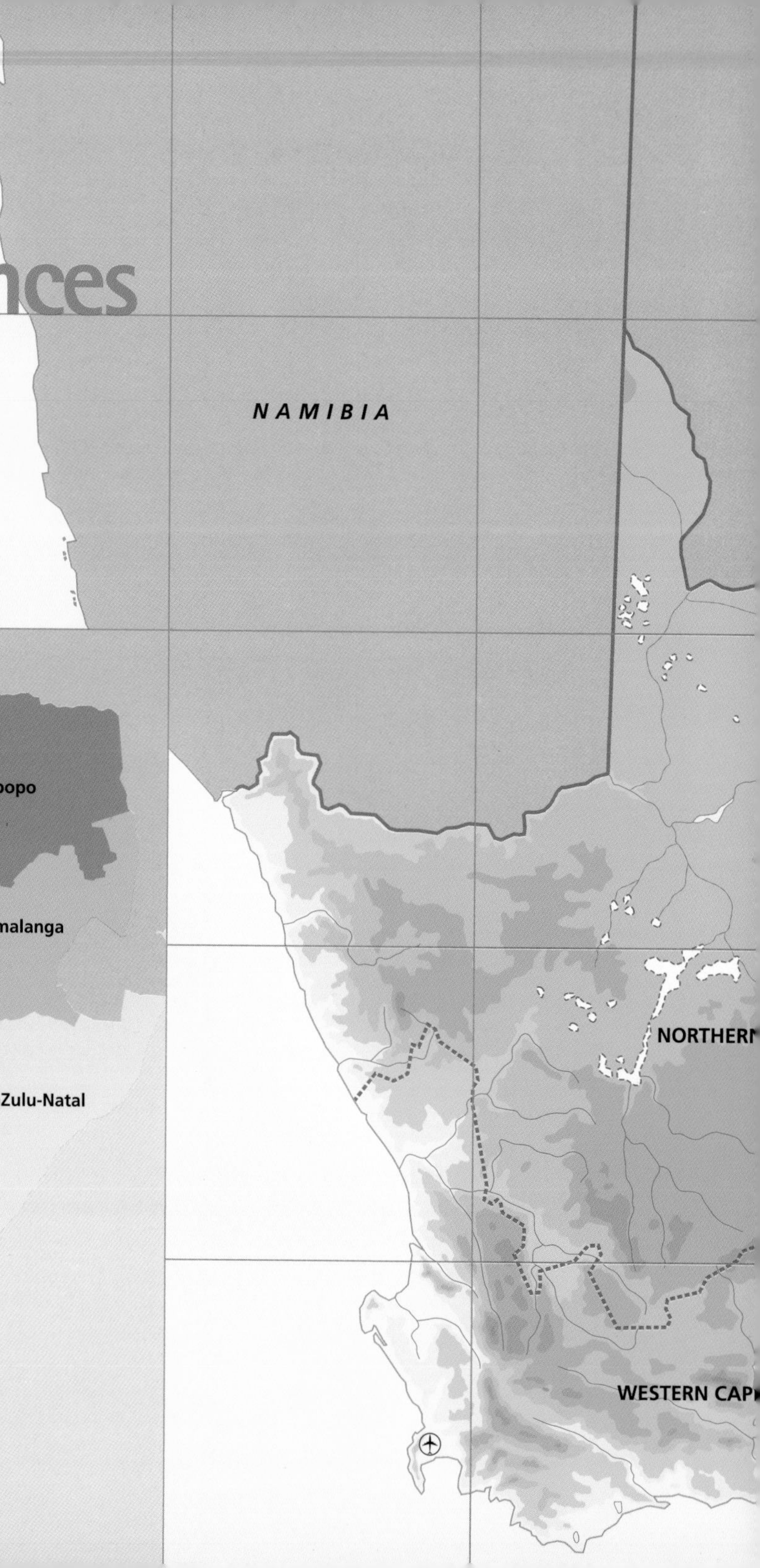

southafrica**by**chapter

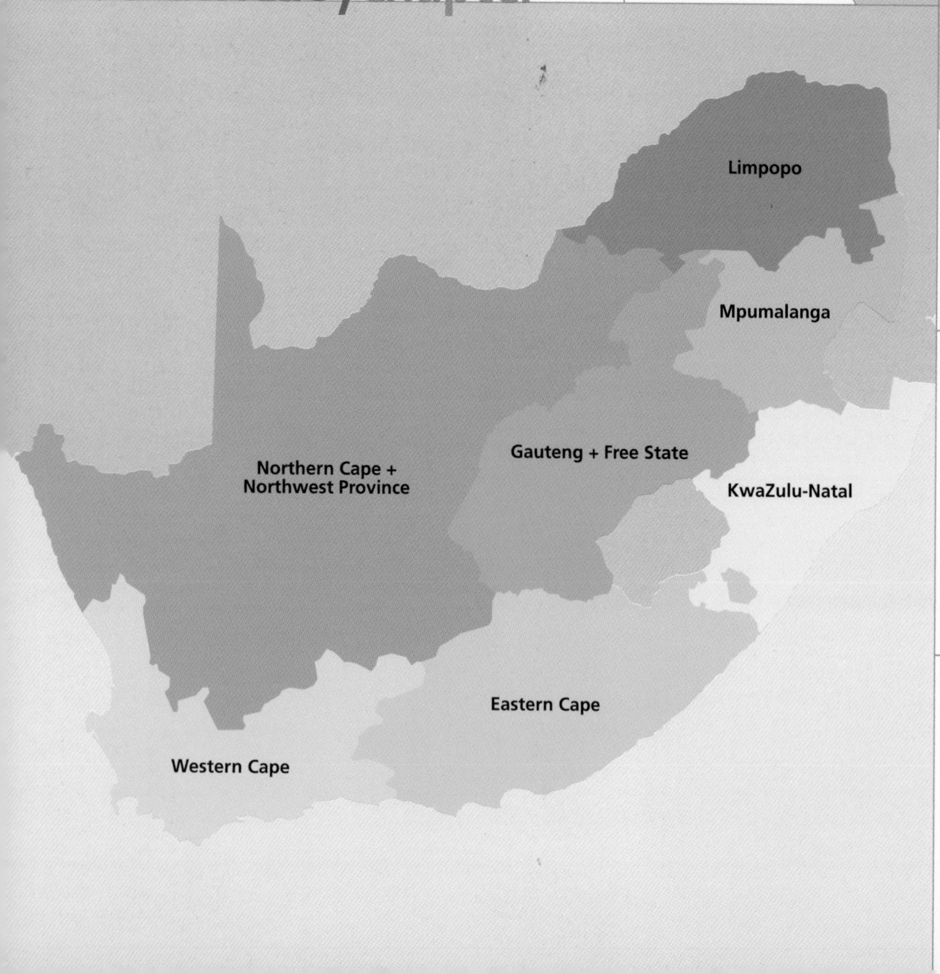

NAMIBIA

Limpopo

Mpumalanga

Northern Cape +
Northwest Province

Gauteng + Free State

KwaZulu-Natal

Eastern Cape

Western Cape

NORTHERN

WESTERN CAP

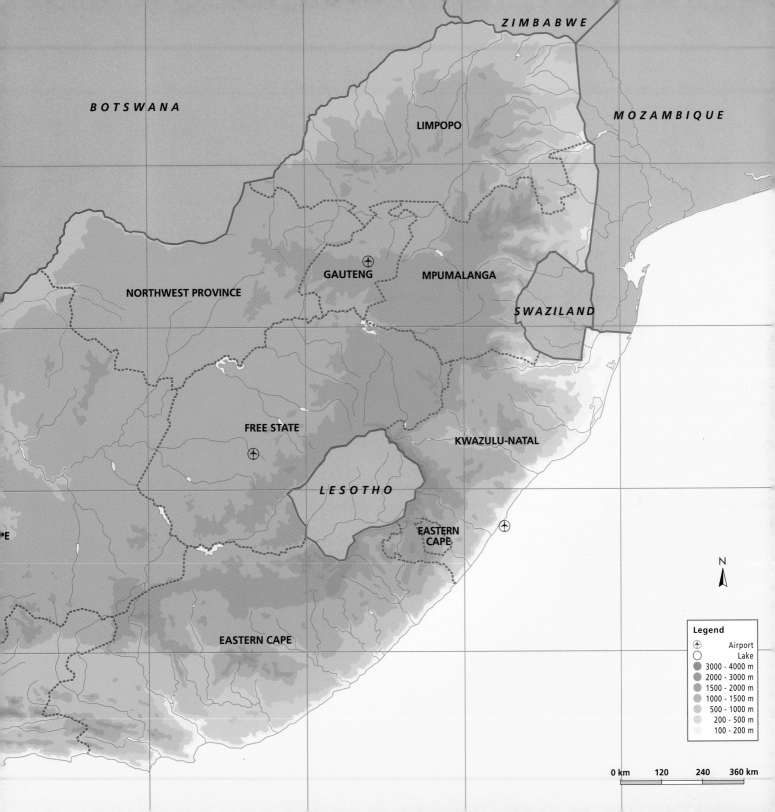

introduction

land of plenty

The increasing influx of eco-tourists, adventurers, business travellers and sports lovers have gone a long way towards establishing South Africa as one of the hottest international destinations in recent years. In addition to its wholesale endorsement by various food, wine and arts cognoscenti who see the region as a fecund land of plenty, the region has garnered award after award for best destination, luxury accommodation and a host of other accolades. Characterised by a tropical climate in the southeast, Mediterranean temperateness in the southwest and the hot, arid Karoo desert and cool mountainous regions in between, South Africa draws avid pleasure-seekers all year round with its rocky and sandy 3,000-km (1,900-mile) coastline, international cuisines, local wines, spectacular wildlife, historic and natural sites, and booming cities with pulsating, sophisticated nightlife and a diverse cultural scene.

With some of the world's most distinctive quality accommodation—often featuring spas, conference centres, golf and spectacular game viewing—and a solid infrastructure that ensures South Africa's continued reputation in successfully hosting major international sports tournaments and other global events, the nation has become a favourite with travellers of all persuasions worldwide.

unparalleled biodiversity

Beaches—from vast and empty stretches of fine sand in the south to hotspots heaving with vibrant restaurants and bars in Cape Town and Durban—are magnets for surfers, whale-watchers, scuba divers, families and honeymooners alike.

It's the extraordinary biodiversity, however, and the famed Big 5 of the African wilderness—lion, leopard, elephant, buffalo and rhino—that have drawn record numbers of visitors almost every year for the last decade or so to what are some of the world's best-managed game- and whale-watching operations. Sensitive to sustaining indigenous wildlife and protecting natural habitat, these eco-aware tour operators provide easy and safe close-up viewing of untamed nature.

THIS PAGE (FROM TOP): A colourfully decked-out participant in the annual Grahamstown festivities; a trio of curious meerkats turn at the snap of a camera while sunning themselves at dawn.
OPPOSITE: Children at play on the waterfront of the Western Cape.

UNESCO has validated South Africa's impressive biodiversity with a network of World Heritage Sites nationwide, including the 553,000-hectare (1.4 million-acre) Cape Floral Region, one of the richest plant areas in the world, that showcases nearly a fifth of Africa's native species of flora. Every province has traditionally offered national parks and botanical gardens, but the recent opening of the Great Limpopo Transfrontier Park, which will eventually cover some 2.6 million hectares (6.4 million acres), opens up new horizons by sharing land and wildlife with Mozambique and Zimbabwe.

rainbow culture

Authentic townships filled with character, historic sites, museums, markets, and modern and colonial European-style architecture are all things to take in if one is to appreciate the many cultures that make up the cosmopolitan Rainbow Nation. Also not to be missed are the African Jazz clubs, classical concerts and multicultural showcases, such as the annual Grahamstown Arts Festival. Bushman rock art is found throughout South Africa, especially in KwaZulu-Natal and the Western Cape. About 20,000 rock paintings at more than 500 sites have been discovered by local and international experts.

discovering the gastronomy

South African food—known as Rainbow Cuisine—is dominated by the rich ethnic origins of its multitude of inhabitants. With over 40 million residents, 11 official languages and growing numbers of immigrants from Europe and Asia, South Africa offers a potpourri of fresh, eclectic gourmet creations. The slave trade brought spicy, fruity, sweet-and-sour Malay recipes to the Western Cape region and Indian labourers introduced curries to Durban and beyond. More recent immigrant waves have added Chinese, Vietnamese, Thai and Japanese restaurants in the larger cities, while Europeans have contributed Dutch baked food and stews, British meat pies, and Afrikaaner favourites including boerewors (sausage) and biltong (dried and salted ostrich, beef or other meat). Although local food is often overlooked or considered bland by tourists used to spicy Asian and rich Western offerings, a number of restaurants dish up tasty maize porridge with beans, and salads with a lively flavour. Outsize steaks are popular with all, including those of Karoo lamb, venison, ostrich, impala and, of course, beef. A significant number of Italian, Portuguese, Greek and French restaurants also offer traditional and contemporary menus.

With such a vast coastline, luxurious amounts of seafood are readily available everywhere: in pubs, restaurants, markets and even the common takeaway. Apart from the ubiquitous fish and chips, one can also find delicious crayfish, prawns, mussels, oysters and the much sought-after delicacy, perlemoen (abalone).

Although beer and brandy have long competed to become the national drink, wine has increasingly been valiantly waving the flag abroad for South Africa. It is now widely seen as being on par with the best in the world. Fifteen of the best-known boutique estates around Cape Town line the official Wine Route, but there are many vineyards new and old that are ideal for tasting tours, wine sales and global deliveries.

There are routes that traverse country lanes, coastal roads and mountain passes. Cheese, brandy, olive and fruit farms compete by offering multi-purpose family spots equipped with modern theatres, luxury accommodation, fine restaurants with European chefs, golf courses and even luxury spas, some dating from Victorian times.

THIS PAGE (FROM TOP): A wide range of international cuisine is now available in the larger cities; a lively dining culture is part of South Africa's cosmopolitan and vibrant urban scene.

OPPOSITE: The Great Limpopo Transfrontier Park will open up borders for migrating wildlife within South Africa's game parks.

outdoor opportunities abound

South Africans' love of outdoor sport is obvious from the menu of exhilarating activities available. Shark watching, paragliding, bungee jumping, kloofing, mountain biking, whitewater rafting, and even flying a supersonic jet at Thunder City in Cape Town are activities that lure adventure-seekers here. As host to the international Comrades Marathon and other major sporting events, South Africa is well-equipped with world-class stadiums, has experience staging international events, and holds an enviable safety record, making it a perfect venue for watching or partaking in outdoor activities.

tapping emerging attractions

A relatively new group of travellers come mainly to see the Cradle of Mankind in Gauteng. The World Heritage Site comprises a network of limestone caves, including the Sterkfontein Caves where fossils dated to millions of years ago have been found. To accommodate rising interest, a new visitors' centre, Maropeng, opened in 2005.

Cape Town and Durban are now popular international conference destinations, thanks to excellent facilities and local attractions that keep delegates and those accompanying them occupied. Medical tourism is another newcomer, with several companies offering specialist cosmetic and plastic surgery, as well as recuperation and rejuvenation holiday packages, with world-class surgeons and facilities, and pre- and post-operative care.

accolades for accommodation

In 2006, UK readers of *Condé Nast Traveller* rated South Africa's hotels and spas among the best in the world, while six scored in the publication's Top 20 Leisure Hotels in the Middle East, Africa and the Indian Ocean Islands category. Indeed, its natural beauty, luxury accommodations and outstanding diversity regularly wins for South Africa such accolades as Best Holiday Destination in Africa, Best Scenery in the World (at the 2005 World Travel Awards) and the Most Affordable Holiday Destination (second place in the 2006 American Express Foreign Exchange Holiday Cost of Living Index).

THIS PAGE: Bungee jumping is a popular choice for those who seek adventure—the Bloukrans Bridge is the world's highest commercial bungee point.
OPPOSITE: Kwandwe Private Game Reserve offers luxury accommodations in the heart of the South African bushland.

...natural beauty, luxury accommodations and outstanding diversity...

heart and soul of the rainbow nation

At the geographical heart and deeply rooted in the soul of South Africa, the provinces of Gauteng and Free State contrast with and complement each other. Brash, diverse and forward-looking, cosmopolitan Gauteng has embraced many cultures and drives the country's thriving economy, while big blue-sky Free State—with its ancient rock art, war history and rolling farmlands—clings to its rural traditions, slowly accepting change as it adapts to the new South Africa. Both provinces, however, share strong links to the lucrative mining industry and bloody strifes that helped create the nation.

Gauteng is the smallest of South Africa's nine provinces, and the most dynamic and diverse. From the wild and remote regions of Magaliesberg and the Cradle of Mankind at Sterkfontein to the urban sprawl of Johannesburg and Pretoria, the Place of Gold, as Gauteng is known by its Sesotho-speaking residents, is the business capital of southern Africa—multicultural and compact, with its museums, galleries, historical battlefields, game viewing, top restaurants, shebeens, designer shopping and international entertainment.

Between the surging Orange and Vaal rivers, meanwhile, the spacious and rural Free State is a hiker's and four-wheel driver's dream of parks, reserves and wildlife. Boer War museums and memorials, San rock art, modern gold mines and flat farmland detail the province's place in history and offer solitude, beauty and intrigue.

gauteng: dynamic and diverse

Created in 1994 from part of the former Transvaal, Gauteng has six diverse regions with many historical, cultural and natural attractions linked by a solid infrastructure of efficient road and rail networks. It is also home to Africa's most modern international airport, along with several smaller ones. Under construction and scheduled for partial completion by 2010, when South Africa hosts the FIFA World Cup, is the Gautrain, an ambitious 80-km (50-mile) rapid rail service that will link Johannesburg, Pretoria and OR Tambo International Airport, travelling at up to 180 km (110 miles) per hour and stopping at several stations.

PAGE 18: *A modern skyscraper in Johannesburg reflects the blue skies and bright clouds typical of a clear South African day.*

THIS PAGE: *The suburban streets of Gauteng are lined with profuse blooms of purple jacarandas.*

OPPOSITE: *Johannesburg's striking city skyline just before a storm.*

South Africa's largest city, Johannesburg, is characterised by its many towering mine dumps that spire up into the skyline, symbolising the city's rich history. Cast a wider look over the urban sprawl to see modern skyscrapers loom over the private pools of exclusive residential enclaves, the classic Dutch architecture of the older sections of town, and swanky shopping malls, such as those in the prosperous financial hub of Sandton, the richest square mile in Africa and a 15-minute drive from the Apartheid Museum that stands in moving testament to the nation's turbulent history.

Its slightly more staid close cousin Pretoria, some 50 km (31 miles) north, is catching up as it evolves into a major rival business and tourism hub, while to the northeast lies Dinokeng, with many cultural and historical attractions.

Gautengers of all cultures share a positive, confident, outgoing and ambitious character, keeping busy working and playing hard with a down-to-earth sense of humour and warm welcoming smile for everyone.

cultural tourism

Just south of Johannesburg is the township-turned-satellite-city of Soweto, with its rowdy shebeens, lively churches of many denominations and numerous apartheid memorials. There's nowhere quite like Soweto to show how cultural tourism is an exciting and rapidly growing market that benefits residents and visitors. Tourist arrivals have grown substantially recently, and Soweto is the fifth most popular destination in Gauteng, despite its squatter camps and often less than sanitary conditions. Most visitors stop by the Mandela Museum, the former home of Nelson Mandela and Winnie Madikizela-Mandela. It is three blocks from a memorial marking where a 13-year-old boy was shot dead by police on 16 June, 1976, sparking the mass riots that first put the country in the international spotlight. Similar memorials are scattered throughout Soweto, drawing mostly tour groups of foreign visitors, who are encouraged to mix with the friendly locals who hail from all over southern Africa.

Battlefield sites are scattered throughout the region. Some of the more important ones are around Magaliesberg and Bronkhorstspruit—a farming town 50 km (31 miles) east of Pretoria, near where the Boers defeated the British in the First Boer War (1880–1881).

THIS PAGE (FROM TOP): Despite a rise in affluence in Soweto, the black township still has a name as a squatters' backwater settlement; South African president Thabo Mbeki stands to attention during the national anthem, at the 30th anniversary of the Soweto riots.

OPPOSITE: Jo'burg, as Johannesburg is colloquially known, glows at night—the hip new Melrose Arch development at Christmas time.

addictive attractions and adventures

Spas have mushroomed around the province in recent years, from those at luxury Sandton hotels for stressed city workers to health resort getaways with luxury detoxification programmes in the mountainous Magaliesberg region of colourful birds, flowers and wildlife, less than an hour's drive from Johannesburg. Most have indoor or outdoor hydro facilities—including jet pools, heated swimming pools, steam baths, saunas, Turkish baths and sitzbaths—and offer diet and health advice and aquarobics. Some even operate within private game reserves, making for a unique ecological experience that combines personal wellness with raising environmental awareness.

train travel in style

A luxury train journey is an unforgettable way to experience travel anywhere in the world, and Gauteng is the main departure and arrival point for many routes throughout southern Africa, whether it's west to Cape Town, southeast to Durban, along the Garden Route on the south coast, or over the border to Namibia, Botswana, or Zimbabwe. Several luxury trains make the trip through the country's most popular and beautiful tourist regions in six-star style—deluxe suites with private facilities and 24-hour room service. Rovos Rail and the Blue Train take passengers through the lowveld into the Kruger National Park and the Karoo from Pretoria as they feast on fine wines and cuisine, past wild and beautiful ever-changing scenery. Less formal are the mainline passenger services of the government-run South African Railways—comfortable, affordable and no less exciting.

nature never far away

Just a short drive from Johannesburg, one can turn adventure tourist. A limited number of self-drive or guided four-wheel-drive trails in Gauteng include camping or bedded accommodation extremely close to nature, with barbecues (called braais) around the campfire, and varying degrees of challenge in negotiating roads and dirt tracks, depending on the terrain and weather. Despite thick sand, damp clay, loose soil, deep mud, heavy rocks, surging rivers and steep inclines, otherwise-inaccessible areas are quite easily navigable, and feature breathtaking scenery, exceptional game viewing and guaranteed excitement. For example, the Berakah 4x4 Eco Trail near Parys and a day-trip from Johannesburg alternates flat stretches of savannah with dense bush, adrenaline-charged river crossings and challenging rocky slopes.

THIS PAGE: *A spectacular day to night panorama of Pretoria.*

OPPOSITE: *A baby rhinoceros tries its legs for the first time—one of the many sights one can expect on the various nature drives.*

Water-sports enthusiasts, meanwhile, flock to two popular and huge dams within about an hour's drive from Johannesburg. The 11,595-hectare (28,700-acre) Suikerbosrand Nature Reserve is populated by eland, zebra, wildebeest and hyena, and its hiking, mountain-bike and motor vehicle trails include the Suikerbosrand Mountain Range, boasting a peak 1,917 m (6,300 ft) above sea level. The Vaal Dam, with over 800 km (500 miles) of coastline—making it bigger than Luxembourg—hosts many international water-sports events.

staying in the cities

Barely a month goes by without another glitzy shopping mall opening in booming Gauteng. Menlyn Park in Pretoria has over 300 local and international shops, 15 cinemas and dozens of food outlets. Johannesburg has more than 20 major malls, as well as the popular Sunday open-air market on the top of Rosebank Mall. Sandton Square is one of the biggest and oldest, and the newer pedestrian-friendly Melrose Arch is a sprawling multi-use development with open spaces and sidewalk cafés. For those seeking the essential Africa, though, the Mai-Mai bazaar in central Johannesburg is the oldest market in town. Most of its 170-plus vendors sell traditional healing products, but it's also a great spot to pick up authentic Zulu clothes made from animal skins and feathers, as well as walking sticks, sandals, masks and beads. Animal parts hung up to dry are sold as tonics to stave off illness, bad luck and nightmares, or ensure popularity and wealth.

Cities and major towns compete to have the best botanical gardens, displaying a rich diversity of South African plant life and a variety of birds and mammals along with

picnic spots and hiking trails. The sprawling Johannesburg Botanical Gardens and Emmarentia Dam are near the trendy suburb of Melville and provide a relaxing escape from the bustle. There are 10 hectares (24 acres) of rose and herb gardens, filled with arbours, statues, fountains, and ponds; and open-air music concerts often provide the backdrop for wedding parties. The Walter Sisulu National Botanical Gardens in Roodepoort has cascading waterfalls and winter concerts, while Pretoria offers the largest botanical garden in South Africa—more than 5,000 species of plants and over half the country's tree species can be seen from paved nature trails.

all-night action and entertainment

With large-scale musicals and operas, protest theatre, sophisticated jazz, African music, international acts, or the local bar's resident rock band, Pretoria and Johannesburg match most big cities in the world for options and variety in nights out.

There is an endless number of bars, pubs and clubs, many in otherwise unremarkable suburbs that are often rather out of the way. However, Melrose Arch is a chic Jo'burg spot for celebrities, with gourmet restaurants and contemporary bars filled

THIS PAGE: Jo'burg comes alive in the evenings with a spread of glittering city lights and neon.

OPPOSITE (FROM TOP): Morning mist rises through the air as a man jogs with his dogs in a park in the middle of an urban sprawl; the entertainment and partying carries on until the early hours.

with the financial and showbiz elite. Closer to the city centre, it's best to avoid sleazy Hillbrow, but Melville, Yeoville and Brixton are cosmopolitan, relaxed and friendly, with eateries and bars favoured by artists, the media, entertainers and students. Some places are so popular that drinkers often spill out and block the road. It is not advisable to visit Soweto day or night unless with a tour group. This can be arranged through major hotels and includes shebeens, clubs and casual dining.

early times

The 47,000-hectare (116,140-acre) Cradle of Humankind at Sterkfontein is the nation's most renowned World Heritage Site—where nearly half of the world's hominid fossil discoveries have been made. Today's caves began as coral reefs in a shallow sea 2.3 billion years ago and provide a scientific window on when our earliest ancestors began developing. More modern history revolves around the traders, colonists, fortune-seekers and adventurers who have been arriving since gold was first found by outsiders in the 7th century and in 1886, when the Main Reef on the Witwatersrand was discovered. This led to Africa's first gold rush and the founding of the city of Johannesburg.

The Magaliesberg mountain range commands a presence in human history that reaches back to the earliest records, and physically extends from Pretoria to south of the Pilanesberg, reaching 1,852 m (6,076 ft) at its highest point. The area is believed by experts to have the longest unbroken human occupation. Recently, Hartbeespoort Dam has become a popular vacation and weekend spot for Gautengers and foreign visitors, particularly because of its water sports. The Kgaswane Mountain Reserve is one of the largest nature reserves in the Magaliesberg area and attracts its fair share of visitors.

free state: nation's colourful breadbasket

With so many places to enjoy in South Africa, many travellers have traditionally avoided the Free State because of its undeserved reputation as an uncultured, bland backwater with little to do or see. But it would be a great pity to forego the many unique pleasures of this charming place of deep beauty and history.

Formerly the Orange Free State, this sparsely populated, unhurried province between the surging Orange and Vaal rivers is also known as the region's breadbasket—peaceful and tidy, with a very sunny, yet often harsh, climate of bitter winter cold in the mountains and fierce summer thunderstorms; and a long history of feuding. Battle sites and San rock art dot this land of magnificent flat plains. Corn, sunflowers and other colourful harvests dominate, along with sandstone cliffs and the country's two biggest dams, while brightly painted Sesotho houses decorate the grasslands. Little has changed since the early Afrikaaners first farmed here some 150 years ago. The cities they built include the well-established and friendly provincial capital of Bloemfontein—the City of Roses—and Welkom that, in the heart of the fascinating Goldfields region, is one of the few completely pre-planned cities in the world. The Qwa-Qwa region is known for the exquisite handcrafted African items produced by the local people and there are some excellent golf courses and spas, particularly around Bloemfontein.

wilderness of surprises

Extensive parks and reserves—including the 11,600-hectare (28,700-acre) Golden Gate National Park with its wildebeest, zebra and springbok—rolling hills, spacious multi-hued plains and sandstone cliffs give travellers on the main N1 route between Johannesburg and Cape Town much variety. Small towns are rich in indigenous and European history, including fascinating museums that detail Basotho War and Boer War battles and skirmishes with Voortrekker settlers, as well as 13 battlefield sites, eight military monuments and three war and concentration camp cemeteries.

Several attractions have been launched in recent years for the tourism market. The Sandstone Steam Rail Company has restored trains that make short journeys along the Bethlehem-Bloemfontein railroad in the historic and fertile Maluti Mountains valley. There are side excursions to Maseru, capital of tiny, landlocked Lesotho, Ladybrand's rock art, and other places of interest. For eco-tourists, the 50-km (31-mile) Riemland Wine Route in the northern Free State is a comfortable and colourful day out.

THIS PAGE: *A blazing yellow field of bright sunflowers typify the Free State's agricultural vistas.*

OPPOSITE: *The iconic sheer cliff face that represents the Golden Gate National Park in various media.*

The world's oldest and largest meteorite impact site, the Vredefort Dome, was formed about 2,000 million years ago when a huge meteorite opened up a crater that today measures about 40 km (25 miles) in diameter. The Vredefort Dome Conservancy region is one of great scenic beauty: a finely balanced ecosystem of vast plains, wild bush, snow-capped mountains, ravines and rare flora and fauna. The area is home to rare animals such as the rooikat, aardwolf, leopard and the endangered rock dassie. River rafting, river tubing, abseiling, horse riding, mountain biking, archery and hiking are popular activities.

The Basotho Cultural Village in Qwa-Qwa, at the foot of huge sandstone mountains, is somewhat commercialised, but provides first-time visitors with the chance to observe a working African village. Occasionally, art exhibitions and stage performances are held at the sandstone amphitheatre and the customs, traditions and culture of the South Sotho people are explained at the centre, which is located in the heart of the Qwa-Qwa National Park, very near the Golden Gate National Park. Several four-wheel-drive rental operators have developed routes for guided or independent tours.

THIS PAGE (FROM TOP): An orange cat peers out of a traditional house of the Basotho people while its brightly garbed owner looks on; ancient artifacts are discovered all throughout the Free State.

OPPOSITE: Rock paintings that date back to the dawn of humans tell fascinating stories of the region.

rock art revival

The Ladybrand area, near the Lesotho border, has the most and best San rock art sites in the province, including some of South Africa's 12 Rock Art National Monuments. Archaeological excavations have established that bushmen lived here for at least 1,000 years. Since many of the best-preserved examples of rock art are on private land, they are less likely to have been damaged by humans or the elements. There are hundreds of paintings depicting people and animals. Running antelope, ostriches, baboons, elands and human figures in a trance during a shamanic experience are common depictions, as are women herding animals. Farms, resorts and guesthouses have opened up near strategic rock art sites to accommodate the growing number of people, from home and abroad, interested in this fascinating anthropological phenomenon.

...hundreds of paintings depicting people and animals.

mount grace country house + spa

...South African country living at its best.

THIS PAGE: *Tranquil pools abound in the grounds of The Spa, which offers hydrotherapy treatments.*

OPPOSITE (FROM TOP): *A quiet spot to relax and spend an hour or two; a picturesque water feature and rock pool are indicative of the peace found at Mount Grace.*

Set in acres of exquisitely landscaped gardens in the mountainous and picturesque Magaliesberg region of Gauteng, Mount Grace Country House & Spa is only an hour's drive from the bustling cities of Johannesburg and Pretoria, and exemplifies South African country living at its best. Spacious and private, the well-known and award-winning country house hotel boasts 81 sumptuously decorated guestrooms and suites arranged in variously themed villages over more than 4 hectares (10 acres) of verdant land.

At Thatchstone, orderly English-style country gardens complete with trimmed lawns, well-kept beds of daffodils and other spring flowers border the rooms, each of which possess their own distinctive character. Quaintly thatched, the rooms exude a quiet charm, and are located at a convenient distance to the main hotel building and its facilities.

Over at Grace Village, the rooms and suites are endowed with either a verandah or balcony with truly spectacular views to the north and west of the mountain range in the distance. At Treetops Village, spacious rooms are adorned with life's little luxuries, such as underfloor heating, air-conditioning and a separate dressing room, so that guests should never want for anything while at Mount Grace. Rooms come with a generous balcony or verandah, and enjoy a magnificent, uninterrupted view of the deep ravine below, dotted with trees and inhabited by abundant and colourful bird life.

Golf carts are available to transport guests efficiently around the property, especially to and from Upper Mountain Village rooms, which are set slightly further from the other accommodations. Those who take accommodation here, however, are amply rewarded with a breathtaking view of the Magaliesberg mountains from their private verandah. Situated on an elevated plateau, each suite has private access. Guests can enjoy a languid dip in their suite's private plunge pool, then curl up inside with a cup of hot tea and choose from a wide selection of movies to watch on the in-room DVD player.

A special treat and a perennial favourite with all guests is Mount Grace's Sunday lunch, which is served in The Copperfield Grill. To make the most of the glorious African sunshine, Mount Grace Country House & Spa conducts its lunch and afternoon tea service out on the shady verandah or in the fresh, verdant garden. Intimate meals can be taken at The Stoep, the hotel's elegant à la carte restaurant, which seats only 35 guests, preserving an exclusive air. The food is characterised as 'country with French flair', and paired with a wine list featuring a choice selection of international vintages. A light and healthy lunch menu is served at the Spa Café.

THIS PAGE: The Spa's brine flotation pool is one of the vast selection of treatments available to guests.

OPPOSITE (FROM LEFT): The outdoor jacuzzi is set amongst the lush vegetation of the hotel grounds; the knopkierie is a traditional Zulu instrument once wielded as a weapon, now an instrument of relaxation at the hotel spa.

The Spa complex at Mount Grace is to be considered a complete destination unto itself. It has, after all, been the recipient of various glowing accolades from the beauty and spa industry over the years, and continues to draw visitors—who often return more than a few times. The complex is built from organic, natural materials like stone, clay and thatch, which blend in soothingly with the surrounding landscape. Like a secret playground for adults, the outdoor hydrotherapy spa garden instantly relaxes work-weary muscles and stressed-out minds. Who can resist the lure of heated al fresco rock pools and cool gushing waterfalls? For the ultimate in relaxation, guests are encouraged to spend some time in the indoor brine flotation pool. This experience is enhanced with soothing underwater music, which induces a state of ultimate repose and calm. Hydrotherapy is a recurring theme in the spa's treatment menu, which has recently grown to include the signature Thaba (translated as 'mountain' in the native Sotho tongue) massage, where two therapists working together skilfully wield the knopkierie—a knobbly rod traditionally used by the Zulu tribes as a weapon—to relieve tension. A range of body wraps and skincare treatments are also offered at the 12 treatment rooms, including six double suites for couples and friends.

There is no lack of activities at Mount Grace Country House & Spa. History buffs will be gratified to discover the historical sites of the Old English Block House, Battle of Nooitgedacht and the Cradle of Humankind. Cheese connoisseurs should make a pit stop at the Van Gaalen Kaasmaker, a cheese factory that still makes cheese the traditional Dutch way. Sports enthusiasts can get their adrenalin flowing with tennis, mountain biking or swimming, while nature-lovers have a wealth of options including bird-watching, fly-fishing and nature walks, while thrill-seekers have hang-gliding and hot air balloon safaris. Mount Grace is the perfect place to rejuvenate a weary soul.

ROOMS
81 rooms

FOOD
Copperfield Grill: buffet •
The Stoep: French country •
Spa Café: light healthy meals

DRINK
Hartley's Bar and Billiard Room

FEATURES
3 pools • library • spa • hydrotherapy garden • snooker and pool tables • croquet lawns • bowling green • tennis courts • picnic grounds

NEARBY
Pecanwood Golf Estate • Battle of Nooitgedacht site • Old English Block House • Cradle of Humankind • Van Gaalen Kaasmaker • microlighting • balloon safaris

CONTACT
Private Bag 5004
Magaliesburg 1791, Gauteng •
telephone: +27.14.577 5600 •
facsimile: +27.14.577 1202 •
email: mountgrace@mountgrace.co.za •
website: www.mountgrace.co.za

fairlawns boutique hotel + spa

The beautiful grounds and Palladian architecture are reminiscent of a stately home...

THIS PAGE: *The Fairlawns Boutique Hotel & Spa warmly welcomes its visitors with open arms.*

OPPOSITE: *In fine weather, nothing appeals more than lunching out by the pool, amidst the hotel's well-kept landscaped gardens.*

The Fairlawns Boutique Hotel and Spa attains a splendid level of luxury while maintaining a good-natured old-fashioned feeling of hospitality. The beautiful grounds and Palladian architecture are reminiscent of a stately home and its gardens—which it once was. Visitors are still treated as if they are in fact personal houseguests of owners Anne and John Tucker—guests at a magnificent and palatial home, no less. From the moment one walks in, every need that comes to mind, and indeed even some previously unthought of, are catered to with an exquisite attention to detail. This includes the standard array of treats expected at hotels of this calibre, such as complimentary tea, turn-down service and airport pick up. At Fairlawns, however, things are taken several crucial steps further, so that guests are picked up in a Rolls Royce, are served, along with tea, complimentary glasses of sherry, and invariably find everything in the room ideally situated for a stay defined by maximum comfort and functionality.

The Fairlawns occupies a sumptuous 4-hectare (10-acre) property, whose rolling green swathes of manicured turf have given the hotel its name. Done up in an 18th century European style with Roman pillars and statues lining its shady courtyard, the graceful, classical atmosphere transports mind and body to a different world, far away from the bustle of Sandton City, which is in reality a mere 5 minutes' drive away. Fairlawns actually delivers on the promise of being a refuge from the city, while still keeping it within easily accessible distance, in a way which few other havens actually have done. The garden is more like a park, with plentiful and varied botanical specimens of South African flora and towering arbores. There are other ways to get around besides walking—horses are also available for the more sedentarily inclined guest keen to explore the grounds. Otherwise, the Rose Terrace is a perfect vantage point from which to survey the beautiful surrounds in comfort and style, sipping a cool beverage or enjoying a light lunch while enjoying the soothing sounds of a waterfall trickling below. There is also a large sparkling outdoor pool which allows guests to enjoy some respite from the midday heat, while still commanding excellent views of the Fairlawns estate.

Each one of the 19 exclusive suites in the hotel is fit for a king—or at the very least a world-famous dignitary—and come to suit all tastes and preferences. The suites have all been done up in a different style and each one boasts a surprising size, grandeur and—for the architectural purists—accuracy in its decorative elements. Guests can opt for one of the original 12 Courtyard Suites, which represent The Windsor or The Empire period, amongst others, and are bathed in rich lengths of gorgeous fabrics, with beautiful hand-painted murals and authentic custom-designed period furniture. The Premier Suites (also known as junior Presidential suites) will appeal to those with an inclination or interest in the historio-political, being named after South African

heavyweights of the genre such as Mahatma Gandhi or Nelson Mandela. The crème de la crème has to be the Presidential suite, which is a European-style villa which spares no luxury or pleasure to match the exacting standards of those who grace its rooms.

While all the rooms are designed with understated glamour and complete refinement in mind, they are surprisingly comfortable and warm in their personal touches. One feels truly welcomed and well cared for with rooms providing fireplaces, individual jacuzzis, balconies overlooking the finely pruned shrubbery, and personal lounges and working spaces. At the same time, one is still thoroughly connected to all the advantages of modern technology and communications with the provision of satellite TV, wireless Internet, and direct international dialling. The rooms seem designed to make guests want to spend as much time as possible enjoying all the finer details in them, and even the spacious bathrooms are sanctuaries of tranquillity with scattered mood candles and massive relaxing baths.

THIS PAGE: High ceilings and lush, sumptuous furnishings give the suites a rare touch of exclusivity.

OPPOSITE: Oriental accents, such as the gilt-etched fan over the silk headboard and armchairs upholstered in brocade, make for an exotic and luxurious stay.

If guests actually do decide to leave their rooms for food and beverage, they can partake in the Fairlawn's modern international cuisine which is served in the elegant and glittering private dining room, the stylish restaurant or on the outdoor terrace. On summer nights, guests may also take the opportunity to dine romantically beneath a bright canopy of stars out on the lawns or near the atmospherically lit fountains. The Fairlawns can also lay claim to a world-renowned bar, named by Diners Club as having the wine list of the year.

Further indulgence and pampering is positively encouraged in the hotel's Balinese-style spa and spa garden which erase modern day anxieties and stress through a wide range of natural and healthy organic treatments. Those in search of more high-intensity activity can chase away their workaday worries in the state-of-the-art gym and steam room or the tennis and squash courts and golf courses. Transportation to Johannesburg's commercial district of Sandton and its myriad of shopping malls is also easily available, so guests can satisfy those retail urges before inevitably returning to the welcoming arms of Fairlawns.

Whether one is a visitor to Johannesburg or a local, the Fairlawn's exuberance in décor, style, and generosity make it perfect for a weekend retreat or a special trip. Prepare to leave the mundane daily routine behind for utter elegance and gracious living.

ROOMS
19

FOOD
private dining room • Restaurant • Rose Terrace • By pool or on lawn by request

DRINK
Colonial Bar

FEATURES
full service spa • gym • sauna • outdoor pool • landscaped gardens • satellite TV • high-speed wireless Internet access • conference centre • free transfers within Sandton area

NEARBY
golf, tennis and horse-riding • upscale shopping centres • casinos • Sandton

CONTACT
PO Box 61, Gallo Manor
Johannesburg 20525, Gauteng •
telephone: +27.11.804 2540 •
facsimile: +27.11.802 7261 •
email: reservations@fairlawns.co.za •
website: www.fairlawns.co.za

melrose arch hotel

Daringly stylish in its creative vision yet assuredly five-star in its execution...

Daringly stylish in its creative vision yet assuredly five-star in its execution, Melrose Arch Hotel offers an interpretation of the modern African aesthetic that's calculated to entice the seasoned global traveller. From the whimsically changing colours of the entrance lobby floor to the works of art scattered unexpectedly throughout the building, this hotel in the upmarket northern Johannesburg development of Melrose Arch is at once playful yet polished, sleek yet surprising.

The guestrooms elect for a classic style, with wood panelling and parquet flooring, and are also equipped with the best of modern conveniences, such as complimentary Internet access, a flat-screen TV with surround sound, satellite channels and even an in-room selection of DVDs. The bathroom area is separated from the bedroom only by a large curtain, and features both deep oval bathtubs as well as walk-in rain showers. Quirky touches make all the difference, such as the oversized polished chrome coat hangers from which the window drapes gracefully cascade, or the cheerful yellow rubber duck in every bathtub.

While the Melrose Arch Hotel is only a short stroll away from the hippest restaurants and bars in Johannesburg, it's also home to sumptuous dining opportunities of its own. March Restaurant specialises in fusion cuisine, serving an eclectic mix of intercontinental flavours in a clean, elegant setting. The Library

Bar is the perfect place to savour a cognac or cigar, while the colonial-inspired Verandah overlooks the busy street and is great for people-watching. Even the daily hotel breakfast is a treat unto itself, with champagne, caviar and oysters to pamper the tastebuds.

Undoubtedly, Melrose Arch's signature establishment is the unassumingly named Pool Bar, where tables and chairs are set in a few inches of water, flanked by trees that have been planted in huge steel buckets. Guests can chill out with cocktails or even enjoy a

light meal in this imaginative setting—reservations, needless to say, are a must—while those who want to take a dip in the pool proper can enjoy the music piped in underwater.

For private parties, the Melrose Arch Hotel has a Sound Room outfitted with luxe furnishings and a state-of-the-art entertainment system. The room is soundproof and available 24 hours a day. Guests can sample the hotel's DVD selection on the extra-large flat-screen TV, or simply

make the most of the high-quality sound system and indulge in a chilled out evening featuring the latest party beats.

With its exquisite service and exclusive location to complete the package, the Melrose Arch Hotel has everything a discerning traveller could want. Its distinctive postmodern sensibility fits right in with the adventurous spirit of contemporary Johannesburg.

ROOMS
117 rooms • 1 penthouse

FOOD
March Restaurant: international fine dining

DRINK
Library Bar: cocktails and drinks • Pool Bar: cocktails and drinks • Veranda: café

FEATURES
business centre • 5 executive boardrooms • auditorium • library

NEARBY
shops • bars and restaurants • city centre • Sandton City

CONTACT
1 Melrose Square
Melrose Arch, Sandton
Johannesburg 2076, Gauteng • telephone: +27.11.214 6666 • facsimile: +27.11.214 6600 • email: info@melrosearchhotel.com • website: www.africanpridehotels.com

ten bompas

Nothing is overlooked at this incredible home away from home.

In the quiet, exclusive Dunkeld suburb of Johannesburg lies a pleasant surprise. Tucked amongst the comfortable upper middle-class homes is a top boutique hotel for leisure and business travellers alike. Ten interior designers were each asked to decorate one of the hotel's 10 suites in their interpretation of an African theme. The result is 10 unique representations of Africa, unified by their use of art and sculpture.

Where this hotel has really made its mark, however, is in its unparalleled personal service. Hotel directors Christoff van Staden and Peter Aucamp were driven to inject intimacy into typically impersonal business travel. Fuelled by their own disappointing business travel experiences, they created service that instantly makes a traveller feel cherished.

The close-knit staff greet guests by name, and personally see them off to work in the morning when the keys are handed in at the reception. Upon the evening return, staff are waiting at the end of the driveway with room keys in hand and a friendly smile. Dinner is served in the restaurant if requested—if not, guests are left to the privacy of their suites.

Nothing is overlooked at this incredible home away from home. Staff note which type of wine each guest prefers and have a bottle waiting. Laundry service is complimentary, and if it is noticed that one is running low on shirts, one will be ironed and delivered to one's suite in time for the next meeting. The mini-bar is also complimentary, a gesture unprecedented in the hotel industry. Generously stocked with standard-size bottles, it offers a privilege all guests have respected. With this degree of hospitality, guests almost feel as if they are staying in their best friend's home.

THIS PAGE (FROM TOP): Rooms are all uniquely designed but share the same air of warmth and comfort; cheery colours shine through the night, welcoming guests back in.

OPPOSITE (FROM TOP): A modern, yet subtly ethnic aesthetic is seen in this bathroom at Ten Bompas; enjoy afternoon tea in the plush interiors—or a bottle of wine; the open-air dining terrace.

ROOMS
10 suites

FOOD
Sides: international

DRINK
wine cellar

FEATURES
complimentary mini-bar • in-suite guest lounge and bathroom • complimentary laundry service • fireplaces • Internet connection • in-suite facsimile • boardroom facilities and services • transfers to and from meetings

NEARBY
Johannesburg city centre • Illova • Sandton • Hyde Park

CONTACT
10 Bompas Road, Dunkeld West Johannesburg 8001, Gauteng • telephone: +27.11 325 2442 • facsimile: +27.11 341 0281 • email: reservations@mix.co.za • website: www.tenbompas.com

Suites come with fireplaces, steam showers and complimentary high-speed Internet. Each suite also has a lounge with a guest bathroom. This allows business associates or friends who happen to drop in to use the facilities without intruding upon the bedroom. Wardrobes are big enough to comfortably store large suitcases—an important but highly underrated factor.

Ten Bompas' five-star restaurant, Sides, offers an excellent menu of food and wine. Going right back to basics, it serves classic cuisine and old home-style favourites. Wine comes from the two-storey, 10,000-bottle cellar stocked with a fine selection of vintage Cape Winemakers Guild labels. Order from the personal waiter assigned to each table or browse the cellar in person. At Ten Bompas, such stellar hospitality is only to be expected.

the grace in rosebank

...nothing less than the finest service and hospitality with genuine feeling.

THIS PAGE (FROM TOP): *A fine selection of international dishes is served at The Restaurant at The Grace; rooms are a comfortable blend of luxury and classic furnishings; the lounge gives off a cosy air.*

OPPOSITE (FROM TOP): *The sumptuous buffet spread invites dining in; the hotel's elegant street façade; the rooftop pool terrace is often found to be a favourite with the hotel guests on a hot afternoon.*

Right in the heart of Rosebank, a sun-dappled, quietly elegant suburb of Johannesburg, The Grace extends its warm welcome to all comers. Its motto proudly proclaims it to be far more than just a fine hotel—for fine hotels are many and plentiful in bustling Johannesburg—it is, much more importantly, a gracious home where each and every guest can expect nothing less than the finest service and hospitality with genuine feeling.

The interior décor is defined by the qualities of luxury without ostentation, and an old-fashioned charm that doesn't date. Sweeping oil landscapes in polished walnut frames and tall, ornate gilt mirrors adorn the walls, while overstuffed settees and armchairs with carved legs nestle comfortably before the rosy hearth. Brass chandeliers discreetly updated with electricity maintain the look of their candled predecessors and cast a cosy glow over the furniture. Dark woodwork and subtle lighting feature throughout for a homely feel.

The design aesthetic extends to the rooms, which only begin on the fifth floor, well away from busy street noise, and affording all rooms the advantage of a clear view over the pleasant, tree-lined streets of residential Rosebank. All the rooms are en-suite and temperature-controlled, and come with complete tea-making facilities for one's convenience. The suites have a bathroom with separate shower, and a spacious lounge area, as well as a guest toilet, and

are suitable for private meetings—in-suite dining for up to four can also be arranged. On the very top floor are three deluxe penthouse suites, which have the additional feature of a private balcony that provides commanding views of the surrounding town.

All accommodation comes with a full English breakfast included, and The Grace prides itself on a truly superb first meal of the day. Mouthwatering additions to the traditional full English fry-up unique to The Grace are, among others, Grace Benedict—poached eggs with smoked salmon and red pepper hollandaise on a toasted brioche—and buttermilk waffles served with maple syrup or white chocolate sauce. For the rest of the day, there are plenty of restaurants and cafés within walking distance of the hotel. In the building, however, lunch and dinner are served in The Dining Room, with an acclaimed international menu that has made the restaurant a favourite with local high society, businessmen and the occasional celebrity. In summer, al fresco dining out on the roof and pool terrace becomes a popular option.

After all this surfeit of good food, a session at The Spa is in order. Highly recommended is the Hot Stone Therapy treatment that purportedly re-energises the body through the specific placement of warmed basalt stones. A full range of beauty and wellness programmes are available, and guests can lie back and relax in the hands of the experienced therapists.

The Grace is within walking distance of the town entertainment centre, where cinemas, shops and art galleries proliferate. Nearby, an African curio market attracts souvenir hunters, as does the Rooftop Market at The Mall of Rosebank, directly adjacent to the hotel. At the end of each day, guests return to The Grace with a lively anticipation of a night spent among the hotel's various creature comforts and another fulfilling day ahead.

ROOMS
60 rooms • 10 suites •
3 penthouse suites

FOOD
The Restaurant: international

DRINK
wine list • hotel bar

FEATURES
The Spa • secretarial services •
library • meeting and event facilities •
Internet connection • fitness centre •
disabled access • rooftop pool •
satellite television

NEARBY
Rosebank entertainment centre • The
Mall of Rosebank • Newtown Cultural
Precinct • Apartheid Museum • Lion
Park Tour • Sterkfontein Caves • Rhino
Breeding Centre • Cheetah Research
Centre • Elephant Sanctuary

CONTACT
54 Bath Avenue, Rosebank
Johannesburg 2196, Gauteng •
telephone: +27.11.280 7200 •
facsimile: +27.11.280 7474 •
email: graceres@thegrace.co.za •
website: www.thegrace.co.za

tintswalo at waterfall

...the most preferred residential country estate in Gauteng...

THIS PAGE (FROM TOP): *All the rooms have a unique equestrian theme; al fresco dining is available out on the terrace of The Feedroom; the cool, inviting outdoor pool.*

OPPOSITE (FROM TOP): *Exposed stone masonry features throughout the hotel's architecture and design; dark hues and woods convey a modern, sombre sophistication; the cosy lounge at Tintswalo.*

The classic equestrian aesthetic takes centrestage at Tintswalo at Waterfall, with an imposing main building that evokes at once both the generous space and cosy warmth of a barn. They certainly don't do anything by halves here, from the 7-m- (23-ft-) high wooden front doors to the surprising interplay of polished steel, timber, exposed stone masonry and brickwork that gives the most preferred residential country estate in Gauteng its presence and stature.

Situated in the 200-hectare (494-acre) Waterfall Country & Equestrian Estate, the lodge has a commanding 360° view of the surrounding verdant countryside. In particular, the rooms on the top floor have floor-to-ceiling windows that look out onto the polo fields and, in the distance, the magnificent Magaliesberg Mountains. Thick stone-clad walls, bolted timber beams and sturdy, elegant furniture add to the air of consummate splendour.

Despite its grandiose bearing, Tintswalo at Waterfall houses only 16 intimate suites, each named and decorated after different breeds of horses found worldwide. From Arabian thoroughbreds to palominos, these famous breeds are represented in the individually commissioned paintings of the respective horse in each suite, as well as the suite's colour

scheme and ornamental details. For example, the Lipizzaner suite is decorated in black and white because the foals are born black and turn white only later. Every suite has a private Juliet balcony—the better to take in the picturesque surroundings—and soft furnishings that play with textures and fabrics to create a modern South African sensibility.

The international equestrian theme is also carried on throughout the rest of the hotel in the framed photographs of some of the racing world's most celebrated horses, which were also specially commissioned for the lodge. Outside the lodge, there are full stables, paddocks, a well-kept racetrack and a jumping/dressage arena.

For guests who want a little pampering, there is a Vital Source Spa with a group treatment room, two full treatment rooms, a Vichy shower, hydro bath and steam and sauna facilities. The hotel also has its own private walking trails, where guests can spend an afternoon in a leisurely stroll. Even within the hotel's landscaped spaces, there are more than 2,000 indigenous trees, grasses and fish, all carefully selected to create an ecologically responsible and sustainable environment within the confines of the hotel grounds.

The Feedroom offers sophisticated dining options in an intimate space that seats just 30 guests. Al fresco seating is available, while indoors a stately fireplace and dark wood accents create a distinguished setting in which chef Ryno Durant and his team serve up a hearty contemporary repast created from only the freshest local ingredients.

Since its opening on 1 February 2007, Tintswalo at Waterfall has unerringly brought its unique brand of five-star service to both business and leisure travellers alike. The region's famous game reserves are no more than two hours' drive away, making this the perfect pitstop on the way to or from a safari experience. There's plenty of room here for everyone to catch their breath and luxuriate in an atmosphere of quiet gentility.

ROOMS
16

FOOD
The Feedroom: international

DRINK
The Cellar • The Bar

FEATURES
executive boardroom • Vital Source Spa • stables • nature trails

NEARBY
Johannesburg • Gold Reef City theme park • Rhino and Lion Park • Wondercaves • Pretoria

CONTACT
Maxwell Drive, Kyalami Midrand 8001, Gauteng • telephone: +27.11.464 1070 • facsimile: +27.11.464 1315 • email: info@tintswalo.com • website: www.tintswalo.com

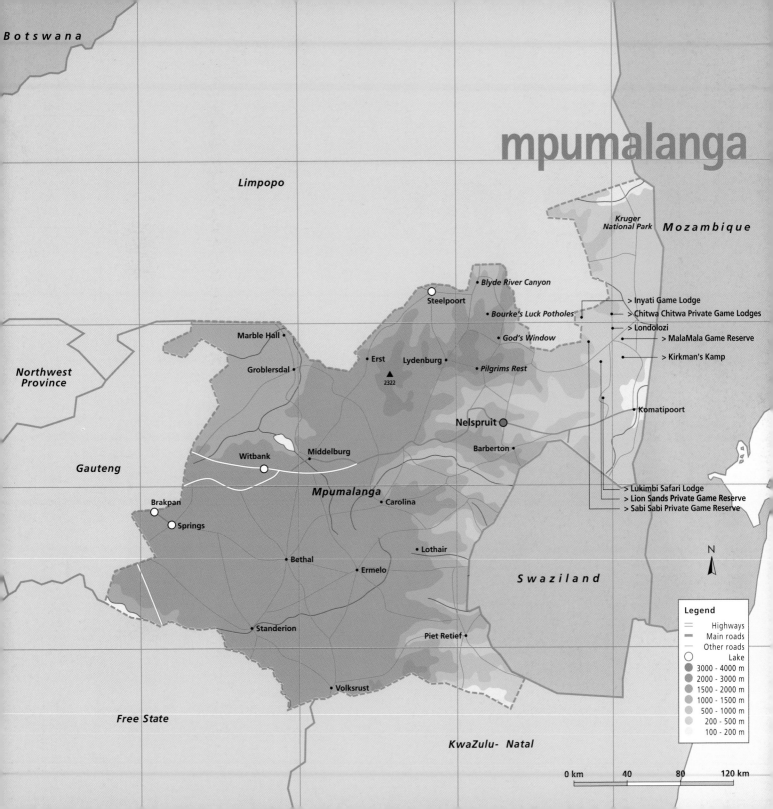

mpumalanga

Botswana

Limpopo

Kruger National Park

Mozambique

● Blyde River Canyon

○ Steelpoort

● Bourke's Luck Potholes

> Inyati Game Lodge
> Chitwa Chitwa Private Game Lodges
> Londolozi
> MalaMala Game Reserve
> Kirkman's Kamp

Marble Hall •

● God's Window

Northwest Province

● Erst

Lydenburg •

● Pilgrims Rest

Groblersdal •

▲ 2322

Nelspruit ○

● Komatipoort

Barberton •

Witbank

● Middelburg

Gauteng

Mpumalanga

> Lukimbi Safari Lodge
> Lion Sands Private Game Reserve
> Sabi Sabi Private Game Reserve

Brakpan
○ Springs

● Carolina

● Lothair

Bethal ●

Ermelo ●

Swaziland

● Standerion

● Piet Retief

Free State

● Volksrust

KwaZulu- Natal

N

Legend

Highways
Main roads
Other roads
○ Lake
3000 - 4000 m
2000 - 3000 m
1500 - 2000 m
1000 - 1500 m
500 - 1000 m
200 - 500 m
100 - 200 m

0 km   40   80   120 km

playground of the rich and famous

The preferred holiday province for many international celebrities, not to mention foreign dignitaries, royals and the moneyed elite, undeveloped and unspoiled Mpumalanga is most remarkable for its exclusive bush accommodation, diverse natural scenery and abundant Big 5 and other wildlife populations.

Besides the world-famous Kruger National Park—now a part of the Great Limpopo Transfrontier Park—there are several other secluded natural havens that make for very attractive weekend (or longer) retreats. One such location is the nature lover's restful paradise of the Highlands Meander, with its reputation for rich fly fishing, rare bird species, challenging rock climbing and swathes of colourful flora, just a two-hour drive from Gauteng's hectic cities. Ruined forts, graves, trenches, artillery placements and other vivid artifacts from the Boer War are still easy to find around quaint little hamlets like Dullstroom, and more of the endangered but well-protected black leopards and cranes can be found here than anywhere else in the country.

Out of South Africa's nine provinces, Mpumalanga is also arguably the greatest spot for high-adrenalin sports. Paragliders, abseilers, hang gliders, bungee jumpers, mountain bikers, whitewater rafters and hot air ballooners dot the vista of the province that is known by some indigenous peoples as 'Where the Sun Rises'. On the several winding rivers, lakes and huge dams in the region, leisure activities such as skiing, parasailing and windsurfing are available too.

God's Window, Bourke's Luck Potholes, Bridal Veil, Lone Creek, Horseshoe and the fascinating gold-rush town of Pilgrim's Rest are some of the memorable place names that capture the region's riveting history, environment and cultures, while the vibrantly coloured houses, beads and crafts of the Ndebele and other peoples are proudly showcased at several cultural villages. After energy-sapping activity in a climate that ranges from the dry highveld region's cold winters to the hot, humid lowveld, it is difficult to resist an indulgent soak in one of the many spas at the luxury health resorts and wellness centres found variously around the region.

PAGE 48: Hot air ballooning is the newly popular way of taking in spectacular views of the region.

THIS PAGE: Bird watchers will find plenty to like in Mpumalanga; Pilgrim's Rush has a fascinating history of gold-rush prosperity.

OPPOSITE: A breathtaking sunset illuminates a number of zebras and just one lone wildebeest.

protecting, promoting nature's best

The most part of the remarkably diverse flora and fauna found in Mpumalanga is protected by a special network of government-managed nature reserves. The Great Limpopo Transfrontier Park, an international game park with some of the richest, best managed and most established wildlife areas in the whole of Africa, operates across three international borders, and incorporates South Africa's Kruger National Park, Mozambique's Limpopo National Park and Zimbabwe's Gonarezhou National Park.

The Wild Frontier, meanwhile, borders Mozambique and Swaziland, promoting a variety of heritage routes of great interest, pleasant hiking, four-wheel-drive trails, hot springs and hydro spas. With geological discoveries and some of the oldest evidence of life on earth, such as the Mkonjwa Mountains—said to be the oldest in the world—the Wild Frontier truly lives up to its dramatic name.

The relatively flat and subtropical lowveld is home to Nelspruit, the provincial capital of Mpumalanga, the Sudwala Caves—the oldest dolomite caves in the world—and a botanical garden with cycads and rainforest well worth the visit. The Panorama Route's rich cultural heritage and dramatic vistas play host to an astoundingly wide variety of adrenalin activities, even gold panning. Bird-watching, game-viewing and trout-fishing opportunities are many and plentiful. The Blyde River Canyon Nature Sanctuary hosts diverse specied of wildlife, birdlife and plant life, with the world's third-largest canyon, powerful waterfalls, clear trails left by the Voortrekkers, and the artistic and cultural footprints of the ancient Africans.

Where the Blyde River and the Treur River join is a peculiar natural phenomenon that draws visitors and is one of the more-photographed sights in the province. Water erosion caused by swirling water has created a spectacular geological quirk: Bourke's Luck Potholes, which took thousands of years to form bizarre cylindrical sculptures with smooth red and yellow banded rocks contrasting starkly with the dark pools of water in their depths. South Africa's five primates are seen in the nature reserve and the hippo and crocodile live in the rivers and wetlands of the Swadini Dam.

jewel in the crown

By far the most popular activity the province offers is game viewing in one of a number of game reserves that preserve the natural habitat of the indigenous wildlife. Whether you prefer a self-drive tour, allowing you to determine the pace of the trip, a guided tour, with the knowledge of an expert tracker and an increased chance of seeing what you want, or to travel on horse or (in true safari style) by elephant, you are practically guaranteed wonderful memories of South Africa's Big 5 and much more.

Night drives conducted by park rangers in the private game reserves are great for spotting game not usually seen during the day. Even though the province offers some of the best chances to view leopards, with one of the highest concentrations of the reclusive animals in the country, they are hard to spot as they spend most of the day hiding in trees. However, a couple of days with an experienced guide should give you several sightings worth a detailed reminiscence or two.

cultures explained through history

The lifestyle and culture of the Shangaans, who live mostly between the Kruger National Park and the Drakensberg mountain range, can be enjoyed by visitors at an authentic traditional village near Hazyview, located between the Blyde River Canyon and the southern part of the Kruger National Park. Set under groves of ancient trees amongst the lush forest and flat grassland, a busy, noisy traditional African market and a cultural village were built by the Shangaan people to preserve their rich heritage and craft skills. As a legendary battle site of warring African tribes, it is said to have provided the direct inspiration for H Rider Haggard's best-known work, the genre-establishing King Solomon's Mines, the first English-language fictional adventure novel set in Africa and responsible for many of the romantic, swashbuckling notions of colonial Africa.

In the eastern escarpment is the historic village of Pilgrim's Rest—with its many places of natural and cultural interest, such as museums and historical sites that vividly capture the brief, but intense, prosperity and tough lives of its residents before and during the gold rush era of the 1800s and early 1900s. Since being declared a National Monument in 1986, large numbers of historians, architects, curators and special-interest groups have ensured that several interesting buildings and historicically significant sites in the village are maintained and open to the public.

The evolving history of a former refuge for Christians that later became perhaps the most influential place where the Bible was taught to Africans is on display at the Ndebele village in Botshabelo, an open-air 'living' museum near Middelburg. Here, visitors can glimpse the initial clash of profoundly different cultures through the colourful decoration of houses and abstract wall paintings, depicting common items—such as razor blades and letters of the alphabet—that people had not seen until they were first introduced to white people The Ndebele people are perhaps most recognised for this— the immediately distinctive style of their dwellings, which are meticulously painted in a geometrically symmetrical framework of black lines, then filled in with bright shades, presenting quite a spectacle under the intense African sun.

THIS PAGE (FROM TOP): *A leopard makes its graceful way down; Ndebele women and children in front of their distinctive houses.*
OPPOSITE: *Christianity made early inroads into Africa through such churches, painted in local style.*

capital city, small town

Mpumalanga has no really large cities, but its traditional gateway is Nelspruit, where farmers from the surrounding regions trade citrus and tropical fruits, such as mango, banana, avocado, and macadamia and pecan nuts. The botanical gardens' rare collection of plants and the first man-made rainforest draw visitors from afar, but the city also has a comfortable eight-cinema complex, lively casino and entertainment centre.

Friendly and set in lush surroundigs, Nelspruit's streets are lined with jacaranda trees and the town has good sports facilities. Nearby, the historic town of Barberton is where the 19th century gold rush started, and the façade of Africa's first stock exchange, built in 1887, still stands today. About 200 km (124 miles) east of Pretoria is the cattle-farming city of Belfast, said to be the coldest town in South Africa. Despite the frigid associations, its trout- and bass-fishing in the clear and freezing cold rivers and streams pulls in the visitors. There are also Boer War-related places of interest and the country's biggest tulip farm, which draws thousands of people in the spring.

action spot for adventure seekers

Mpumalanga has no beaches or oceans, but where else in the world can you view game from an agile kayak, boisterous booze cruise or bobbing river tube? There is also powerboating, cave diving, and whitewater rafting, or simply cooling off after a long day under one of many waterfalls. You can even warm up at a subtropical hot spring. The region's roughest rapids slice through the tropical jungle of the 700-m- (2,300-foot-) deep Blyde River Canyon, and the nearby Sabie River specialises in 'bum-sliding' down shallow waterfalls. The province's largest river, the Oliphants River, is excellent for game-viewing and exhilarating whitewater rafting. Kloofing, or canyoning, involves joining small groups going down streams that feed into rivers, such as the Sabie, Blyde and Oliphants, in a wild ride involving abseiling, canoeing and swimming. Leaping between rocks, sliding down mini-rapids, and jumping from waterfalls into clear pools before swimming to canoes or kayaks fills a typical action-packed day.

THIS PAGE: *Colourful swathes of tulips take centre stage in the city of Belfast, where South Africa's largest tulip farm is.*

OPPOSITE: *Lush greenery is on all sides in the tropical jungle with its cascades of mini-rapids.*

The region's roughest rapids slice through the tropical jungle...

chitwa chitwa private game lodges

At Chitwa Chitwa, the African wilderness calls...

Chitwa Chitwa Private Game Lodges are openly unpretentious, and their homely atmosphere is the first thing that strikes guests. Situated in Sabi Sand Game Reserve and owned by Charl and Italian-born Maria Brink, Chitwa Chitwa began life as a family home. The transformation from family premise to luxury game lodge took eight years, with the addition of a bar, lounge, dining and entertainment area, sundeck and pool. Maria added her personal touch by painting Italian phrases on the screed stone floors. Indeed, her vibrant Italian personality and heritage are gently reflected in the large-than-life paintings and murals on the walls.

To up the chic factor, Lantis Bain Scorgie, an interior decorator with a highly individualistic style, installed a graphic monochromatic theme throughout the lodge. He added to that a dash of European and African influences to create a cocktail of styles that is quirky yet harmonious. In tune with this eclecticism, flea-market treasures are mixed with family silverware, and heirloom antiques with slick, chrome furniture. The result is a comfortable setting where a healthy sense of humour is always appreciated, and where guests are beckoned to chill out.

The accommodations at Chitwa Chitwa are split into two camps: Chitwa Chitwa Safari Lodge and Game Lodge. The Safari Lodge, once a hunting lodge, is a group of five chalets nestled beneath a luxuriant blanket of knobthorn trees. In unwavering African tradition, the chalets are thatched and seem to melt seamlessly into the surrounding bushveld. This makes Safari Lodge a prime location for animal- and bird-watching.

Game Lodge, its sophisticated sibling, peeps over a glassy lake—one of the Sabi Sand Game Reserve's largest. Here, guests are rendered practically invisible to the animals which gather on the open plain on balmy evenings. Luxury suites are fitted with glass-walled showers

THIS PAGE (CLOCKWISE FROM TOP): Stark monochromatic décor highlights the modernistic design aesthetic; the tranquil outdoor pool and shady sundeck overlook one of the largest lakes of Sabi Sand.

OPPOSITE (FROM TOP): Simply not to be missed is the awe-inspiring game-viewing at Chitwa Chitwa; a luxury suite at Game Lodge; lean back and enjoy an evening cocktail at the cosy lodge bar.

ROOMS
Safari Lodge: 5 chalets •
Game Lodge: 5 rooms, 3 suites

FOOD
dining room and boma: African-
Mediterranean • poolside lapa: lunch

DRINK
Game Lodge: wine cellar •
Safari Lodge: bar

FEATURES
pool • rangers

NEARBY
game-viewing spots

CONTACT
PO Box 781854, Sandton
Johannesburg 2146, Gauteng •
telephone: +27.11.883 1354 •
facsimile: +27.11.783 1858 •
email: info@chitwa.co.za •
website: www.chitwa.co.za

which offer splendid views of the surroundings. Among the other outstanding features of Game Lodge are elevated baths and private sundecks. Honeymooners have the exquisite Boulders Suite all to themselves, which boasts a private dip pool that overlooks the savannah, a lounge area and a luxurious corner bath by the window.

Like any self-respecting family-run lodge, food is the focal point of the Chitwa Chitwa experience. The cuisine is a hearty mouth-watering fusion of Mediterranean and African fare, often in the form of Maria's speciality dishes. Meals are a social affair where guests mingle with rangers and staff to catch up on the day's game sightings.

Sabi Sand Game Reserve borders world-famous Kruger National Park. With no fences between the two, animals wander around as they please and graze on vast plains. Home to the Big 5, Sabi Sand offers ample opportunities for visitors to rub shoulders with these majestic animals during safari drives. Dozens of other species can be observed from the comfort of the lodge. At Chitwa Chitwa, the African wilderness calls.

inyati game lodge

...a pristine quality about the surrounding land...

THIS PAGE: *The sumptuous yet cosy suites at Inyati open out onto a spacious and private verandah.*

OPPOSITE (FROM TOP): *A leopard, the solitary big cat of Africa, on the prowl through its bush habitat; the outdoor freeform pool is the ideal spot for relaxing, with the magnificent South African bush landscape in the background; come together after a long day on safari for a hearty dinner of local cuisine in the lodge boma.*

Located on 65,000 hectares (160,600 acres) of savannah vegetation is Inyati Game Lodge. Set in the picturesque Sabi Sand Game Reserve roamed by powerful buffalo, elephants, rhinos, lions, leopards and many other species, this is nature as it should be. There is a pristine quality about the surrounding land, which hearkens back to a time before people, pollution and mass rapid civilisation came to define much of life on earth.

Inyati has taken this to heart, doing its part towards responsible safari travel by engaging in eco-friendly practices which protect the bushveld from alien species and processes. The result is a game lodge that blends with the environment in a concert of man-made and natural, as the chalets hold their own against the arresting backdrop of the reserve.

Guests enter into a deep and rewarding commune with nature in these gorgeous chalets infused with equal parts of exotic languor and pampering hospitality, complete with thatched roofs, flowing muslin curtains and colonial furniture in warm hues. Warm afternoons can be whiled away here in a glorious rush of leisurely laziness. All of the chalets come equipped with all modern conveniences, such as in-room temperature control for guests who may need a buffer against the African heat. The staff at Inyati are known for their lavish attentions towards visitors, and individual preferences are always taken into account, given the exclusivity of the lodge.

The highlight of the Inyati lodge experience is indisputably the chance to experience first hand the varied and diverse animal and plant species in their natural habitat. Coming eye to eye with a wild lion or watching a herd of elephants make their way across the bushveld is sobering and exhilarating in its novelty but also produces a sense of sharing this landscape with these graceful beasts. After all, this territory has belonged to them since time immemorial. The game drives conducted by Inyati's experienced guides and trackers allow visitors to experience either a bush sunrise or sunset, while the prospect of drifting down a barge on the Sand River while sipping sundowners promises to be a defining moment of one's stay.

Inyati also provides premier authentic African cuisine, which is served on the river patio, overlooking the hippopotamus habitat, or in the bush, where one can dine under a star-filled sky. Diners can also enjoy world-famous South African wines from Inyati's private cellar.

This is an unmistakable chance to experience an awe-inspiring world up close while maintaining the highest standards of luxury and refinement, as the staff and gorgeous surroundings of Inyati welcome guests time and time again into the South African heartland.

ROOMS
10

FOOD
outdoor venues: modern African

DRINK
Warthog Wallow Bar • wine cellar

FEATURES
outdoor pool • gym • curio shop • conference centre

NEARBY
Sabi Sand Game Reserve • fishing • Sand River • game viewing

CONTACT
PO Box 38838, Booysens Johannesburg 2016, Gauteng • telephone: +27.11.880 5907 • facsimile: +27.11.788 2406 • email: inyatigl@iafrica.com • website: www.inyati.co.za

londolozi

...the tantalising promise of an unforgettable adventure...

THIS PAGE (FROM TOP): *A cosy little fireplace adds atmosphere and extra warmth on cold nights; dusk overlooking the Sand River; accessories give a rustic touch.*

OPPOSITE (FROM TOP): *Nature is all around at Londolozi Reserve; an open-air verandah lets the surrounding lush greenery in; serenity is found at the end of a long day with a relaxing soak.*

Londolozi, one of South Africa's pioneering game reserves, is the ideal place to reconnect with Mother Nature and all her wild inhabitants. With the Sand River and the Sabi Sands Game Reserve right at its doorstep, the tantalising promise of an unforgettable adventure is almost guaranteed in this 14,000-hectare (34,600-acre) safari utopia.

A widely recommended way to start one's day here is to go on a Land Rover game drive at the break of dawn to view freely roaming white rhinos, buffalo, antelope and lions. In particular, Londolozi is famous for its magnificent leopards, and guests are often delighted to spot these usually elusive creatures. An interpretive bush walk with a knowledgeable ranger is another option for those who prefer to savour the great wilderness at a more engaging pace. Whatever the case, getting up close and personal with the awesome creatures in their natural habitat is a life-transforming affair for many visitors to the reserve. After all, part of the vision of Londolozi, which means 'protector of all living things' in Zulu, is to leave all guests instilled with a deep sense of reverence and awe for the animal kingdom and its denizens.

Londolozi's distinctive style of luxurious sanctuary is one that comfortably complements the secluded copses of towering trees on the banks of Sand River. At the Tree Camp Suite, one is pampered with chocolate plaited leather beds, fine linen, Ralph Lauren wallpaper, a private pool and contemplation decks, creating the perfect setting to appreciate the pristine surroundings. Their wellness centre, Londolozi Life, offers a holistic range of massage services, yoga classes and exercise equipment to ensure the body, mind and soul of a guest is well-aligned with the harmonious, healing forces of nature. Dusk is a celebrated daily affair at Londolozi, with crystal flutes of chilled champagne served at sunset decks below magnificent skies dyed in brilliant swathes of fuchsia and mauve. This awe-inducing spectacle of nature gives way to the romance of open-air campfire dining under a sky profusely studded with stars.

Unsurprisingly, Londolozi is the first game reserve in South Africa to have been accorded the prestigious Relais & Châteaux status. At the same time, there is an inspiring sense of idealism that pervades the atmosphere as this family-run private game reserve is committed wholeheartedly to conservation efforts. Londolozi is a unique paradise, and does not simply indulge guests with extravagant luxuries—it is also a place that restores one's faith in the intrinsic relations between the earth and the people and animals that roam it.

ROOMS
Tree Camp • Pioneer Camp • Varty Camp • Founders Camp and Private Granite Suites

FOOD
camp dining room: Pan-African food • campfire or bush banqueting

DRINK
wine list

FEATURES
specialist leopard safari • yoga • game drives • Londolozi Life wellness centre • interpretive walks • outdoor pools • Jon Varty cinematography centre • library

NEARBY
Shangann Cultural Village • Sabi Sand Game Reserve • Kruger National Park

CONTACT
PO Box 41864, Hyde Park Johannesburg 2024, Gauteng • telephone: +27.11.280 6655 • facsimile: +27.11.280 6610 • email: reservations@londolozi.co.za website: www.londolozi.com

malamala game reserve

...the heart of the South African lowveld.

The largest privately owned game reserve in South Africa, MalaMala Game Reserve covers 16,000 spectacular hectares (39,500 acres) in the heart of the South African lowveld and is regularly featured in award-winning National Geographic films. It's also one of the most exclusive, undisturbed locations, accessible only to guests at its luxury accommodations on the banks of the Sand River. Small wonder that it was named one of the Top Ten hotels worldwide on Fodor's Choice 2006 list, the only African destination to be selected.

THIS PAGE (FROM TOP): Enjoy a meal in MalaMala's outdoor boma; each suite is furnished in luxury.

OPPOSITE (FROM TOP): A maximum of six people in each safari vehicle means a closer bush experience; MalaMala is by no means short of luxurious touches such as this deep-soaking bath with bubbly.

MalaMala Game Reserve shares an unfenced border with Kruger National Park and sees animal herds migrating regularly to the Sand River. The first outfit to make the transition from hunting safari to photographic safari in 1964, the Reserve operates safaris both during the day and at night, and can even arrange walking safaris with an experienced armed ranger. More than three-quarters of guests have had close contact sightings of Big 5 game, which have been seen on the reserve almost every day of the year for the past five years.

Guests have a choice of three camps at MalaMala, each with its own brand of bushland hospitality. The Main Camp has been located at the same site since 1930 and today offers 18 thatched bungalows with no more than 36 guests at a time, ensuring a quality experience. Every guestroom is air-conditioned, with insect-proof screens, and enjoys a stunning view of the surrounding landscape. There is also a fully equipped disabled suite with an elevated deck and specialised furniture and bathroom fittings. At

ROOMS
MalaMala Main Camp: 18 suites •
Rattray's on MalaMala: 8 suites •
Sable Camp: 7 suites

FOOD
dining room: international • authentic
dining bomas

DRINK
wine cellar • safari bars

FEATURES
business services • DVD library •
disabled access • gym

NEARBY
Kruger National Park

CONTACT
PO Box 55514
Northlands 2116, Gauteng •
telephone: +27.11.442 2267 •
facsimile: +27.11.442 2318 •
email: reservations@malamala.com •
website: www.malamala.com

the southern end of the MalaMala Camp, Sable Camp offers a more private experience. With only five luxury suites and the two-bedroom Lions Den, it never has more than 14 guests. From the large wooden deck surrounding the camp, there's a clear view of the bush on all sides, while the outdoor pool and cosy safari bar provide restful alternatives for guests between the exhilarating game drives. The most exclusive of accommodations on the reserve is Rattray's on MalaMala, with just eight plush and spacious suites nestled on an elevated location overlooking the Sand River. Every suite has its own plunge pool, garden and outdoor dining area, giving guests ample opportunity to soak up the sights and sounds of the reserve and its incredibly diverse wildlife from the comfort of their own lodgings.

Despite its isolation, MalaMala Game Reserve is served by a daily flight service from Johannesburg and every camp has Internet connectivity and satellite television. But with over two hundred different species to watch out for from a beautiful verandah or the comfortable seat of an open safari vehicle complete with an experienced guide, guests will certainly be tempted to forget about the outside world for the duration of their stay.

sabi sabi private game reserve

...a wildlife oasis in the heart of the bush.

THIS PAGE (FROM TOP): *A private pool and deck hint at the pleasures to be found in Sabi Sabi's suites; outdoor dining amongst fellow guests is the perfect opportunity to swap the day's bush stories.*

OPPOSITE (FROM TOP): *Expert guides offer some fascinating insights; the relaxed open lounge area provides ample space to kick back and enjoy a quiet day in; the Amber Suite at Earth Lodge.*

Situated in the world famous 65,000-hectare (160,620-acre) Sabi Sands Reserve, on the southern edge of the famed Kruger National Park, Sabi Sabi, with its four five-star lodges, is a wildlife oasis in the heart of the bush. The reserve is blessed with a great diversity of habitats and wildlife, giving guests plenty of opportunities to have a close encounter with the Big 5—lion, leopard, elephant, buffalo and rhino—as well as cheetah, wild dog and all other species indigenous to this richly inhabited area. Experienced guides in open safari vehicles conduct a wide range of tours in various habitats, introducing guests to the many facets of this wildly beautiful, unpredictable landscape in an unparalleled safari experience.

Within this untamed environment, Sabi Sabi has created the luxurious worlds of Yesterday, Today and Tomorrow in its accomodations. Reminiscent of a bygone era, Sabi Sabi offers 'Yesterday' in the form of Selati Camp, infused with memorabilia, vintage décor and an old-world charm. Selati's beautifully appointed suites offer intimacy with a dash of colonial opulence—all set against a background that is unashamedly seductive and romantic.

The 'Today' experience is found at Bush Lodge, which remains a firm favourite with visitors looking for a vibrant and companionable visit, combined with excellent personal service and the lodge's legendary hospitality. Furnished with mementos from all over Africa, the lodge exudes a charm that makes guests feel instantly at home. Little Bush Camp provides an

extension of the 'Today' experience. The lodge is small—just six comfortable suites—and carries on the warm, contemporary feel of Bush Lodge—an ideal retreat for small groups and families seeking an idyllic hideaway amidst spectacular views of African wildlife.

Earth Lodge represents 'Tomorrow' by way of a unique, ultra-luxurious lodge inspired by the concept of Earth Shelter Architecture from the Middle Ages. Sculpted into a slope of the earth, the lodge uses texture, space and light to present a lodge like no other. Its organic architecture literally merges with the environment, creating an earthy vitality that pervades every room. Earth Lodge reflects Africa's immense artistic talent and is, quite simply a world's first, breaking from the traditional style of lodge to set a new standard in design.

At Sabi Sabi, these seemingly disparate guest lodges come together in what is widely said to be one of the most rewarding experiences of South Africa's pristine wilderness. After a day spent out in Sabi Sand Reserve—where the animals enjoy an open border with Kruger National Park—guests return to an open-air boma to partake in a convivial and hearty African dinner and swap bush stories from the day's exploration. As the stars emerge, slowly filling the sky, another day has passed at Sabi Sabi, sanctuary of the South African spirit.

ROOMS
Earth Lodge: 13 suites • Bush Lodge: 25 suites • Little Bush Camp: 6 suites • Selati Camp: 8 suites

FOOD
authentic bomas: African

DRINK
bar • wine cellar

FEATURES
outdoor pools • private airstrip • curio shop • library • viewing decks • spa

NEARBY
game-viewing spots • savannah, bush and scrub habitats

CONTACT
PO Box 52665, Saxonwold Johannesburg 2132, Gauteng • telephone: +27.11.447 7172 • facsimile: +27.11.442 0728 • email: res@sabisabi.com • website: www.sabisabi.com

kirkman's kamp

...one of the best-loved lodges in the Sabi Sand Game Reserve...

This gem of a find is located in the heart of one of South Africa's most prestigious reserves, the Sabi Sand Game Reserve, renowned for having the best Big 5 game viewing in the country. Thanks to the 65,000-hectare (160,620-acre) reserve sitting on highly enriched soil—perfect for grazing and browsing habitats—spotting the solitary leopard and majestic lions roaming the grounds here is more common than one might imagine.

Accommodation at Kirkman's Kamp is just as impressive, offering spectacular views as far as the eye can see. Widely regarded within the travel community as one of the best-loved lodges in the Sabi Sand Game Reserve, its 18 cottages offer a throwback to the 1920s when colonial luxury and gracious style met to satisfy the most discerning of travellers.

Marrying modern-day comforts and the wild and rustic natural beauty surrounding the lodge, each cottage boasts its own private verandah (doing double duty as patio and viewing terrace) and bathroom with separate showers and freestanding baths. Of course, the outdoor infinity-edge pool is also a welcome respite to weary travellers at the end of the day.

One particular room that stands out at the lodge is its large sitting area, which has a 1920s ambience about it. Plush overstuffed sofas are set against pristine whitewashed walls where an open, crackling fireplace exudes cheerful warmth, inviting a good post-dinner sit-down read or evening chat. Meals, which feature succulent venison specialities from the bush and other hearty examples of South African cuisine, are practically special events on their own—lunch is served on shady verandahs and dinners in romantic lantern-lit bush settings under the starry African sky.

However, the undisputed highlight of Kirkman's Kamp has to be its spectacular location, which borders the Kruger National

THIS PAGE (FROM TOP): Breakfast can be taken on the verandah, or if the weather is fine, in the open; the sitting room is a highlight of the main lodge, warm and cosy.

OPPOSITE (CLOCKWISE FROM RIGHT): The luxury of a relaxing bath awaits; faded photographs add a quaint old touch to the bedroom walls; spectacular views from the pool.

ROOMS
18 cottages

FOOD
various indoor and outdoor venues: pan-African

DRINK
full bar and wine list

FEATURES
outdoor infinity-edge pool • open safari vehicle • guided bush walks • butler services

NEARBY
Sabi Sand Wildtuin • Grahamstown • Port Elizabeth

CONTACT
Conservation Corporation Africa
Private Bag X27, Benmore 2010
Gauteng •
telephone: +27.11.809 4441 •
facsimile: +27.11.809 4400 •
email: information@ccafrica.com •
website: www.ccafrica.com

Park. It is at this park that restricting fences are done away with so animals can roam freely just as nature intended. It's no wonder that the Sabi Sand Game Reserve is best known for having some of the most spectacular Big 5 game viewing in Africa.

Thanks to its history of sensitive game viewing practices, visitors are likely to spot packs of hyenas, various antelope species, white rhino, and the magnificent leopard and lion. Nocturnal sightings on thrilling night game drives are no less exciting when the white-tailed mongoose, African civet and large-spotted genet make their appearances.

Game viewing is spectacular throughout the year—in summer wildlife flourish because of the rain, and impala lambs are born, the staple diet of all predators. The winter season, on the other hand, is the dry season when the grass is low, and spotting game becomes much easier.

lion sands private game reserve

...impeccable service adds that personal touch to every element of the bush experience.

Imagine a safari experience that comes with all the comforts of being treated like one of the family—that's the promise to guests made at Lion Sands Private Game Reserve. Family-owned and managed since 1933, it offers exquisite service that makes every stay all the more memorable at the only private reserve located on the perennial Sabie River.

The Reserve covers just 4,000 hectares (9,885 acres), but because the Sabie River borders Kruger National Park, guests can be assured of spectacular wildlife sightings all year round. Lion Sands is also the only reserve in the Sabi Sand Game Reserve with a full-time ecologist who ensures that the bushveld environment is properly conserved and cared for.

Where a family camp once was, today stands River Lodge and Ivory Lodge, built after 2000 when an unprecedented flood washed away the previous buildings. River Lodge is located on a site with trees dating back almost 800 years and offers 18 luxury thatched guestrooms, each with its own private viewing deck. As the Lodge was designed

THIS PAGE (FROM TOP): Room interiors at Ivory Lodge feature crisp lines and light hues with exotic hints; a pool with a magnificent view.

OPPOSITE (FROM TOP): Get up close and personal with native fauna; a welcoming fire in the lounge; the Chalkley treehouse at Lion Sands is a very popular option.

to face due east, guests can enjoy a golden sunrise over Kruger National Park every morning. Recreational facilities offer alternative ways of enjoying the sweeping landscape, from outdoor pools and a health spa, to more quiet retreats on the River Island deck or secluded bird hide.

A more exclusive option is the international award-winning Ivory Lodge. Inside each of its six suites is a sumptuous sitting area separated from the bedroom by a patio, with selected glass walls allowing light and air to circulate freely. Outside, a private infinity-edge plunge pool awaits, from which guests can spot all manner of wildlife, not to mention a breathtaking view of the nearby Sabie River. The Peregrine suite offers the ultimate in privacy, though each and every suite enjoys careful touches such as having morning tea discreetly served through a small service hatch or providing a range of spa treatments in the suite itself.

Lion Sands also boasts a treehouse with its own bush-style bedroom. One couple each night can sleep on a platform built above the tree line, with a four-poster bed with mosquito net, dining area and simple bathroom facilities. Between the time they are dropped off at sunset and picked up in the early morning, guests are left in absolute privacy, with only the sounds of the African night and the illumination of the stars for company.

Given Lion Sands' proximity to roaming herds of native wildlife drawn to the Sabie River, there's certainly no shortage of opportunities for animal sightings. Whether it's a lavish breakfast served on an open plain overlooking the animals, an interpretive bush walk or a river tour that brings guests closer to see a hippopotamus or Nile crocodile, Lion Sands' impeccable service adds that personal touch to every element of the bush experience.

ROOMS
River Lodge: 18 bedrooms • Ivory Lodge: 6 suites • Chalkley treehouse

FOOD
conceptual outdoor venue dining: international • private in-suite dining

DRINK
full bar • wine cellar at Ivory Lodge

FEATURES
spa • gym • conference rooms • curio shop • authentic boma • game drives • private outdoor pools • bush walks • river island deck

NEARBY
Kruger National Park • game viewing • Skukuza Airport • Hazyview • Paul Kruger Gate • Sabie River

CONTACT
Sabi Sand Game Reserve
PO Box 2667
Houghton 2041, Gauteng •
telephone: +27.11.484 9911 •
facsimile: +27.11.484 9916 •
email: res@lionsands.com •
website: www.lionsands.com

lukimbi safari lodge

...a snug refuge in the pristine wilderness.

THIS PAGE (FROM TOP): *Complimentary champagne welcomes couples on their honeymoon at Lukimbi; dining in the authentic boma; a suite with a bath overlooking a private plunge pool below.*

OPPOSITE (FROM TOP): *The perfect spot to spend a hot afternoon; the main lodge epitomises the quality of rustic chic as seen throughout the rest of Lukimbi; the lounge with its exotic décor.*

The most southerly-located safari lodge in the Kruger National Park, Lukimbi Safari Lodge may also be the most romantic. The property combines exclusive access to 15,000 hectares (37,000 acres) of prime game territory with luxe accommodations and signature amenities like a wedding chapel, creating a snug refuge in the pristine wilderness.

The main lodge is a charming celebration of wooden accents and earth tones, vividly animated by carved wall panels depicting mythical creatures and traditional African patterns. Capitalising on its elevated riverfront location, the lodge has covered open decks from which guests can admire the view of the meandering river Lwakahle. The raised walkways also lead to the 16 suites nestled discreetly amidst the placid vegetation.

While every guest suite is designed for absolute privacy, they all enjoy a view of the nearby river from their private decks. Inside, a contemporary African aesthetic infuses the spacious rooms with a vivid, lively style. Guests have at their fingertips every modern convenience in a space designed with imaginative flair. The luxury Giant Eagle Owl and King Cheetah suites also have a dining room, second bathroom and their own private plunge pool—the last being the perfect place for guests to take in the sights and sounds of the surroundings without leaving the comfort of their own accommodations.

Spectacular game viewing abounds at Lukimbi. The heavily wooded landscape and lush riverine habitat attract both the white and black rhino as well as the rest of the Big 5 game. Elephants, for instance, are commonly seen at the river in front of the lodge, sometimes lingering for hours at a time with their young. For a closer encounter with nature, guests can try any of the game drives or guided walks led by knowledgeable rangers, who have a wealth of bush anecdotes which they are always more than willing to share.

To relax and unwind at the end of the day, the lodge hosts wine tastings where local wines take centrestage and guests can sample a variety of estates' offerings before dinner. In the summer, there are special Swazi evenings that showcase the culture and history of the Swazi people; guests can even borrow traditional costumes to wear for the evening.

Lukimbi also makes for an unusual wedding venue, with an airy baroque-style chapel, all the more romantic that it's set in the dramatic African bushland. Alternatively, couples may choose to be married under a Jackalbery tree, to the harmonies of an African choir.

Whatever the occasion, the staff are always up to the task, delivering meticulous, professional attention to every need. Whether guests are looking for a romantic getaway, a family vacation or simply a chance to get in touch with nature, Lukimbi's cosy air and beautiful environs present a welcome opportunity to relax and rejuvenate.

ROOMS
16 suites

FOOD
boma and dining area: South African and international

DRINK
bar • wine cellar

FEATURES
pool with jacuzzi • viewing decks • library • curio shop • gym • children's play area • wedding chapel

NEARBY
wide variety of game • golf courses

CONTACT
PO Box 2617, Northcliff Johannesburg 2115, Gauteng • telephone: +27.11.431 1120 • facsimile: +27.11.431 3597 • email: info@lukimbi.com • website: www.lukimbi.com

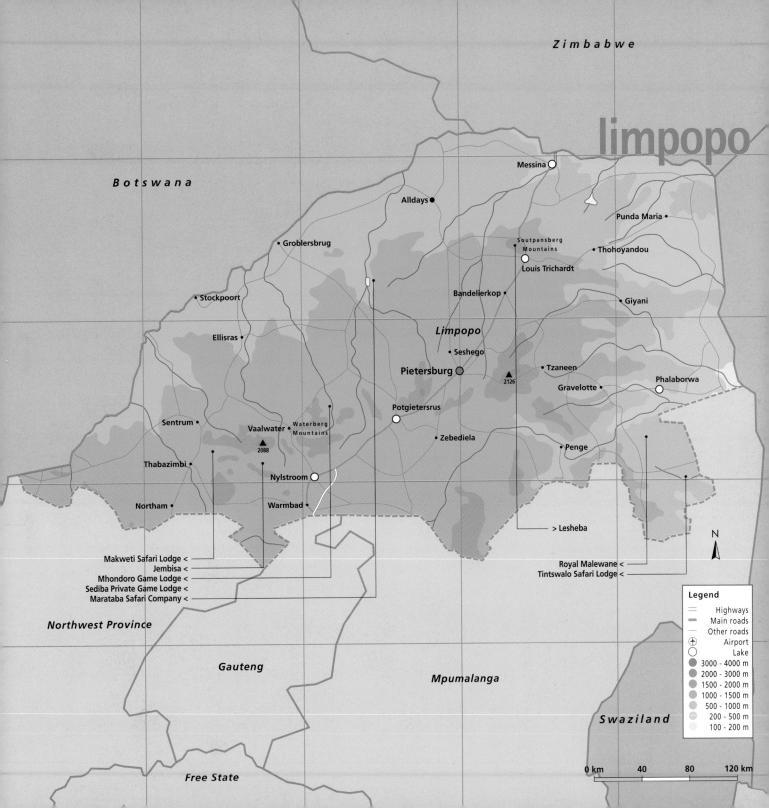

Z i m b a b w e

limpopo

B o t s w a n a

Messina ○

Alldays ●

Punda Maria ●

• Groblersbrug

Soutpansberg
Mountains

• Thohoyandou

Louis Trichardt ○

Stockpoort •

Bandelierkop •

• Giyani

Ellisras •

Limpopo

• Seshego

• Tzaneen

PIETERSBURG ●

▲
2126

Gravelotte •

Phalaborwa •

Sentrum •

Potgietersrus ○

Vaalwater •   • Waterberg
                  Mountains

▲
2088

• Zebediela

Thabazimbi •

• Penge

Nylstroom ○

Northam •

Warmbad •

> Lesheba

Makweti Safari Lodge <
Jembisa <
Mhondoro Game Lodge <
Sediba Private Game Lodge <
Marataba Safari Company <

Royal Malewane <
Tintswalo Safari Lodge <

Northwest Province

N

Legend

═══ Highways
── Main roads
── Other roads
✈ Airport
○ Lake
● 3000 - 4000 m
● 2000 - 3000 m
● 1500 - 2000 m
● 1000 - 1500 m
● 500 - 1000 m
● 200 - 500 m
● 100 - 200 m

Gauteng

Mpumalanga

Swaziland

Free State

0 km   40   80   120 km

vast, remote wilderness wonderland

Endless bushveld and wide skies frame distant mountains and prolific wildlife throughout Limpopo's expanses. Natural hot-springs for therapeutic healing and holistic rejuvenation ensure that the country's most northern province is the ideal antidote for frenzied lifestyles. Nature conservation is key to preserving the magnificent conditions for hiking, fishing and four-wheel-drive adventures, and Limpopo is remarkable for its history, with rumours and legends adorning its past and adding an intriguing twist to any visitor's itinerary.

The Makapans Valley is a prime historical and cultural heritage spot, with sites as old as 3 million years that provide much evidence of how ancient Africans lived well before the first Europeans arrived. Limpopo's landscape has inspired a number of well-known poets and writers. The various faiths practiced here mirror the province's diversity and deep spirituality, and include the Dutch Reformed Church of Voortrekker descendants and the Zion Christian Church, one of the biggest churches in South Africa. This romantic land of legends and ancient civilisations also has modern towns and infrastructure, with resorts, spas and conference centres. Limpopo's four regions are characterised by mountains, forests and savannahs that delight the increasing number of visitors. Local yarns and mysteries are still fiercely debated and today's peaceful aura contrasts with the province's turbulent history, marked by war monuments, vivid legends and tragedy.

conservation through responsible hunting

Commercial hunting geared towards wildlife preservation is, controversially, widely practiced in Limpopo. It is strictly controlled through a system of licensing hunters who tender for quotas of the most prized and dangerous Big 5 trophy animals and other wildlife that would otherwise be culled to control numbers. Although critics consider hunting to be anti-conservation, Limpopo's experience appears to indicate otherwise. Trophies and accommodation that create hundreds of jobs and rake in millions of rand each year provide substantial revenues to conservationists through direct funding. Cattle farmers with overgrazed land have embraced ecological hunting in recent years by

PAGE 74: *A lone giraffe grazes on the Limpopo plains at moonrise.*

THIS PAGE: *Tintswalo Safari Lodge is one of the many game lodges offering luxurious bush holidays.*

OPPOSITE: *Faithful followers of the Zion Christian Church represent the deep spirituality of Limpopo.*

switching to lucrative, environment-friendly operations, generating hard currency that helps ensure the survival of many endangered species. There is more game in the province now than at any time in the last 40 years. Attracting less criticism is fishing, perhaps the hunting activity for which Limpopo is most renowned. With the meandering Limpopo River along the province's northern border depositing dams and clean, clear well-stocked streams throughout the province, the fishing tourism industry is flourishing and hosts several major annual tournaments.

many ways to safari

A most rewarding way to experience and learn about bush culture, wilderness and wildlife in Limpopo is by hiking. Guided walks in Big 5 areas are a great way to spot elements of the unpredictable, abundant natural habitat. Excursions into the wild with expert rangers are recommended. They provide informal tuition and advice along the routes; identify animals, flora, insects and birds of note; explain local folklore and medicinal uses of plants; and teach basic tracking and survival skills.

Hiking is also perfect for observing flying feathered species in the Limpopo Valley, a bird-watcher's haven with its African fish eagles, bateleurs, martial eagles, black eagles, crowned eagles and giant eagle owls. As a major crossover point for the desert birds of the west and tropical birds of the east, more than 400 species have been identified in the Limpopo Valley's Mapungubwe area.

Horseback safaris enable riders to see more panoramic views. Overnight trails in the Lapalala Wilderness Area, Mabula Game Reserve and the Atherstone and Mabalingwe nature reserves are an institution, with fast-changing landscapes with plentiful wildlife.

The latest Big 5-related adventure in Limpopo is hot-air balloon flying over prime lowveld wildlife spots by the Kruger National Park, the Kapama Game Reserve and other lodges and reserves with suitable terrain. Passengers are served pre-dawn coffee as the aircraft is prepared and inflated. In flight, it affords those on board a bird's-eye view of up to eight storeys high of the teeming wilderness below.

THIS PAGE: Experienced rangers can offer tips on tracking and survival in the bare wilderness.

OPPOSITE: An elephant goes for a quick dip on a blazing afternoon.

...a great way to spot elements of the unpredictable, abundant natural habitat.

The four-wheel-drive multi-terrain vehicle is strictly monitored in Limpopo, but widely available throughout the province. Craggy roads, deep sand traps, slippery riverbanks and steep hills await novice and experienced drivers, with good game-viewing along many routes of all grades, starting from just a three-hour drive from Johannesburg in Gauteng. Further afield, the Great Limpopo Transfrontier Park takes you deep into very remote parts of Mozambique to explore villages and camp in unfenced wilderness. One route follows the Limpopo River deep into the park, crossing the Shingwedzi and Buala rivers before crossing back into South Africa's Kruger National Park. For such an adventure, though, travellers must be totally self-sufficient in terms of food, drinking water and bedding. Conditions can get very hot and sticky (in more senses than one), and malaria prophylactics and passports are essentials for a hassle-free experience.

heritage preserved and showcased

Europeans fought with local tribes over land in several bloody wars, of which many

memorials remain; and missionaries brought Western faiths and education, adding a contrasting dimension to the ancient traditions of Africans. These diverse populations have since created a formidable presence. A good place to start understanding the cultural make-up of such a cosmopolitan melting pot as Limpopo is its capital. Polokwane, a major commercial and agricultural regional hub halfway between Pretoria and the Zimbabwe border, has wide, clean jacaranda tree-lined streets and beautiful parks and fountains. The Polokwane Museum presents various themes that highlight the different regional peoples

and their impact on the harsh but delicate environment. Contemporary art by locals is exhibited at Polokwane's Library Gardens Complex, especially in the high season from August to December.

The cultural heritage sites in the Makapans Valley near Mokopane date back three million years. With the Makapans Cave National Heritage Site at its centre, it has excited many scientists and experts with hints of how Africans lived long ago. Some researchers are convinced that the Iron Age sites of Mapungubwe, a World Heritage Site on the southern banks of the great Limpopo River, were capital cities of powerful African kings. Graves found in the 1930s containing gold, pottery, iron and glass artefacts led to much speculation concerning a new theory that a technologically advanced tribe had once existed on that very site.

tracing ancient culture through nature

The 15,000-sq-km (5,800-sq-mile) Waterberg Biosphere is a UNESCO-designated Biosphere Reserve with Stone Age sites and impressive rock formations formed by hundreds of millions of years of erosion. Among the treasures preserved here are rock paintings at Lapalala by bushmen who arrived 2,000 years ago, illustrating rhino and antelope, and dry-stone walls built by the Nguni to fortify their Iron Age settlements.

Thought by some to be South Africa's most spectacular region, the craggy, mountainous, mysterious Soutpansberg is located in the apartheid-era independent homelands of Lebowa and Venda, where African lifestyles have thrived since the Iron Age. Massive tea estates, tumbling waterfalls and the sacred lake of Fundudzi welcome tourists, as do a number of local art galleries. Original works by the Venda people,

THIS PAGE: Venda mud huts are ingeniously built to resist heat.

OPPOSITE (FROM TOP): Missionaries made their mark among the locals, bringing Christianity to the various peoples of Limpopo; young children busy at play in a Polokwane neighbourhood.

considered to be among the finest artists in Africa, are highly sought after by international collectors. The attractive and historic town of Louis Trichardt serves vast ranches and huge citrus and subtropical fruit farms. Among the 340 species of indigenous trees in this diverse region is the baobab, said to be one of the most useful plants to animals and humans. The baobabs here average 300 to 500 years old, with the oldest tree aged 3,000 years and measuring 43 m (141 ft) in circumference at its base.

Perhaps the most elusive and exotic draw, is the world's highest concentration of the shy, cunning and solitary leopard, found near dense thickets on mountain slopes and along streams and rivers. Deadly and powerful, the leopard quickly climbs trees to hide large prey from rivals and scavengers, and its only predator is man.

rain queen's fascinating story

No chapter on Limpopo is complete without an explanation of the revered Rain Queen of Balobedu—the hereditary head of the South African 'royal family' believed to have special powers, including the ability to control the weather, particularly rain. As with many aspects of Limpopo's ancient history and traditions, there are conflicting tales about Rain Queen culture. Some say the 400-year-old dynasty originated in Egypt, but others trace it to Zimbabwe in the 1500s. According to custom, the Rain Queen must shun public functions, and can only talk with her subjects through male advisors; her eldest daughter must always succeed her. Highly respected throughout southern Africa, the Rain Queen often blesses or consults with political and tribal leaders of the region. However, since Makobo Constance Modjadji VI died in 2005, traditionalists are said to be unlikely to accept her daughter as rightful heiress, because her father was a commoner. This puts the future of the clan in serious question.

THIS PAGE: The late Rain Queen Modjadji left behind a powerful legacy which is left in doubt as succession disputes continue.

OPPOSITE: A magnificent baobab tree, with its spreading boughs, commands the endless bushveld.

...the baobab, said to be one of the most useful plants to animals and humans.

royal malewane

...total immersion in the pinnacle of South African luxury...

Prepare for a total immersion in the pinnacle of South African luxury at Royal Malewane. This exclusive safari retreat lies in a private reserve on the western fringes of Kruger National Park in Limpopo Province, and has played host to countless celebrities, Arab sheiks, Indian princes and American tycoons alike. At Royal Malewane everyone is treated like royalty, and all visitors are guaranteed a warm, red-carpet welcome.

Eight separate luxurious suites dot the property. Nestled among native acacia-thorn trees and other bush vegetation, the suites are connected by a network of elevated walkways to allow guests to get as close to the bush as possible, while preserving it almost entirely. Infinity-edge pools and thatched gazebos with loungers provide ample opportunity for outdoor relaxation, while opulent colonial-style interiors hearken back to a bygone era. Sleep in a canopied king-size four-poster bed lined with crisp white linen, and step into a freestanding Victorian-influenced cast-iron bathtub in one's own bathroom.

The two top suites are the Royal and Malewane Suites. Regularly requested for by the property's VIP guests, these two-bedroom suites accommodate up to four guests each. There is also a private lounge with dining facilities, and those staying in these suites get to enjoy the dedicated services of a private butler, chef, private game drive and up to four private massages a day per suite. An outdoor jacuzzi and pool allow guests to commune with nature in the total privacy of their own private verandahs.

Royal Malewane is situated in the unspoilt Thornybush Private Game Reserve. South Africa's Big 5 are well-known residents here, and the resort's Master Tracker has an uncanny ability to spot them. He is after all the only working Master Tracker in the entire country, and specialises in tracking dangerous game.

Fine dining is the order of the day here. Executive Chef John Jackson delights in full-flavoured, colourful cuisine made with only the freshest of local ingredients. Vegetables and herbs come from his own

THIS PAGE (FROM TOP): A refreshing plunge in the outdoor lap pool; dine under a South African sky.

OPPOSITE (CLOCKWISE FROM TOP): Enjoy a relaxing massage treatment in a secluded open-air sala; bathrooms utilise a palette of earthy hues to convey a close affinity to the natural elements; candles add just the right touch of romance to a luxurious suite.

ROOMS
6 Luxury Suites • Royal Suite •
Malewane Suite

FOOD
private chef: international

DRINK
wine cellar

FEATURES
spa • library • private gazebos and
pools • open-top game-drive vehicles

NEARBY
game-viewing spots • Nelspruit •
White River

CONTACT
PO Box 1542
Hoedspruit 1380, Limpopo •
telephone: +27.15 793 0150 •
facsimile: +27.15 793 2879 •
email: info@royalmalewane.com •
website: www.royalmalewane.com

garden, and everything else is delivered from nearby towns. Breakfast is a buffet spread, including many of John's exotic homemade jams. Lunches are light and healthy, while dinners can be formal affairs served on china, crystal and silver, or a sumptuous cookout in the boma.

With its impeccable tradition in hospitality and an unmatched standard of luxury and comfort, it's easy to see why so many illustrious people count themselves among the property's patrons—they know that this is nothing less than the best of what South Africa has to offer.

tintswalo safari lodge

...distinctively decorated to hark back to the romance of African travel and exploration...

Imagine a place where guests need only look out the window to see an elephant passing by, where they may encounter curious baboons on the patio—that's the type of intimacy with nature that Tintswalo Safari Lodge revels in. Located on the banks of the seasonal Nwaswitsontso river amidst an ancient cluster of sycamore trees and other vegetation, the Lodge offers unparalleled access to the richness of the Manyeleti Reserve, Great Kruger National Park. Big 5 game abounds here, to be enjoyed in an environment that takes care of every creature comfort.

Tintswalo's emphasis is on privacy and indulgence, with only seven exquisite suites available, charmingly linked to each other by raised wooden walkways. Each suite is named for intrepid figures like Livingston or Burton, and is distinctively decorated to hark back to the romance of African travel and exploration in the 19th century. Evoking a dignified, genteel air,

THIS PAGE (CLOCKWISE FROM BOTTOM):
Rooms open out onto a private viewing deck with plunge pool; interiors are furnished with such luxuries as deep soaking tubs; the lush, well-stocked wine cellar.

OPPOSITE (FROM TOP): Enjoy vistas of open South African bushland in the privacy of one's own bath; the spa is a welcoming haven; the ultimate in luxurious safari experiences—here at Tintswalo.

the accommodations bring an added luxury to the safari experience—all the more so as each suite has its own private plunge pool and a deck on which guests can sit back on a mild evening and take in the exquisite view of South African bushland.

For guests who prefer more exclusive lodgings, there is the two-bedroom Presidential suite, which has a spacious living area and open plan kitchen. Alternatively, the thatched Manor House, located just a five-minute drive from the main lodge, is designed for private parties of 4–10 guests. It has its own swimming pool, deep patio and traditional open boma for meals, and guests can still take advantage of the services of the main lodge.

Game viewing is the cornerstone of Tintswalo's many offerings—the main lodge area even overlooks a waterhole favoured by elephants and other big game. Viewing schedules are led by highly experienced, accredited guides and completely tailored to guests' requirements. Whether it's a pre-dawn expedition, afternoon exploration or late-night activity, there are game drives or bush walks to meet all different interests, while bringing guests as close to the animals as possible. Guides also conduct stargazing sessions; Manyeleti, after all, means 'place of the stars' in the local Shangaan language.

The Lodge also has its share of civilised pleasures, with an imaginative range of beautiful al fresco and indoor dining venues, and a menu embracing both South African and international cuisine. A vintage wine cellar and a library stocked with rare books provide cosy little nooks where lodge guests can unwind, not to mention the on-site Vital Source Spa.

With Johannesburg a distant five-hour drive away, Tintswalo Safari Lodge thoroughly immerses its guests in the various wonders of the great outdoors. From big game and spectacular bird life to the secluded comforts of a home away from home, it has all the essentials and more for a satisfying modern safari experience.

ROOMS
7 suites • Manor House

FOOD
dining room: South African and international • al fresco venue dining

DRINK
wine cellar • bar

FEATURES
Vital Source Spa • game viewing • library • stargazing

NEARBY
Manyeleti Reserve • Sabi Sands Reserve • Timbavati Reserve

CONTACT
PO Box 70406, Bryanston Johannesburg 2021, Gauteng • telephone: +27.11.464 1070 • facsimile: +27.11.464 1315 • email: info@tintswalo.co.za • website: www.tintswalo.com

lesheba

...captivating combination of magnificent natural surroundings and rich cultural heritage.

Be prepared to be magically transported to an ancient Venda village at Lesheba. Tucked away in a hidden valley near the cloud-wreathed peak of Soutpansberg Mountains in Limpopo, Lesheba offers that sublime travel experience with its captivating combination of magnificent natural surroundings and rich cultural heritage.

Upon entering this luxury lodge, visitors are first struck by the intricate artistry of its sculpted walls, seating areas, figurines and showers. What is fascinating about this architectural vision of a re-created Venda Village is that it first appeared to internationally renowned artist Noria Mabasa quite literally in the form of a series of inspired dreams. Lesheba actively promotes and preserves indigenous practices such as carving, storytelling and traditional healing, and has been accredited by Fair Trade in Tourism in South Africa. Pay a visit to its Center for Indigenous Knowledge, to gain insights into the unique Venda style of craftsmanship and ways of life.

The Greater Soutpansberg is one of South Africa's most unique and biodiverse environments with over 340 species of trees and an impressively rich mix of animal life, and Lesheba is part of the movement to establish it as a UNESCO Biosphere Reserve. Stroll under dense canopies of lush green forest, discover ancient rock art sites, hike down breathtaking rocky gorges and swim in crystal-clear rock pools, and one may just begin to get a full appreciation of its raw, majestic beauty. For those who fancy some good old safari animal spotting, game drives and horse rides provide some excellent and rewarding opportunities to get up close and personal with the roaming rhinos and

THIS PAGE (FROM TOP): Private suites are ideal for a romantic stay; the gorgeous landscape goes on for miles around Lesheba.

OPPOSITE (FROM TOP): A clay statue forms a unique outdoor shower; a bath with a breathtaking view; The Greater Soutpansberg offers incredible biodiversity and is an ideal spot for hiking activities.

ROOMS
2 Luxury Suites • Hamasha Bush Camp • Venda Village Lodge

FOOD
dining room: African and international

DRINK
wine list

FEATURES
game drives • horse trails • bushmen paintings • woodcarving and beading workshops • nature trails • massage services • African drumming

NEARBY
Johannesburg

CONTACT
PO Box 795
Louis Trichardt 0920, Limpopo •
telephone: +27.15.593 0076 •
facsimile: +27.86.689 4790 •
email: lesheba@mweb.co.za •
website: www.lesheba.co.za

zebras. However, a truly unforgettable African Eden experience is the chance to catch the mesmerising sight of a wide variety of animals, reminiscent of old Africa, gathering together around the vleis during the early mornings and evenings.

Lesheba is powered by solar energy, and one is constantly in close communion with nature. Staying at Mwedzi, one of its luxury lodges, is pure secluded bliss, with its flourishing bush surroundings and a patio overlooking grazing giraffe and rhinos on the plains. For an added dose of indulgence, enjoy a soak in Lesheba's delicious bath hut which also offers some splendid panoramic views of the mountains. Meanwhile, at Hamasha Bush Camp, one can be treated to some spectacular views of high cliffs and dramatically plunging gorges. Whatever the case, nature's pure magnificence and its populace of teeming wildlife unfolds before one's very eyes at every turn at Lesheba, whether one is sipping a sundowner by the deck, sunbathing in a private plunge pool, tucking into a delectable meal at a lively African kitchen or sharing stories with fellow guests by the fireplace under the night sky. More than just a malaria-free wildlife reserve, Lesheba gives visitors an opportunity to fully immerse in a uniquely African way of life, surrounded by luxury and hospitality.

marataba safari company

...a pristine wildlife sanctuary like no other.

THIS PAGE (FROM TOP): **The exquisite tented suites come with no lack of luxuries and conveniences; a hammock beckons from the deck on those lazy afternoons.**

OPPOSITE (CLOCKWISE FROM TOP): **Suites are immersed in scenes of great natural beauty from all around; the entrance to the main lodge utilises a slick blend of modern design and traditional materials; an awe-inspiring evening view of the Waterberg mountains.**

There are plenty of places that claim to epitomise all that is Africa—only a few actually live up to this promise. Marataba is one of these rare gems, nestled deep in Limpopo's Marakele National Park. Within this dramatic terrain that encompasses vast plains, dense bushveld, winding rivers, deep gorges and majestic mountains, Marataba's 23,000 hectares (56,800 acres) offer an unsurpassed opportunity to experience a pristine wildlife sanctuary like no other.

The concept of African Renaissance is central to the Marataba aesthetic, coming together in a concordant union of innovative architecture, design and technology, embracing both the contemporary and the ancient. The luxurious lodge features heavy use of stone masonry and glass, evoking a strong affinity with nature while showcasing the gorgeous views for miles around, which include the awe-inspiring Waterberg Mountains and Limpopo River. The Ladies Bar is situated such within the lodge so as to take full advantage of the surrounding panorama, and The Wallow, in the adjoining stone tower, boasts a bird's-eye view.

Of course, one of the distinguishing features of Marataba is its emphasis on quality malaria-free game viewing. With access to Africa's Big 5 and a multitude of other animal species such as rare antelope and prolific birdlife, Marataba is certainly in a uniquely gifted position to do so. Open vehicles are available for this purpose, as are highly experienced and knowledgeable guides who will lead drives or walks. Guests are always aware of their propinquity to nature at its most primal, and never more so than during these walks and drives that bring the various denizens of this habitat into close focus.

Dinner is served between 7.30 and 8.00, modern gourmet cuisine infused with fresh African flavours, in the elegantly appointed dining room. Alternate dining venues include the dining verandah, or out under the evening sky fading to a starry night. Post-dinner, cocktails and conversation are favoured, when visitors sit back to recount the day's adventures.

The exotic tented suites are a haven to which to retreat at the end of the evening, creations of canvas, timber and stone that recall the lavish safari expeditions of the 19th century. Each of the 15 suites have their own private verandahs overlooking the sweeping plains and river below, not to mention outdoor showers, air conditioning and exquisite furnishing.

Marataba is a dream come true for those who crave a break from life's hectic routines, a place where eager sunrises and glorious sunsets are the only markers of each day's passing. For total immersion in the solitude of the African landscape and the comfort and luxury of an exclusive safari hideaway, there is scarcely need to look any further.

ROOMS
15 suites

FOOD
indoor and outdoor venues: modern
African

DRINK
The Ladies Bar • The Wallow

FEATURES
game-viewing • outdoor pool •
curio shop • private outdoor
showers • library • private airstrip •
business centre

NEARBY
Thabazimbi • Rustenburg • Lephalale •
Waterberg Mountains • Marakele
Endangered Species Project

CONTACT
PO Box 454, Plettenberg Bay 6600
Western Cape •
telephone: +27.44.501 1111 •
facsimile: +27.44.501 1100 •
email: res@hunterhotels.com •
website: www.hunterhotels.com

mhondoro game lodge

...a perfect complement to the pristine South African wilderness...

THIS PAGE (CLOCKWISE FROM BOTTOM):
An open safari vehicle waits at the ready for a post-breakfast drive through the African bush; interiors come in soft earth hues; a verandah with a great view.

OPPOSITE (CLOCKWISE FROM TOP): Views of the surrounding landscapes; the dining boma, set and ready; the ultimate relaxing evening.

The secluded luxury of Mhondoro Lodge is a perfect complement to the pristine South African wilderness surrounding this intimate game lodge and its grounds. Set on a rocky outcrop of Welgevonden Private Game Reserve, Mhondoro means 'spirit of the lion', and guests most appropriately feel like jungle royalty here, with the lodge's hallmark personal service and sweeping views of this 42,000-hectare (103,800-acre) reserve.

Mohndoro comprises four elegant chalets and one master game lodge chalet, each overlooking a large waterhole frequented by various wildlife species, and the vast plains of the bushveld in the distance. The private viewing verandah is an ideal spot on which to sit back with a pre-dawn coffee or an evening cocktail and watch the sun rising or setting, or simply to observe animals resting and drinking by the waterhole. However, for the ultimate visual treat, one can always remove to the larger viewing terrace at the master game lodge chalet, where a private jacuzzi ups the indulgence factor that extra notch.

For more up close and personal encounters with the wild, game drives are organised for guests to explore this unspoiled, malaria-free African bushveld. From an open game vehicle, one can encounter a variety of magnificent natural landscapes, from rocky outcrops to the open, limitless savannah. There is plenty of native fauna to spot too, with over 75 species of animals and 350 species of birds roaming this nature reserve. Besides elephants, leopards and rhinos, a few of the less well-known animals the friendly and knowledgeable ranger is likely to

point out are the smaller but no less exotic impala, waterhog, kudu and eland. Tuck into a sumptuous 'Bush Breakfast' while stopping for a break atop a mountain ridge, and enjoy the spectacular views of Waterberg Mountains and the abundant forestry below.

Alternatively, a hike with an experienced guide allows a more intimate experience of this magical eco-system. While out spotting the reserve's smaller creatures and some of the more interesting insects, such as the elephant shrew, leopard tortoise, rhino beetle, buffalo weaver and ant lion, one may also view ancient rock art done by the indigenous San people.

After all that outdoor activity, the urge to stay may strike, and there's plenty within the compounds of Mhondoro itself for those who like to keep occupied. The library is well stocked with reading material for all tastes, and the crystal-clear plunge pool is hard for anyone to resist, even simply to read by while catching some rays. Work off the hearty meals provided by the lodge's talented chefs at the fully equipped gym and relax in a radiant glow in the sauna. In the evenings, dinner at Mhondoro is quite literally a star-studded affair if choosing to dine in the authentic outdoor boma. Enjoy a delectable four-course meal with a glass of vintage South African Chardonnay, all while taking in the nocturnal sights and sounds of the bush.

With all these pleasures at one's fingertips, the stage is set for a perfect five-star getaway, and Mhondoro, the majestic Spirit of the Lion, ensures that every guest here will be embraced with the quintessential African sense of beauty, geniality and comfort.

ROOMS
4 chalet lodges

FOOD
outdoor boma: international • bush breakfast • private dining

DRINK
beverage and wine list

FEATURES
game drives • gym • outdoor pool • entertainment centre • library

NEARBY
Johannesburg

CONTACT
PO Box 1120, Rivonia
Johannesburg 2128, Gauteng•
telephone: +27.73.819 4233 •
facsimile: +27.16.364 2470 •
email: reservations@mhondoro.com •
website: www.mhondoro.com

sediba private game lodge

...the quintessential African getaway...

Nestled within the pristine foliage of Welgevonden Private Game Reserve lies Sediba Private Game Lodge, a plush forest haven that gives seclusion a sense of style and indulges guests with the best that the African landscape and wildlife have to offer.

Emulating its namesake, which means 'spring' or 'source' in the Soho language, Sediba Private Game Lodge places a strong emphasis on the renewal and restoration of one's physical being and state of mind. This is definitely accomplished at least in part through the magnificent panoramas of the majestic Waterberg Mountains, abundant animal and plant life, and all the extravagant services a luxurious safari lodge can conceivably lavish upon its guests.

Sediba's surrounding malaria-free bushveld is a wondrous adventure waiting to unfold from the back of an open-air jeep. Africa's Big 5—the lion, the leopard, the elephant, the rhino and the buffalo—roam freely around this fertile area teeming with life. Bird lovers will also have a field day with over 270 species of bird fluttering around this 37,000-hectare (91,400-acre) unspoiled reserve. If fortunate, there may even be a sighting of the rare brown hyena during these game drives, which are organised twice daily.

There are two main lodges to choose from—Letlapala ('place of the sun') and Letlalpa ('rock') which together house 15 double suites. Each suite's intimate set-up ensures that guests attain much-needed moments of introspection within its minimalist, African-inspired interiors. Soak in a jacuzzi on the private viewing deck while taking in panoramic vistas of rock valleys and sunsets. During chilly winter evenings, there is a warm fireplace for guests to cosy up to.

For a memorable experience, dining at Sediba's traditional African boma, made of natural rock, will simulate the fascinating primitivism of eating a meal in a cave lit by the starry sky. Of course, the excellent cuisine served by in-house chefs and a bottle of fine wine from Sediba's impressive vintage wine cellar will definitely up the indulgence factor on this occasion by a few notches.

Besides a thorough pampering of the tastebuds, there are plenty of wellness treatments and services on offer at Sediba's

THIS PAGE (FROM TOP): The stunning Letlapa lodge, plunging down to a crystal-clear outdoor pool; dine out in a traditional boma.
OPPOSITE (CLOCKWISE FROM RIGHT): The open, airy main Letlapala lodge; natural fabrics, aged timber and muted hues dominate interiors; relax and enjoy panoramas of the surrounding landscape from the comfort of a long, hot bath.

renowned Health & Beauty Centre to restore each guest's glow and energy levels. A soothing Hot Stone Massage is nothing short of pure bliss after an active day of safari exploration and game viewing, while frazzled, newly arrived guests might prefer to opt for a purifying Lymph Drainage Special Treatment or calming Aromatherapy Massage to start their holiday retreat on just the right note of relaxation and inner tranquillity.

Sediba Private Game Lodge is the quintessential African getaway with its opulent solitude harmonising perfectly with the best of nature's untouched beauty. If the heart yearns to rest in a place where time exists only with the unhurried, diurnal rise and fall of the sun—Sediba is the place where one can find that rare, precious form of refuge.

ROOMS
15

FOOD
dining room: international • various al fresco venues

DRINK
wine cellar • lodge bars

FEATURES
helicopter landing pad • health and beauty centre • 2 outdoor pools • 3 meeting rooms • fitness and steam room

NEARBY
Johannesburg International Airport

CONTACT
PO Box 938
Vaalwater 0530, Limpopo •
telephone: +27.11.958 2914 •
facsimile: +27.11.958 2913 •
email: reservations@sediba.com •
website: www.sediba.com

jembisa

...the ultimate in personal safari experiences...

THIS PAGE (FROM TOP): *Jembisa glows warmly in the early evenings; the pool beckons on a hot day.*

OPPOSITE (CLOCKWISE FROM TOP): *An all-inclusive family policy means children are always welcomed; young twin rhinos in the bush; take in the breathtaking scenery from one's own private balcony.*

For the ultimate in personal safari experiences, Jembisa is the place to make one feel right at home in the bush. A former family home that has now been converted into an idyllic five-star safari lodge, Jembisa is uniquely exclusive in the sense that it is one of the rare lodges that comes with its own private game reserve—the beautiful Palala River Reserve, a paradise of rivers, forests, cliffs, gorges and plains in the very heart of the magnificent, malaria-free Waterberg, three hours north of Johannesburg.

As only single party bookings are accepted, a stay in Jembisa with a small group of family or friends promises to be a hospitable and intimate one with a personalised programme to discover the beauty of the bush precisely according to one's own desires. Nighttime game drives give an interesting twist to the usual daytime safaris, and allow one to catch glimpses of rarely-sighted nocturnal creatures such as the brown hyena, aardvark, civet cat and the shy porcupine. Bush walks with one of Jembisa's knowledgeable rangers may result in having a rhino as a strolling companion or a chance discovery of bushman paintings from ancient times. For unmatched bonding with the great outdoors, however, guests can spend a night out under a blanket of stars, only to wake up to the majesty of a South African sunrise.

Jembisa's commitment to being an authentic 'African Bush Home' means that guests will never feel out of place in this cosy stone and thatch lodge with plush interiors and an impeccable reputation for excellent service. A personal chef is always ready to whip up a meal using only the very freshest ingredients. Guests can then choose to have an intimate picnic breakfast in the bush or a romantic al fresco dinner lit by flaming torches. A day in the lodge is like a stay in one's dream home—a tennis court at one's disposal and all-day lounging at the natural saltwater pool with a glass of South African wine and a book from the library.

Beyond Jembisa and Palala, there is still plenty to do to gain a greater appreciation of this beautiful country. For those craving retail therapy, the surrounding Waterberg region has plenty of curio shops selling African art and souvenirs. The seasoned equestrian may want to visit Horseback Adventures where one can pick up or brush up on riding skills and spend an afternoon game viewing from horseback and exploring the Waterberg Mountains. For a quieter and more educational itinerary, visits to the Waterberg Museum and Rhino Museum will provide much insight into the evolution of the people and animals from this region.

However, for a more informal version of history and life in this beautiful country, do not hesitate to talk to the wonderful, friendly staff at Jembisa, who are intent on giving each and every visitor the most hospitable and unforgettable stay in South Africa.

ROOMS
6 rooms

FOOD
personal chef: local and international

DRINK
wine list

FEATURES
child friendly • game drives • bush walks • camping trips • library • reading room • tennis court • games room • natural saltwater pool • in-house masseur • archeological visits • private air strip

NEARBY
elephant-back safaris • Horseback Adventures • Waterberg Museum • Rhino Museum • curio shops • white lion breeding project

CONTACT
PO Box 162
Vaalwater 0530, Limpopo •
telephone: +27.14.755 4415 •
facsimile: +27.14.755 4444 •
email: info@jembisa.com •
website: www.jembisa.com

makweti safari lodge

...the gateway to a thrilling, malaria-free safari experience.

All over the Waterberg wilderness lie spiny candelabra trees. With bright orange or red fruit and large crowns of spindly branches that curve upwards, these trees are impossible to miss. So characteristic is the candelabra tree of Waterberg vegetation that it has lent its name to Makweti Safari Lodge. Makweti is Sotho for 'candelabra tree', and this lodge promises to be the gateway to a thrilling, malaria-free safari experience.

This safari lodge perched on the side of the rugged Makweti Gorge is crafted from natural rock. Teak decks overhang the gorge, which in the summer is a graceful waterfall, and in the winter is a sculptured stone wall. Birds and animals abound, and their presence is often heard before it is seen. The gorge is like an echo chamber, projecting baboon barks and melodic bird calls from black-headed orioles, babblers and starlings into the crisp, clean air.

The atmosphere of peace here is never disturbed. Makweti Lodge accommodates a maximum of 10 guests in five secluded thatch-and-stone suites. Each suite is decorated with an array of antique treasures, hand-beaded fabrics and rich, dark woods. All suites come

THIS PAGE (FROM TOP): Suites offer a unique seclusion, being shielded about by the natural bushveld; rich African textiles and opulent accessories furnish each suite.

OPPOSITE (CLOCKWISE FROM TOP): Enjoy a luxurious bath in your suite; traditional local cuisine is on the menu at the lodge dining boma; unique objets d'art and earthen colours blend in harmoniously; it's common to catch glimpses of wildlife around the lodge.

ROOMS
5 suites

FOOD
dining room and boma: local

DRINK
Zebra Bar • Indaba Lounge •
wine cellar

FEATURES
watering hole • game viewing •
rock pool • African art

NEARBY
Marakele National Park

CONTACT
PO Box 310
Vaalwater 0530, Limpopo •
telephone: +27.11.837 6776 •
facsimile: +27.11.837 4771 •
email: makweti@global.co.za •
website: www.makweti.com

with indoor and outdoor showers, Victorian bathtubs, open fireplaces and decks with uninterrupted views of the bushveld. Scattered throughout the Lodge are antique African art, khelim (flat-woven) rugs and comfortable leather couches.

Meals are expertly prepared by a private chef. She will delight guests with homemade soups, game and other native fare infused with local spices. Dinner may be served either by candlelight in the formal dining room, or out under the stars in the African boma.

The Indaba Lounge, which overlooks the Makweti Gorge and undulating landscapes beyond, is an ideal place to sample one of the lodge's exquisite South African estate wines from its own cellar. Guests can watch animals drinking at the lodge's waterhole from the comfort of the lounge or laze in the sun at Makweti's filtered rock pool.

Makweti Lodge is set in the midst of the pristine Welgevonden Private Game Reserve. Proclaimed a UNESCO Natural Heritage Site, it shares the Waterberg's Biosphere status, meaning that it is recognised as a unique centre of biodiversity and cultural heritage. An expert guide takes visitors on game drives or bushveld walks through this unspoiled landscape, comprising 33,000 hectares (81,550 acres) of Highveld woodland savannah. The largest crash of privately-owned white rhino roam alongside 16 species of antelope, giraffe, zebra, wildebeest, lion, leopard, elephant, buffalo, brown hyena, cheetah and wild dog, complemented by sightings of over 254 bird species. At Makweti Safari Lodge, one's experience in the Waterberg can only be described as unforgettable.

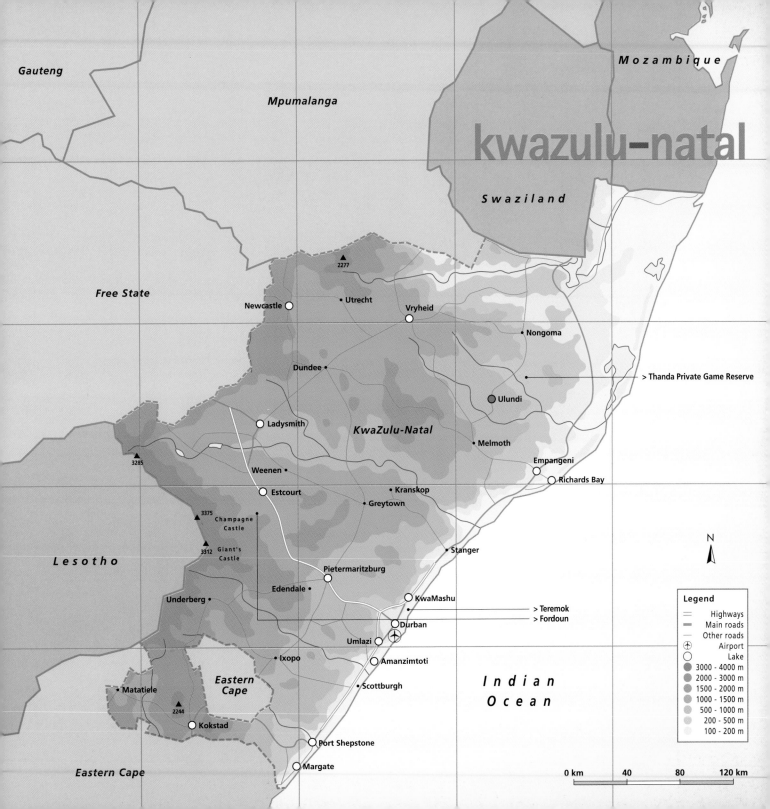

land of legends and pelagic pleasures

The warm Indian Ocean and perennial hot climate help multicultural KwaZulu-Natal welcome discerning visitors year round to its rocky and sandy stretches of coastline, sophisticated and bustling cities and verdant inland with heritage showcases of Indian, African and European cultures and history.

The ancient Zulu Kingdom is a veritable kaleidoscope of colour, characterised by a variety of breathtaking hilly and wetland World Heritage Sites and three separate, distinct regions: a central undulating hilly plateau with moist grassland and forests; subtropical coastal lowlands; and cooler mountainous areas west and north. This is a land alive with a history tapestry-rich in tales and legends of heroic deeds, tragic and bloody battles and dramatic reconciliations, fiercely protected and preserved with a deep-rooted pride in an intricate network of war memorials, ancient art, colonial architecture and traditions of the indigenous Zulu tribes.

It's the pristine coastline, however, of expansive golden sand beaches and luxury properties perched on rocky cliffs above waters teeming with diverse sea life that inspire most people's memories of this lively, cosmopolitan province. A spectacular natural event occurs every June and July, when millions of sardines migrate north en masse in a great silvery bank of iridescence. Driven by cooling waters, thousands of dolphins, Cape gannets and other types of game fish follow the shoals, offering delighted anglers bountiful catches, even from the shore.

Coastal KwaZulu-Natal is an area with a strong affinity with the sea, and it shows. Surfers, divers, sunbathers and boaters all flock to the Indian Ocean's clean waters, enjoying also the simple but plentiful beachfront traditional arts and crafts stalls and exclusive wharfs with private moorings for high-end luxury yachts in laid-back Durban's prime downtown waterfront area, just a block or two from the fine shopping, vibrant entertainment and bustling business districts. The nearby International Convention Centre regularly hosts important global events and the Indian Market's stalls, restaurants and temples heave with shoppers and tourists from early morning to late evening.

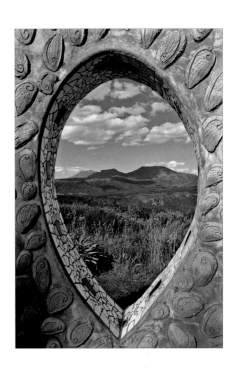

PAGE 100: *Dolphins frolick in the waves just off the coastline.*

THIS PAGE: *A carved wall reveals views of inland KwaZulu-Natal.*

OPPOSITE: *Downtown Durban comes alive in the evening with a multitude of electrical lights.*

preserving provincial eco-diversity

The Greater St Lucia Wetland Park's unique features and immense range of eco-tourism activities were finally recognised in 1999 and awarded the coveted UNESCO World Heritage Site status. Large game popular with wildlife-spotters here are the leopard, hippo, antelope and crocodile, while the smaller warthog, bush pig and especially birdlife also flourish in great numbers, thanks to the park's commitment to sustaining habitats such as mangrove and forest swamps, sweeping coastal dunes and lush open grasslands. In Sodwana Bay's coral garden, keen-eyed scuba divers can spot the shadowy manta ray and swim alongside the smaller sharks. On land, visitors come from all over the world just to catch a glimpse of the endangered loggerhead and leatherback turtles laying their eggs in the dunes.

The province's other UNESCO World Heritage Site is the 200-km (124-mile) and 243,000-hectare (600,500-acre) Khahlamba–Drakensberg Park's range of mountains. The area is doubly remarkable because it was actually recognised for both its historical claims and significant biodiversity. Fly fishermen, golfers, watersport enthusiasts, equestrians, polo players, mountain-bikers, bird-watchers and also botanical enthusiasts flock to the southern Drakensberg, staying at lodges, cottages, cabins and guesthouses, many of which come with modern health spa facilities. Wilderness trails can take from a couple of hours to several days on foot, by horseback or by four-wheel-drive.

THIS PAGE (FROM TOP): Zulu warriors engage in a ceremonial dance; the Drakensberg range rises up majestically in the distance.

OPPOSITE (FROM LEFT): The city of Pietermaritzburg shows its old-world influences in architecture.

meandering routes of many themes

Dubbed 'a little piece of the Old Country' due to its Victorian and Edwardian architecture, Pietermaritzburg—the City of Flowers—has elegant living and is the starting point for the picturesque hamlets and hideaways of the Midlands Meander Route's artist havens, cottage industries, antique shops, quaint taverns and fine dining. This city of glorious parks and gardens, with seasonal blooms and a variety of trees, has at least 50 National Monuments. Some of South Africa's most celebrated country homes, exclusive hotels and most popular health hydros are within easy reach, offering plush surroundings, sumptuous cuisine and superior service amid thick woodlands and gentle streams.

In the southern Midlands, Richmond reverberates with Zulu lifestyle and settler touches, and near Ixopo is the country's oldest Buddhist retreat, a semi-monastic, non-denominational establishment that teaches bird listing, Japanese brush painting and the psychology of meditation on 125 hectares (310 acres) in a lush valley. Inland, Magwaqa Mountain scores high marks internationally for hang-gliding and paragliding, while Underberg and Himeville are tranquil with fern-carpeted forests, secluded valleys and spooky caves.

There are other routes, for those seeking peace and quiet, unique sights and good country fare, that pass by the highest pub in Africa at 2,874 m (9,430 ft) above sea level on the Drakensberg escarpment, as well as traditional medicine shops, tea plantations, cattle ranches and Victorian therapeutic sulphur-spring spas. The Beer Route, based on the famous wine routes of the Western Cape, showcases a number of micro- and large breweries that offer tastings, tours and lectures to those who enjoy their drink and want to learn more about the processes involved. The well-planned Battlefields Route among picturesque hills and

rocks comprises the sites and monuments of the spear-wielding Zulus and heavily armed Boer and British soldiers who fought here for decades. The Zululand Birding Route is the first of its kind in South Africa. This 200-km (124-mile) trail drops to the coast at Mtunzini and ends in Richards Bay, traversing the habitat of at least 10 species.

city of beaches

Quite grubby in places, friendly Durban is easygoing and alive with nature and culture. The Golden Mile, as the beachfront is called, has a tinge of a once-grand British seaside resort, evoking memories of modest bathing suits, rickety gaming arcades and fish and chip shops just metres from modern and colonial-style hotels overlooking the golden beach, lapped by the welcoming Indian Ocean. Protected by shark nets and lifeguards, surfers and body-boarders are kept apart from swimmers.

Cinemas, restaurants, pubs, fast-food shops, amusement arcades and flea markets vie for business, especially as dusk breaks and people of many races stroll the promenade before gradually filling the various sea-facing balconies of hotels and bars. Southward from here, as far as a gigantic headland called The Bluff, is a series of such safe, pleasant swimming spots as those around the beaches of Brighton and Cave Rock. With relaxing walks through the bush almost to the water's edge, a trail continues to the south's seaside capital of Amanzimtoti. Durban's Botanical Gardens are a particular attraction on fine days, when people sail, swim, run or play tennis, and Music by the Lake evenings feature the famous KwaZulu-Natal Philharmonic Orchestra.

people make places

Famous names with strong political, historical or cultural links to the province include noted warrior kings, military strategists, and human rights activists whose world-changing deeds have been captured in various celebrated movies and documentaries, such as Shaka Zulu, Sir Winston Churchill, Mahatma Gandhi and General Louis Botha, to name only an outstanding few. KwaZulu-Natal bears the imprints of these greats, and it's fascinating for visitors to the region to go around seeing the places where these characters each played what can only be considered as major roles in shaping the history and future of modern South Africa through bloodletting, bravery and ultimate

THIS PAGE (FROM TOP): Streets have been renamed to reflect their history of apartheid struggle; the KwaZulu-Natal Philharmonic Orchestra during a concert.

OPPOSITE: Sandy beaches stretch on into the sunset—coastal Durban's famed Golden Mile.

reconciliation. Battlefield sites, historic towns, national monuments and museums portray the bravery and sacrifices made by many.

Knowledgeable guides talk you through battles, explaining strategies and naming and numbering those who perished and the medals awarded for bravery. A wreath-laying ceremony is regularly held at the scene of Churchill's capture by Boers in 1899, and you may recognise several spots around Durban where the movie *Shaka Zulu* was filmed and memorials where he is said to have spent time. The magistrate's court, where Mahatma Gandhi had his first 'brush with the law', is now a national monument with a local history museum; and at the Old Durban Railway Station, there is a bust of Gandhi where, in 1893, he began the train journey that was to influence the course of world history. Humiliatingly ejected from the train at Pietermaritzburg Station for refusing to move from a 'Europeans Only' carriage, he vowed to stay in South Africa and fight racism, an act that he later said motivated his campaign of non-violence in India to end British rule there, and led to the relatively peaceful dismantling of the British Empire.

a coastal kingdom

Whether flanked by time-share resorts or nature reserves at your hotel or guesthouse's doorstep, or skirting a prime golf course, beaches are everywhere in KwaZulu-Natal. Some transform into huge entertainment venues at night, others attract shy or nocturnal creatures, and a few are as close as most people will ever get to whales or dolphins. The province has beaches for the angler who wants seclusion and quiet, the four-wheel-drive enthusiast equipped for a mission, devil-may-care water sports fans, and large tour

THIS PAGE: *The Elephant Coast offers far more in its variety of wildlife than its name implies.*

OPPOSITE (FROM TOP): *Zululand is a flowering paradise of fields; a surfer swims up for air.*

groups that want a quick lunch before moving on. That KwaZulu-Natal promotes its
healthy beach culture to visitors should not be surprising, given that it is where ancient
San hunters wintered to escape the harsh snow-capped mountains, and where
shipwrecked sailors and Zulus have for centuries marvelled at the crashing waves and
diverse sea life. But the coastline has many other draws and eco-adventure is a
speciality. The Elephant Coast alone has no less than 21 ecological systems with some
of the world's highest natural dunes, stunning coral reefs and rolling acacia bushveld.
Home to the friendly Zulu and Tsonga people, Elephant Coast accommodation includes
luxury game lodges, tribal homestays and camping. After following a wilderness trail on
foot or horseback, a great change of pace and way to cool off is to canoe, scuba
dive or snorkel to enjoy the 1,200 species of marine life in the sea, rivers and lakes, or
to go whale- and turtle-watching along the 200 km (124 miles) of unspoilt beaches.

From July to November, whales move north to breed off the Mozambique coast,
returning between September and November to the nutrient-rich Antarctica. Up to 15 m
(49 ft) long and weighing 60 tons, they perform spectacular
high leaps out of the water, best enjoyed from specially licensed
boats, although whale-watching towers in Cape Vidal, Amatikulu
and Mpenjati allow the mammals to be observed—albeit from a
greater distance—from land. Meanwhile, playful bottlenose
dolphins patrol the coastal areas all year in groups, called pods,
up to 50-strong just beyond the breakers.

The South Coast's subtropical forests, shimmering lagoons,
soft-sand beaches and warm Indian Ocean ensure it is a year-
round holiday destination. Ramsgate may sound like an old
British resort that's seen better days, but in fact it has International
Blue Flag beach status, along with nearby Marina Beach and
Lucien. The so-called Golf Coast has nine superb 18-hole
courses, including two rated amongst the country's top 12, and

'Noble and beauteous, she stands midst the sea...'

some 400 bird species are known to thrive along part of the coastline. With excellent deep-sea diving at Aliwal Shoal and Protea Banks, international-standard surf spots and abseiling in the plunging Oribi Gorge, the area has developed into a major adventure sport region for local and foreign visitors.

The Zulu Kingdom's prime northern spot, called the Dolphin Coast, stretches from Zimbali to the Tugela River, offering luxury, beauty, sport and, naturally, dolphins. Fine dining or clubbing at night are the favoured ways to relax after a session on one of the many golf courses, or fishing, microlight flying, rock climbing or horse-riding at low tide to spot interesting sea life. One unusual activity to consider is the Muti Walk. The trail, with a name incorporating the Zulu words for medicine and tree, is in the Harold Johnson Nature Reserve and takes people through an area developed to promote a system of African traditional healthcare that includes plant and animal parts—and sometimes even those of humans. Sangomas, often called witch doctors, who dispense the treatment claim that muti brings luck and health to consumers. As one will find, the warm and friendly Zulu people are ever proud to explain their beliefs to anyone who displays a genuine curiosity and interest.

The North Coast also accommodates a thriving Indian community. Just north of Durban, the Mediterranean-style Umhlanga Rocks area pulsates with designer-shopping frenzy, friendly taverns, hardcore gambling, fine dining and sophisticated clubs. By day, the Indian community's presence is felt at serene temples, happy festivals and aroma-filled markets, while Hazelmere Dam is a spot for serious water sport enthusiasts.

uplifting, enlightening

From the steamy metropolis of Durban along the coastal highway and into the heart of Zululand, fields of waving sugarcane and landmarks of military history reveal how trade and tourism is helping to stimulate and preserve the province. Formerly disadvantaged communities are marketing their traditional skills to tourists, with many destinations offering a chance to live the Zulu lifestyle. Township tours and less frenetic rural

THIS PAGE (FROM TOP): Abseiling is a popular choice among travellers seeking out adrenalin activities.; a witch doctor, locally known as a sangoma, casting the bones OPPOSITE: Zulu children traversing the undulating grassy lands.

homestays are easily arranged. Be a guest of honour by sleeping in a mud and thatch hut, trying indigenous cuisine, learning the language or the drums, or having your fortune told by a throw of the bones in a number of small villages.

At another major gateway to Zululand is one of the most unlikely successes of the region yet—industrial tourism. In the busy port of Richards Bay—South Africa's largest harbour—sand mining, mineral processing and other operations have opened to the public with extraordinary success. This was a small fishing village until 1976, but today it boasts the world's largest coal terminal. Marine buffs come to see the special ships that take raw materials around the world to be used in the manufacture of metals, paper, automobile safety products and paint. As one of the closest sea destinations to Gauteng, tourism is flourishing, helped by its promotion of commercial plants and mines. Fed by the profits of rapid industrial expansion, its vibrant business centre now has modern recreational facilities, with stunning wetland scenery close by. The 350-km (217-mile) coastline, from the mouth of the Tugela River in the south to the Mozambique border in the north, includes unspoilt beaches and conservation areas that incorporate the largest estuarine system in southern Africa.

Meanwhile, the Richards Bay Game Reserve features many aquatic birds, hippos, crocodiles and other threatened species that are increasing in numbers as a result of efforts by conservationists and eco-tourism developments.

ultra marathon challenge

For a memorable South African-style spectacle, try to take in the Comrades Marathon, a ferociously tough annual ultra marathon run every June over about 90 km (56 miles), with the direction of the race alternating each year between the up-run starting in Durban and the down-run from Pietermaritzburg. The world's largest ultra marathon has attracted up to 23,000 international runners, and takes in The Big Five of Cowies Hill, Field's Hill, Botha's Hill, Inchanga Hill, and Polly Shortts, with even the down-run offering exceptionally daunting hills to climb.

THIS PAGE: *A young frog perches precariously in the open jaws of a hungry crocodile in the Richards Bay Game Reserve.*
OPPOSITE: *The Comrades Marathon starts just before dawn; runners compete in a challenging race to push the limits of endurance.*

...the Comrades Marathon, a ferociously tough annual ultra marathon...

thanda private game reserve

...guests experience luxury resort living in the very midst of the bush.

A vibrant, pulsing drumbeat beckons guests into Vula Zulu, a traditional kraal and the setting for the performance of ancient Zulu dancing rites. An army of 50 to 100 impi (Zulu warriors), trained by an associate of a Zulu prince, engage in a spirited battle dance that pays tribute to their tribal roots.

The thumps and beats of native rhythms are at the very heart of Zulu heritage, which is wholly embraced by Thanda Private Game Reserve. Elements of this age-old tradition are smoothly integrated into many aspects of the lodge, and guests are greeted with countless ways to appreciate the rich and still very much alive spirituality of the Zulu people.

THIS PAGE (FROM TOP): Commune with nature in Thanda Private Game Reserve's open outdoor showers; the understated entrance lounge leading in to the main lodge.

OPPOSITE: A luxurious bedroom with an open fireplace and a four-poster bed romantically draped with gossamer netting.

Subtle references to Zulu culture can be found everywhere by the observant guest at Thanda, from the décor to the cuisine and activities on offer. A large plaque in the form of a Zulu shield proudly presides over the entrance to the lodge. It was unveiled by the Zulu king His Majesty King Zwelithini in appreciation and recognition of the Reserve's commitment to promoting the Zulu nation and its fascinating culture. When the lodge was being built, over 200 native Zulu workers were engaged, many of whom are now fully employed by Thanda. Crafts by local artists decorate the public areas, and are also on sale at the curio shop.

Nine sprawling bush villas are the very embodiment of decadence. In each, a wooden platform reaches out like a hand to the surrounding vegetation. A thatched sala, complete with a plush lounge seat, perches at the end of the platform and is a superb spot from which to enjoy the panoramic tranquillity of nature. A splash pool, viewing deck, lounge, fireplace and a fully kitted-out bathroom with an outdoor shower complete each spacious villa. With exquisite four-poster beds draped in soft, rustling fabrics—inviting night after night of uninterrupted, refreshing slumber—and freestanding bathtubs placed strategically by a bay window, guests experience luxury resort living in the very midst of the bush. The pièce de résistance is a private boma in each villa where guests can chill out or dine in privacy. Even the food served embraces the colourful culture of the Zulu people. Thanda's signature fusion menu of Western

and traditional Zulu cuisine can be relished in the dining room in front of a roaring fire in winter, or, if the weather is fine, under the stars in the boma or the bush. Alternatively, guests can ask for meals to be served right in the privacy of their own boma.

To get more intimately acquainted with the bushveld, a camp built on the slope of a hill offers four tents as alternative lodgings. With viewing decks and spacious bathrooms with showers, the tents are rustic yet luxurious. They have no electricity, and guests have meals in the dining tent or by the glow of the boma's fire.

Game drives are a popular way to see the plants, animals and landscape of the reserve. Set just north of Hluhluwe in the province of KwaZulu-Natal, the diverse Thanda landscape encompasses rolling hills, valleys and aloe forests. A drive with one of the lodge's experienced rangers in an open game-viewing vehicle gives guests a clearer understanding of Thanda's wild heritage. For those who prefer to get up close and personal with the flora and fauna, bush walks led by knowledgeable trackers allow for more intimate interaction with nature.

Thanda is 'love' in the Zulu language—a concept that is immediately apparent in this meticulously put together game reserve. The philosophy that drives every detail at Thanda is 'for the love of nature, wildlife and dear ones', aiming to create a harmonious relationship between man and nature. To this end, Thanda Private Game Reserve is equal parts a nature reserve and purveyor of luxury accommodation. To satisfy the former criterion, the land is currently undergoing a process of rehabilitation to return it to its original state.

Looking at it now, it is hard to imagine the degeneration it once went through. Invasive alien plant species, which infested the soil when the land was first bought, have been thoroughly cleared and replaced with flora indigenous to the area. Animals which freely roamed the expansive grounds in the past— buffalo, cheetah, duiker, impala, giraffe, hyena, warthog and reedbuck—have been reintroduced in large numbers. Now birds and wildlife flourish, as a healthy balance has been newly restored to the eco-system. In this natural setting, the Big 5 and the Super 7 are thriving like never before.

THIS PAGE (FROM TOP): In each villa, a thatched sala sits at the end of a raised wooden walkway and is furnished with a circular sofa and plush cushions for a panoramic view of nature.

OPPOSITE (FROM TOP): Freestanding baths by bay windows provide an excellent view from the tub; the main lodge's opulent lounge with its Zulu-inspired décor.

Guests will find a wide array of activities to fill their days after the ubiquitous safari. The eastern shores of KwaZulu-Natal are prime spots for whale-watching between the months of June and November. Sodwana Bay, South Africa's most exciting diving destination, boasts a proliferation of Indo-Atlantic species of coral and marine life. Bottle-nosed dolphins, turtles and sharks swim here. Non-divers can feast their eyes on various reefs, pinnacles, buttresses, caves and blowholes. Leatherback and loggerback turtles, the stars of Sodwana Bay, lay their eggs here every year as they have for the last 200 million years. Sodwana Bay forms part of the Greater St Lucia Wetlands, South Africa's first World Heritage Site. Home to an abundance of unique plant and animal species, St Lucia Lake has about 1,500 species of fauna, the highest number in all the animal parks this side of Africa.

While in the area, guests should also make a detour to the Elephant Coast, so named for being the habitat of the largest herd of African elephants, living and foraging in the sand forest. Twenty-one eco-systems thrive on the Elephant Coast, including sand forests, lagoons, lakes, wetlands and pristine beaches that are host to animals such as hippopotamuses and birds.

After guests have had their fill of tourist magnets, Thanda offers a variety of activities, ranging from freshwater and deep-sea fishing to horseback-riding and bird-watching safaris. Because five superb golf courses pepper the surrounding areas, golf enthusiasts can tee off amidst the serenity of the savannah. The spotless beaches of the Indian Ocean are particularly inviting for leisurely evening beach walks and private barbecues.

Cultural tours and visits to a nearby Zulu tribal village can be arranged, and bring guests on an informative journey into the daily lives of the indigenous community. To see first-hand the close connections forged between the surrounding nature and the Zulu people, guests will

THIS PAGE: A private pool and sundeck boast uninterrupted views of the unspoilt Thanda Private Game Reserve lands.

OPPOSITE (FROM TOP): Zulu warriors, impressively decked out in full battle regalia and weaponry; a playful herd of elephants stop by a watering hole for a drink; tents offer unmatched levels of intimacy with the African bush.

be led through various local historical sites, battlegrounds of note and the present-day village school. Back in the comfort of the lodge, a well-stocked library of glossy reference tomes provides literary insights into fascinating aspects of this ancient people.

If leisurely cruises down estuaries or refreshing dips in private pools are not enough to recharge the batteries, a visit to the wellness centre is sure to soothe body, mind and soul. Crafted from natural ingredients such as plant and marine extracts, the spa's signature treatments have an exotic appeal. Thanda Spirit starts with a rose petal-filled bath for two, followed by a rose petal salt scrub, an African hot stone massage and a pressure point massage. A truly sublime experience, is the Essence of Africa Sala Treatment, administered in the exclusive surrounds of the outdoor sala treatment area. African maize meal and sour milk are used to exfoliate the body. An outdoor bushveld shower if followed by a massage using a cocktail of shea butter massage balm and aromatherapy oil—blended the African way, of course.

Thanda Private Game Reserve is the perfect place to restore weather-beaten, overworked souls. The service and atmosphere of luxury which are its hallmarks are unparalleled, and prevail alongside a mindfulness for the culture and history of the surrounding environment. The spirituality of the Zulu people echoes strongly throughout Thanda Private Game Reserve. Many guests have spoken of a sense of rejuvenation they feel during their stay, which they just cannot quite explain. Perhaps it is the rhythm of the impi, or simply the magic of this wild, untamed land.

ROOMS
9 bush villas • 4 tents

FOOD
dining room, dining deck and boma: Western and traditional Zulu

DRINK
wine cellar

FEATURES
private splash pools • indoor and outdoor showers • private bomas • library • viewing decks • Big Five • wellness centre • Vula Zulu Cultural Experience • conference facilities • facsimile • Internet facilities

NEARBY
Zulu villages • Hluhluwe • Greater St Lucia Wetlands • Elephant Coast • Sodwana Bay • Cape Vidal

CONTACT
PO Box 652585, Benmore Johannesburg 2010, Gauteng • telephone: +27.11.469 5082 • facsimile: +27.11.469 5086 • email: reservations@thanda.co.za • website: www.thanda.com

teremok

...a warm, memorable experience graced with all the finer comforts one looks for in life.

The name Teremok comes from the Russian word for 'little hideaway', and it's that spirit of restful solitude and unpretentious comfort that pervades the boutique lodges Teremok Marine at Umhlanga Rocks and Teremok Riverside at Gauteng. Both share a reassuring proximity to water—Teremok Marine enjoys splendid views of the Indian Ocean while Teremok Riverside sits in the Fourways area on the banks of the Juskei River—and both were lovingly developed with a respect for the original architecture while allowing for unintrusive modern touches.

Just 1 km (0.6 miles) from Umhlanga Rocks village, Teremok Marine was once a holiday home built around a large milkwood tree. Now renovated to house eight graceful suites, it retains that home-away-from-home feel. The building's exterior has been preserved and the original doors, sash windows and wooden flooring left intact or re-used on the premises. Photographs are on display throughout the house as a reminder of the original Russian owner's family.

Each of the eight suites has been named for some aspect of Teremok or its history, from the common milkwood tree to the flavours of nearby Durban to the colourful names of the former owner's family. Every suite is individually designed, right down to details such as scent,

toiletries, mood music and confectionery. Whether it's the classical accents of the Juliet suite or the rich intensity of the Zodiac or Vladykin suites, every suite evokes a distinctive mood of quiet sophistication. Subtle embellishments like hand-crafted ceiling fans or antique mirrors provide just the right finishing touches to each carefully customised room.

At Teremok Riverside, just opened in October 2007, the same philosophy of personalised, understated elegance applies. Each of the nine suites here is also decorated according to a singular inspiration, such as the soothing hues of the Kilimanjaro suite, the rich gentility of the Vladykin suite or the contemporary extravagance of the Bushwillow suite.

Where the suites at both Teremok properties are similar is their spread of modern amenities such as an Internet connection, LCD screen televisions, an extensive DVD library and a wide selection of music CDs, as well as individual iPod docking stations. Every suite has open-plan bathrooms, with large raindance showers and freestanding baths for maximum luxury.

The final flourish is Teremok's signature service, which includes thoughtful little touches such as the daily weather report slipped under the door of each suite and a different breakfast prepared every day in an open-plan kitchen. For the guests' convenience, there are complimentary tea and coffee stations and an honesty bar in each lodge, as well as a range of books and binoculars available for loan, the latter absolutely essential for appreciating in close detail the lodges' park-like environs and wildlife. Both Teremok properties also have their

own on-site wellness centre, with a gym with all the latest equipment and a full-time experienced spa therapist.

As a reaffirmative testament to its continued excellence in hospitality, Teremok Marine won the coveted Zulu Kingdom Service Excellence Award for three consecutive years—from 2005 to 2007. Plush and cosy, Teremok is an ideal complement to any journey through South Africa, offering a warm, memorable experience graced with all the finer comforts one looks for in life.

ROOMS
Teremok Marine: 8 suites •
Teremok Riverside: 9 suites

FOOD
dining rooms: international

DRINK
wine list

FEATURES
wellness centres • Internet connection • DVD libraries • reading libraries • gyms • outdoor pools

NEARBY
Teremok Marine: Umhlanga Rocks Village • Gateway Shopping Centre • Durban Central • Durban Airport

Teremok Riverside: OR Tambo Airport • Montecasino • Sandton • Rosebank • Johannesburg • Midrand • Lanseria Airport

CONTACT
Teremok Marine: 49 Marine Drive Umhlanga Rocks 4320 KwaZulu-Natal •
telephone: +27.31.561 5848 •
facsimile: +27.31.561 5860 •
email: marine@teremok.co.za •
website: www.teremok.co.za

Teremok Riverside: 3–10 Riverside Road Beverley 2191, Gauteng •
telephone: +27.11.467 7791 •
facsimile: +27.11.467 7137 •
email: riverside@teremok.co.za •
website: www.teremok.co.za

fordoun

...a holiday experience unlike any other.

THIS PAGE (FROM TOP): *A dairy farm once occupied the grounds; now the sprawling estate hosts guest after satisfied guest as Fordoun; rooms come uniquely decorated in a colonial and African blend.*

OPPOSITE (CLOCKWISE FROM TOP): *Fine international cuisine is served at Fordoun's Skye Restaurant; the heated indoor pool offers guests a chance for relaxation; Fordoun's award-winning spa.*

Where once a dairy farm thrived, Fordoun now sits at the end of a tree-lined avenue in the KwaZulu-Natal Midlands, basking in an air of pastoral tranquility. This family-run hotel and spa complex exudes the promise of warm hospitality and exquisite service, capped with its unique range of traditional medicine and healing methods alongside contemporary spa treatments.

The original homestead that today houses the hotel and spa dates back to the 1860s, while 1950s buildings have found new life as the restaurant and conference centre. Much of the property's charm comes from staying true to the original layout of the farm and using old materials inventively, as well as the sprinkling of old framed photographs, newspaper clippings and notes detailing historical information about the buildings to evoke the romance of a bygone era. Even a butler who has been associated with the owner's family for over 50 years remains on the hotel staff, extending his personal welcome to the guests.

As a luxurious boutique establishment, Fordoun boasts 17 plush suites, each with its own private verandah, not to mention a large bathroom and dressing area. The decorative theme for each suite ranges from various local flora and fauna, to families who lived on the farm, to historical battlefield sites of the area. Many of the suites still retain the building's original stone walls, accentuated with artwork by local artists, local fabrics and accessories to achieve a sumptuous, elegant blend of colonial and African styles.

All staying guests have free use of the large indoor heated pool, the flotation pool with underwater music and starry ceiling, as well as the sauna, steam room and gymnasium. But the real attraction of Fordoun is its African spa treatments, overseen by Dr Elliot Ndlovu, an inyanga (medicinal healer) and sangoma (spiritual healer). Drawing on the botanical richness

of over 130 different healing plants that are cultivated in its traditional African garden, the spa offers an impressive range of traditional treatments and indigenous healing products, and aims to be a hundred per cent African in its spa products one day.

While the spa building has seven therapy rooms and a couple's room for its plethora of modern-day spa and beauty treatments, there are also new African-style treatments available. Carried out in the two traditional rondavels, complete with thatch and cowhide, these include massages such as a Nduku duku stick body massage with a knobkerrie. Dr Ndlovu also conducts tours of the herb garden and gives talks on Zulu spiritual healing for guests.

Besides pampering the body, Fordoun also has its Skye restaurant to indulge the tastebuds. With organic or hormone-free options aplenty, there's something to suit every dietary preference. The international menu is complemented by an extensive wine list.

Confirming Fordoun's meteoric rise as a landmark spa destination is a number of prestigious accolades. It was named a finalist at the inaugural Les Nouvelles Esthetiques Spa Awards 2005 when the hotel was just four months old, and it also bagged the title of Top Destination Spa 2006 at the Professional Beauty Spa Awards. A cosy country getaway rich in local flavours and influences, it certainly offers a holiday experience unlike any other.

ROOMS
17 suites

FOOD
Skye Restaurant: international

DRINK
wine list

FEATURES
conference centre • spa

NEARBY
flyfishing • golf • Karkloof Canopy Tours • horse-riding • hot air ballooning • Midlands Meander • mountain biking

CONTACT
PO Box 17, Nottingham Road Midlands 3280, KwaZulu-Natal • telephone: +27.33.266 6217 • facsimile: +27.33.266 6630 • email: info@fordoun.com • website: www.fordoun.com

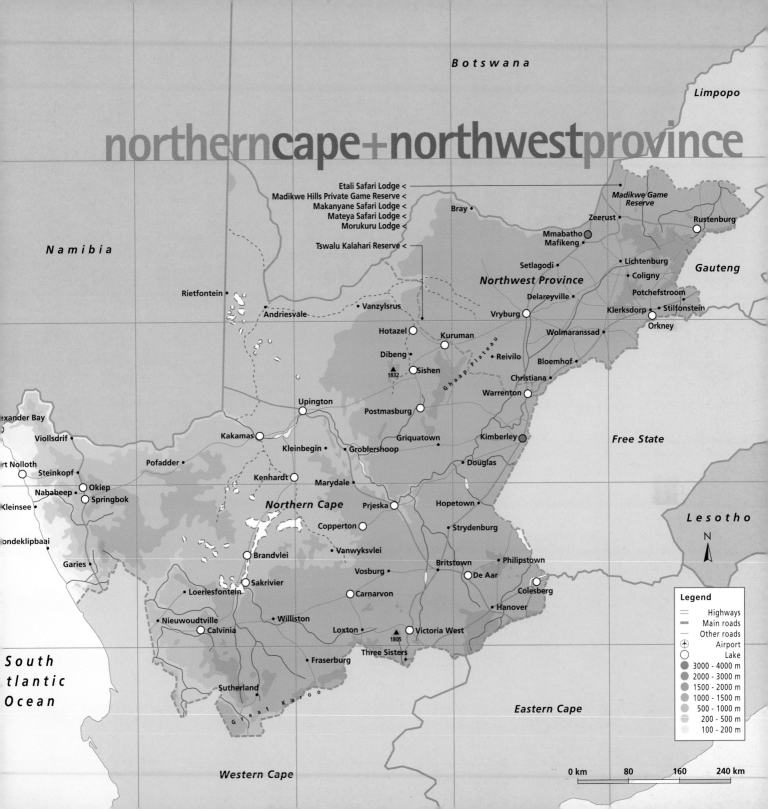

northerncape+northwestprovince

Botswana

Limpopo

Namibia

Gauteng

Etali Safari Lodge <
Madikwe Hills Private Game Reserve <
Makanyane Safari Lodge <
Mateya Safari Lodge <
Morukuru Lodge <

Tswalu Kalahari Reserve <

Bray •

Madikwe Game Reserve

Zeerust •

Rustenburg

Mmabatho ⦿
Mafikeng •

Northwest Province

Setlagodi •

Lichtenburg •
• Coligny

Delareyville •

Potchefstroom •

Rietfontein •

Klerksdorp • • Stilfonstein

• Vanzylsrus

Vryburg •

Wolmaranssad •

Orkney •

• Andriesvale

Hotazel •
Kuruman •

Reivilo •

Bloemhof •

Dibeng •
• Sishen

▲ 1832

Ghaap plateau

Christiana •

Warrenton •

Upington •

Postmasburg •

Griquatown •

Kimberley ⦿

Free State

Alexander Bay
Viollsdrif •

Kakamas •

Kleinbegin •
• Groblershoop

• Douglas

t Nolloth

Pofadder •

Lesotho

Steinkopf •

Kenhardt •

Marydale •

N

Nababeep •
Okiep

Springbok

Kleinsee

Hopetown •

Prjeska •

Northern Cape

ondeklipbaai

Copperton •

• Strydenburg

Garies •

Brandvlei •

• Vanwyksvlei

Vosburg •

Britstown •
• Philipstown

Sakrivier •

De Aar •

• Loeriesfontein

Carnarvon •

Colesberg •

Nieuwoudtville •
Calvinia •

• Williston

• Hanover

Loxton •
▲ 1805

Victoria West •

South Atlantic Ocean

• Fraserburg

Three Sisters •

Sutherland •

Great Karoo

Eastern Cape

Legend

	Highways
	Main roads
	Other roads
⊕	Airport
○	Lake
⦿	3000 - 4000 m
	2000 - 3000 m
	1500 - 2000 m
	1000 - 1500 m
	500 - 1000 m
	200 - 500 m
	100 - 200 m

Western Cape

0 km   80   160   240 km

eco-tourism wonderland

The Northern Cape and Northwest Province share a fascinating frontier mining history of mixed cultures, and offer countless challenges for adventurers, hikers, hunters and four-wheel-drive enthusiasts, with a number of impressive parks featuring countless game and rich, rare plant life that has adapted to the tough climate. The Diamond Fields region's Kimberley Big Hole and Mine Museum is the Northern Cape's biggest draw in terms of tourist numbers, and has just had a major revamp to keep up with the recent increase in visitors. But it's the arid Karoo region and its starkly beautiful architecture—built to withstand the climate—that typifies this area.

With a spectacular climate, Northwest Province is outdoors country at its very best, a wildly popular spot for whitewater rafting, canoeing, diving, hot air ballooning, hiking, fishing, rock climbing, abseiling, hunting and, for the more sedate sportsman, golf. The province also offers game hunting and viewing, and has three major dams that serve excellently for bird-watching and a wide range of water sports, including windsurfing. There are also leisurely cruises on a floating restaurant, picnic spots and spectacular sunsets. Adventure enthusiasts shouldn't miss a ride on the longest zip slide in the world: 280 m (919 ft) high and 2 km (1.24 miles) long, it reaches 140 km (87 miles) per hour and provides a four-minute-long intense adrenalin rush.

The Northern Cape is an eco-tourist's dream of diverse and untouched natural scenery, with rugged mountains, pristine flatlands, deep-red dunes, stunning plant life and plentiful game roaming free. Its open, vast tracts of empty land and brilliant blue sky are seen year round, but the oft-photographed wildflowers of Namaqualand bloom in July and September if there's been a good amount of rainfall, presenting visitors with a spectacular multi-hued display that can almost entirely obscure the grass beneath. Natural fountains empty crystal-clear water into canals and lush valleys that decorate the hinterland with vivid yellows and burnt earthy shades. One can tour an operational diamond mine, visit one of colonial Kimberley's historical sites and enjoy the Karoo desert's original town dwellings built by early missionaries.

PAGE 22: A multi-terrain vehicle makes short work of massive sand dunes, dyed crimson in the last rays of the setting sun.

THIS PAGE: Scenic rock formations draw travellers with a keen eye for natural beauty and solitude.

OPPOSITE: Brilliant azure skies and open spaces typify the region.

over and above—the sky's the limit

The landscape that formed naturally over millions of years, however, has changed dramatically thanks to the effects of mankind; not least at Sutherland, one of the coldest towns in southern Africa, with an average winter minimum of -6°C and snow often blanketing surrounding mountains. Sutherland is set to be more famous, though, for a man-made creation, as it is where an international team of experts is building the largest single telescope in the southern hemisphere. It is set to be the epicentre of the International Year of Astronomy 2009—a global celebration of astronomy and its many and varied contributions to society and culture. Expected to stimulate worldwide interest in astronomy and science in general, especially among the younger generation, the event will mark huge strides made in astronomical observations and research. The Southern African Large Telescope (SALT) will record very distant stars, galaxies and quasars—up to a billion times too faint to be seen with the naked eye—on a desert hilltop away from interfering lights and pollution. The South African Astronomical Observatory operates tours here conducted by experts.

THIS PAGE: *The South African Large Telescope (SALT) looks set to be the focus of much astrological research and study in 2009.*

OPPOSITE: *The Kimberley Big Hole is the world's largest manually excavated mine, immediately recognisable from a distance.*

Mining has for a long time played a key role in the development and prosperity of the Namaqua region. Copper was first discovered in Namaqua in 1685, and visitors flock to the world's only guided tour of an operational diamond mine, kitted out in full miners' gear, strapped up with oxygen-generating survival packs. You plunge 840 m (2,760 ft) to the very source of the precious stones, rubbing shoulders with real miners while learning about illicit dealing, diamond markets, and the sensational and romantic tales that thrive in this billionaires' industry.

Everywhere throughout the province, one can see the Karoo desert's original town dwellings erected by early missionaries. They are simply built, with plain covered balconies, or constructed in the Victorian style, with ornate structures. Houses in the little towns of the Karoo have prominent, covered verandahs that give protection from the harsh sun, from the purely utilitarian to more elaborate with Karoo-like touches. Less common are the ingenious corbelled houses, built by the resourceful Voortrekkers, that are entirely made of stone—which has strong thermal properties—even the roof.

The famous Kimberley Big Hole, meanwhile, is the world's largest recorded hand-dug excavation site. Some 215 m (705 ft) deep with a surface area of around 17 hectares (42 acres) and a perimeter of 1.6 km (1 mile), the Kimberley Mine site was begun in 1871. It yielded a staggering 2,722 kg (6,000 lb) of diamonds throughout its lifetime as an operational diamond mine. Today, it is surrounded by old buildings, relocated from their original sites and extensively renovated in 2006, to create a stunning open-air museum showcase for the public.

harsh land

Sweltering summer temperatures sometimes top the 40°C mark and even the winter days are relatively warm, with occasional dew and frost supplementing the low rainfall. Surreal lava mountains and sandy plains of southern Africa's largest mountain desert park make up the Ai-Ais/Richtersveld Park. In August 2003, the presidents of South Africa and Namibia signed a joint international treaty that opened up the way for border crossings within the park. With less than 5 cm (2 inches) of annual rainfall, this is the driest area in the Northern Cape, and as testament to this, the rugged Richtersveld side has about one third of South Africa's succulent plant species. Home to leopards and an assortment of lizards, it is the perfect spot to spend a few days roughing it, exploring from the comfort of a four-wheel-drive, or by paddling along the river. The Transfrontier Park has led to the rapid development of more comfortable accommodation on the South African side, with a number of self-catering camps and wilderness sites offering full ablution facilities.

routes to history, nature and wine

The so-called route phenomenon has caught on here, too, and it is a great way to get to know what the province has to offer. The Northern Cape played a major role in the Boer War, which is commemorated here with a route preserving sites where major battles took place within a 120-km (75-mile) radius of Kimberley.

The Flower Route between July and September runs riot with a thick carpet of flowers every hue and shade of the rainbow, if there has been a good rainfall. Namaqua is the world's only arid biodiversity hotspot, with a surprising amount of wildlife thriving in its climate—more than 6,000 plant species, 250 species of birds, 78 species of mammals and 132 species of reptiles and amphibians, 40 per cent of which are not found anywhere else on earth. The 77,000-hectare (190,300-acre) Namaqua National Park, just 22 km (14 miles) northwest of Kamieskroon, is open all year round, while 15 km (9.3 miles) from Springbok is Goegap Nature Reserve's 15,000 hectares (37,065 acres) of rocky hills and sandy flats supporting some 600 indigenous flower species, 45 mammal species and 94 bird species.

The Orange River Wine Route includes five different wineries in Upington, and grape juice cellars operate from Kanoneiland, Kakamas and Grootdrink. The wine grapes of the Oranjerivier Wine Cellars originate from a total of 794 producers along the Orange River and offer dry white, natural sweet, dry red and dessert wines for those who appreciate fine vintages. The Red Dune Route's creative guest houses, farms and game reserves in the remote, most northerly area of the Northern Cape, en route to the Kgalagadi Transfrontier Park, have a history of excellent hospitality with endlessly entertaining stories, and traditional local dishes like roosterkoek, nabbas, venison and melktert. For a sense of the sheer size and vast wilderness of the province, though, it is hard to beat the aptly named Roaring Kalahari Route. It begins in the oasis town of Kuruman, from where it goes up north to the mining towns of Hotazel and Black Rock, and then continues on to the Botswana border, before turning west to Askham, via the Kgalagadi Transfrontier Park.

THIS PAGE (FROM TOP): *The vibrantly dressed people of Namaqua; a lizard makes its way across the blazingly hot desert floor.*

OPPOSITE: *Daisies are in full bloom in Namaqualand after a good rainfall in the wetter months.*

rich in minerals and reserves

The Northwest Province, which was created more than 10 years ago in 1994 by the merger of two regions—Bophuthatswana, one of the former black homelands, and the western part of Transvaal, now Gauteng—is rich in mineral deposits which include gold, uranium and diamonds. The province borders the Northern Cape with abundant swathes of grassland, maize, golden sunflowers, citrus fruits and tobacco. One should not by any means miss the dramatic Magaliesberg mountain range and the surging currents of the Vaal River. Heritage treats greet intrepid visitors, such as Lotlamoreng Cultural Village near Mafikeng, a traditional African village, and Boekenhoutfontein, a historic Afrikaaner farm, both competing with several national parks for tourists. These national parks include the famous Pilanesberg Game Reserve, located in a long-extinct volcano. It also boasts the internationally reputed entertainment and casino complex at Sun City and Lost City. A popular holiday destination for both locals and tourists of all persuasions, the complex has hosted a number of international events over the years and still continues to draw the crowds today.

About 112 km (70 miles) northwest of Johannesburg and situated at the foot of the Magaliesberg, the jacaranda tree-lined streets of Rustenburg are the hub of regional travel. The Rustenburg Nature Reserve has been gradually expanded over the years, and now covers some 4,500 hectares (11,120 acres) of the Magaliesberg's rocky ridges, not to mention some of the most breathtaking scenery around.

Aukoerebies means 'the Place of the Great Noise' in the Khoi language and refers to the Orange River, which thunders down a spectacular 60-m (197-ft) waterfall, the 5th biggest in the world. The Augrabies Falls National Park's traditional and picturesque domed huts are perfect for all seasons because they are made with stems and culms that shrink to make gaps that cool the huts in summer; in winter the stems expand to prevent cold and rain from penetrating the huts. Moon Rock and Echo Corner are evocative names that perfectly describe the area, with its 18-km (11-mile) deep abyss, craggy outcrops and scrub plains.

THIS PAGE (FROM TOP): *Maize is a common crop in these parts; the entertainment complex at Sun City puts on a grand show.*
OPPOSITE: *A herd of wildebeest are shrouded in morning mist.*

spotting the big 5

Hectares of national parks, nature reserves and game farms dominate the Northwest Province. Self-drive game viewing, guided game drives, guided wilderness hiking trails, game viewing on horseback or from hot air balloons are great ways to spot the Big 5. This 'volcano that gave birth to a game reserve' is otherwise known as Pilanesberg National Park. Formed by landscape-changing eruptions some 1,200 million years ago, this extinct volcano rates highly amongst the world's outstanding geological phenomena. Located between the dry Kalahari desert region that covers much of Botswana and parts of Namibia and South Africa, and the wetter lowveld

vegetation, the topography comprises richly forested ravines, typical bushveld, rolling grasslands and lightly wooded areas. The early presence of man is evident in the many Stone Age and Iron Age sites at Pilanesberg, which accommodates virtually every mammal of southern Africa. The park has many rare and common animals, such as the nocturnal brown hyena, cheetah, giraffe, zebra, hippo and crocodile. Over 300 bird species have been recorded, including migrants and permanent inhabitants, and almost 200 km (124 miles) of solid roads with scenic picnic sites and upmarket lodges and campsites allow prime viewing of the local fauna.

early populations still on show

The attractive cultures of the peoples of the northwest is obvious in their beadwork, pottery, accommodation and music. BaTswana, SeTswana, Ndebele and Sotho people dominate and all have their own cultural villages open to the public. An international favourite is Lesedi, which showcases its mystical culture, folklore and ancestral traditions. At The Lost City of Mogale you can see the remains of Iron Age settlements and are welcome to visit the chief's courtyard, reception, private place of worship and cattle kraal. The Buya Zulu Cultural Kraal is a Zulu Kraal of six huts with traditional utensils and clothes, and displays of shield and spear-making, and frenetic dancing that tells the tales of yesteryear.

Throughout the Karoo are fine examples of engravings left by nomadic people, mostly on low rock ridges. Although they are somewhat time-consuming to reach, the incredibly well-preserved engravings can be seen in completely natural surroundings, rather than from a distance over a fence or through glass in a museum, and are well worth the effort. The early missionaries also left their mark. They had considerable courage and faith in a strange land where they knew precious little about the area or its people. Missionaries built homes, churches, missions and schools—that remain well-preserved—and converted to Christianity the tribal Nama people who were polygamous, worshipped their ancestors and believed in spirits.

THIS PAGE: A dancer performs in a traditional Tokolosh mask at the famous Lesedi cultural village.

OPPOSITE: Early missionaries left their mark on the region and various churches and missions are testament to their efforts.

...considerable courage and faith in a strange land...

etali safari lodge

...combines the traditional safari holiday with a heavenly spa experience.

THIS PAGE: *The elevated pool deck also doubles as an observation terrace, with sun loungers and an infinity-edge outdoor pool.*

OPPOSITE (FROM TOP): *Enjoy the spa menu with hot stone treatments; a fireplace gives warmth to the room—literally and figuratively; don't be surprised to find Etali's native inhabitants dropping by every now and then for a visit.*

Come and discover the natural way to health and beauty at Etali Safari Lodge. Situated in the Madikwe Game Reserve in the Northwest Province, this lodge successfully combines the traditional safari holiday with a heavenly spa experience.

The highlight of this exceptional lodge is undoubtedly its Wellness Centre. Here, a wide range of holistic therapies will rejuvenate and invigorate the mind, body and spirit. Upon entering the spa, guests are greeted with a cup of herbal tea. Soothing background music and aromas instantly create the right mood. A stylish interior decorated with organic elements such as wood, stone and water evoke the tranquillity of nature.

Enjoy Etali's signature spa treatment that begins with a deep massage against the glow of scented candles. After all the knots have been soothed out and muscles are completely relaxed, a textured body scrub is applied to exfoliate one's skin. While fully immersed in enjoying the scrub, a pampering facial and scalp massage is administered. This supreme indulgence of the senses is rounded off with an aromatherapy steam sauna and a shower.

Luxuriate in the spa's other tantalising treatment packages as well. Roll around in the mud—literally—with Etali's Warthog Hour, a fun and revitalising private mud bath. After soaking up one's fill of the mud's beneficial nutrients, slough off the mud and slide into a bath for two with a glass of fruit tea or, if preferred, South African bubbly.

Guests who want a spa treatment in the privacy of their suite will find the Essence package just perfect. This package comes in two parts. First, a warm herbal bath is specially prepared for a long deep soak. Then, a portable plinth is brought to the suite open-air deck to stretch out on while a therapist slowly massages away any tension knots that remain in the body.

For an all-day luxurious spa treatment designed for couples, try Innersence. It begins with an invigorating mud treatment, followed by a sensuous shower for two. The hands get some care next with a manicure—and then take a break for lunch or dinner. After a delicious meal, end the treatment with a languorous massage in the privacy of one's suite.

There are only eight suites at Etali, set apart for total exclusivity and decorated with cool, earthy tones. Each suite's bathroom is designed to double up as an exquisite spa treatment room so that couples may enjoy spa packages in complete privacy. A whirlpool, available on each suite's deck is the perfect spot to laze in between treatments, and an outdoor shower allows guests to bathe in privacy while a view of antelopes or a fiery sunset.

The cuisine at Etali is an exotic fusion of African and Asian. Organically-grown vegetables, fruit and herbs are staples, and the chef uses only the best local produce in season. There is no set menu, and every meal is a gastronomic surprise. Health-conscious guests will find plenty to suit their tastes here. Meals are light and wholesomely appetising, fruit and vegetable juices are served all day and tasty low-fat or low-carb options are available.

Should it appeal to take a few hours exploring beyond the lodge, Madikwe Game Reserve offers plenty to see. Designated a game reserve in 1991, Madikwe covers a pristine 75,000 hectares (185,330 acres) of wilderness and is one of the largest game reserves in South Africa. The reserve consists of different habitats—vast plains of open woodlands and

THIS PAGE: *Luxury isn't scarce here in the bush, with king-size four-poster beds draped in fine linen and polished wood furnishings.*

OPPOSITE (FROM TOP): *A visit to Etali's Wellness Centre is definitely one of the highlights of a stay here; a deep soaking tub is one of the little luxuries Etali offers guests; a succulent beef pie more than satisfies at any time of the day; a band of zebras and one lone wildebeest at a watering hole.*

grasslands, rugged mountain ranges and rocky hills. Since the replenishing of Madikwe's native animal stock in 1991, more than 8,000 animals from 28 species have been introduced in the largest game translocation exercise in the world at that time.

The beauty of Madikwe Game Reserve can be savoured through a full range of safari activities at Etali. Game drives with an experienced ranger will take guests up close to leopards, rhinoceroses, lions, elephants and giraffes. The world's most endangered canine, the African wild dog, is frequently seen here. Over 300 species of birds have been spotted, and more are believed to exist. If there is time for only one game drive, make it the sunset drive to the watering hole. Hordes of game throng the place at this hour, feeding, bathing and preying.

To explore the bush at a more leisurely pace, opt for one of Etali's bush walks. Led by knowledgeable local guides, these walks reveal a treasure trove of secrets about the land, its flora and smaller creatures. Learn about the medicinal value of bush plants and the magical powers attributed to them. Identify grass and bird species and taste the bittersweet fruit of the maroela tree, which is used to produce juice, jam and beer.

Etali means 'a new beginning' in Lingala. With all that this superb safari lodge has to offer, a new beginning certainly awaits guests at Etali Safari Lodge each and every day.

ROOMS
8 suites

FOOD
dining room: African-Asian fusion

DRINK
wine cellar

FEATURES
Wellness Centre • private jacuzzis • Internet facilities • gym

NEARBY
nature habitats • watering hole • game viewing • bird watching

CONTACT
Tshukudi Area in Madikwe Game Reserve 8460, Northwest Province • telephone: +27.12.346 0124 • facsimile: +27.12.346 0163 • email: info@etalisafari.co.za • website: www.etalisafari.co.za

BEEF PIE DELUXE
Serves 12

Pie filling
1 kg (2⅓ lb) cubed beef
3 ml (⅗ tsp) chopped garlic
1 onion, finely chopped
1 celery stalk, chopped
1 carrot, peeled and diced
100 g (3½ oz) chopped leek
5 ml (1 tsp) mixed dried herbs
salt and pepper to season
10 ml (2 tsp) beef stock powder
15 ml (3 tsp) tomato paste
5 ml (1 tsp) tomato puree
1 glass of red wine

Pie crust
500 g (17⅗ oz) puff pastry

Pie filling Season the meat with beef stock, salt, pepper and herbs. Fry garlic, onion, celery and leek until golden brown. Add beef and fry for 5-10 minutes on high heat until just browned. Add

tomato paste and tomato puree and fry for about 5 minutes. Add red wine, half a glass at a time until combined. Add carrots. Simmer for 45 minutes or until the meat is tender.
To serve Roll your pastry according to the size of the dish. Transfer filling into tray and cover with pastry (egg washed). If there are any off-cuts you can use it to decorate the top. Bake at 180°C (400°F) for about 35-40 minutes or until the pastry is golden brown. Serve with green salad or roasted vegetables.

madikwe hills private game reserve

...an evocative landscape marked by impossibly large boulders and age-old trees...

THIS PAGE: *The thatched suites at Madikwe Hills Private Game Lodge are the height of luxury.*

OPPOSITE (FROM TOP): *The lodge is surrounded by greenery, which is emphasised by the decorative motif at the entrance of this suite; a private plunge pool and deck offers views of the surrounding bushveld and various wildlife.*

Set in an evocative landscape marked by impossibly large boulders and age-old Tamboti trees, Madikwe Hills Private Game Lodge offers a sumptuous stay that is appointed with every luxury. From the ten glass-fronted suites in the Main Lodge to the two-bedroom Little Madikwe Hills, guests have splendid wraparound views of the South African plains and can thoroughly soak up nature's showcase while enjoying absolute comfort.

The main accommodation at the lodge consists of ten thatched chalets, scattered unobtrusively amidst an ancient granite boulder koppie (rocky outcrop). Though interconnected by a series of wooden boardwalks and linked to the Main Lodge, the spacious suites are secluded from each other and each has its own broad sun deck with a private plunge pool. Even the outdoor shower and charmingly old-fashioned claw-foot bathtubs are strategically located in order to afford guests a little game-viewing from one's very own bathroom. It's not uncommon for guests to see the odd occasional elephant strolling about near their suites or dassies (rock rabbits) foraging among the nearby boulders.

Every suite is designed for complete relaxation, with soothing white and earth tones applied in a subtle Afro-chic aesthetic. The lower-level lounge area comes with concertina floor-to-ceiling glass doors and a fireplace to cater to those cooler winter nights. On the upper level, the bedroom is superbly furnished, not only offering reassuring privacy but also bringing a little bit of the safari experience into the room, with its cool ochre concrete floors and massive boulders jutting into the interior.

The bathroom is a space that deserves mention all on its own. More than just oversized, it encourages an extravagant state of mind. The free-standing bathtub and separate toilet all boast majestic views to rival those of the rest of the suite, and beyond the shield of a large boulder, the outdoor shower awaits. There's no better way for guests to feel at home in the environment than to indulge in a long shower while surrounded by the sights, sounds and smells of the bush.

Little Madikwe Hills effortlessly amplifies the lodge's experience of luxury, providing personalised service and private indulgence every step of the way. Guests staying in this exclusive suite have a personal butler to take care of their every need, as well as the use of a private safari vehicle and game ranger. Game drives can be scheduled to suit guests' various preferences, as can mealtimes, with a

personal chef, gourmet kitchen and a diverse wine cellar at the ready. For guests with large parties, two nearby standard suites can be reserved as well, forming a private camp for up to eight guests.

Madikwe Hills prides itself on being one of the best in this Game Reserve and that sense of distinction is conveyed in the warm grandeur of its Main Lodge. A giant leadwood tree feature takes centrestage in the reception area, which is lit by three chandeliers and framed by impressive stonework and gleaming sandblasted concrete floors in ochre. The library, lounge, bar, indoor dining room and wine cellar all spill out onto an outdoor wooden deck with an infinity pool. This overlooks a waterhole, making it the perfect spot for a little amateur animal watching.

For the real game spotting, Madikwe Hills has a full complement of experienced bush rangers and trackers who take guests out in four-wheel-drive vehicles. Each game drive leaves with a ranger and a tracker, so that there are two sets of experienced eyes to look out for tracks and other telltale signs of animal movement against the backdrop of acacia savannah and the Marico River. To preserve the bush, only a limited number of vehicles go out at one time and no more than three are allowed at each sighting.

Besides the spectacular Big 5 game, the 67,000-hectare (165,000-acre) malaria-free Madikwe Game Reserve is also known for sightings of the endangered black rhinoceros and African wild dog, with two packs of the latter thriving in the region. Over 8,000 of these animals and other species were introduced into the area in 1991, as conservationists and local communities set

THIS PAGE (FROM TOP): The lodge bar is laid-back spot for a drink or two after a full day in the bush; the bathroom utilises light and space to create an airy retreat.
OPPOSITE (FROM TOP): Evening meals taken in the open air boma are frequently a highlight of a stay; a soft bed dressed in exquisite linen—one of many luxuries in the Madikwe Hills guestrooms; a bath with a spectacular view.

ROOMS
10 suites • Little Madikwe Hills

FOOD
boma and pool deck: international

DRINK
wine cellar • lodge bar

FEATURES
library • spa • gym • curio shop • game viewing • outdoor pool • private pools

NEARBY
Sun City

CONTACT
PO Box 612, Hazyview
Johannesburg 1242, Gauteng •
telephone: +27.13.737 6626 •
facsimile: +27.13.737 6628 •
email: reservations@madikwehills.com •
website: www.madikwehills.com

out to create a game reserve from arid, cattle-grazing land. The newly introduced wildlife populations flourished liberally at this intersection of bushveld and Kalahari vegetation, and the previously barren plains are now literally teeming with game.

After a hot day spent out in the bush, Madikwe Hills has no shortage of ways to help guests unwind. The fully equipped gym is open on all sides, so that guests are never sequestered from the view. Two full-time therapists also offer spa treatments. Evening meals are served in a traditional boma or on the deck beside the infinity-edge pool. The sunset landscape is a befitting setting for the exquisite cuisine and wines that will be served.

Never seeing more than 24 guests at a time, Madikwe Hills Private Game Lodge maintains an exclusive edge while delivering dedicated and friendly service on every count. Whether guests aspire to an up-close encounter with the animals or are contented with savouring the creature comforts of their suites, this lodge has the full spectrum of provisions to cater to them.

makanyane safari lodge

...total immersion into the great African wilderness.

A stay at Makanyane Safari Lodge offers no less than complete and total immersion into the great African wilderness. Situated on over 1,800 hectares (4,450 acres) of private land in the midst of Madikwe Game Reserve, this lodge offers the latest in safari chic. It blends seamlessly into the surrounding bush, yet pampers guests with luxurious facilities and services.

With a capacity of just 16 guests, Makanyane Safari Lodge affords each of its eight one-bedroom thatched suites true seclusion. Suites are situated along a shady path that winds through the bush, and are well hidden from each other. Thanks to the clear glass walls in each suite, guests have unobstructed views of the Marico River and the surrounding forest. Attached outdoor showers afford you the novel chance to bathe amidst the natural surroundings. Alternatively, one can throw open the folding doors of the bathroom to usher in the many sights and sounds of Madikwe while having a luxurious soak in the deep freestanding tub.

THIS PAGE (FROM TOP): A startling visit from one of the native dwellers; the freestanding bathtub is one way to fully experience nature.

OPPOSITE (FROM TOP): The infinity-edge pool draws the gaze out into the spectacular wilderness; spending a night under the stars is the highlight of many a stay; wraparound glass walls provide shelter while displaying nature.

The main lodge, which houses the lounge, dining room, library and curio shop, is dramatically positioned to overlook a stream flowing through a ravine. Ancient leadwood trees, rock fireplaces and thatched roofs ensure the building design integrates naturally with its surroundings.

Guests are given the fullest opportunities to observe wildlife at Makanyane. A prime spot for animal watching is the infinity-edge outdoor pool that seems to flow over into the surrounding bush, and game are often seen drinking from the stream-

fed watering hole below. On the upper level of the main lodge is an elevated den, which offers panoramic views of the wilderness. Massage and other spa treatments can be provided al fresco; guests may choose to have their treatments on the private deck of their suite or out in the wilderness at the sleep-out hide.

Dinner is served outdoors amongst the trees in a lantern-lit boma that brings romance to a new level of exotic. The sumptuous meals are prepared using the finest ingredients and fresh local produce. House wines are included in the room rate, but wine connoisseurs may opt for other South African labels from the cellar. Guests may also feast on the spread available at Makanyane's bush barbecues and breakfasts served out in the bush.

At Makanyane, the wildlife are the stars of the show. The sprawling South African bush can be explored by safari vehicle or on foot, guided by an experienced ranger. Rustic hideouts and lookouts are scattered across Makanyane's private grounds, where guests can sip cocktails while observing herds of grazing waterbuck, zebra, impala and a host of other animals.

Perhaps the ultimate safari experience, however, is a night under the gorgeous star-studded skies, a rarity in this era of urbal sprawl. Guests can set up a bed on the upper deck of a bush-concealed hide, and be lulled to sleep by the nocturnal sounds of the African bush.

ROOMS
8 suites

FOOD
dining room: African fusion • outdoor venue dining • authentic boma

DRINK
wine cellar

FEATURES
private lounge • sundeck • infinity-edge pool • rangers on staff • hide-outs and lookouts • gym • spa treatments • library • curio shop

NEARBY
game viewing • Johannesburg

CONTACT
PO Box 9, Derdepoort 2876 Northwest Province •
telephone: +27.14 778 9600 •
facsimile: +27.14 778 9611 •
email: enquiries@makanyane.com •
website: www.makanyane.com

mateya safari lodge

...a luxurious refuge that prizes intimacy with nature...

THIS PAGE (FROM TOP): *The stunning, exotic décor of the lounge sets the tone for the rest of the lodge; Fire Core boma offers African fusion dining at its very finest; each suite has its own infinity-edge pool deck with a view.*

OPPOSITE (FROM TOP): *The sculpture in the lounge draws all eyes; miles of open skies and pristine bushland surround the lodge; the suites are the epitome of luxury combined with comfort.*

An unforgettable safari experience that is shared by only up to ten guests at one time, a luxurious refuge that prizes intimacy with nature—these are the hallmarks of a stay at Mateya Safari Lodge. Situated on the Gabbro Hills, it offers unimpeded views of the surrounding Madikwe Game Reserve and delivers a bushland encounter like no other.

While every safari lodge has game drives led by rangers and trackers, at Mateya these activities are conducted in small groups, with only a maximum of four guests per vehicle. No more than three of the custom-built four-wheel-drive vehicles are allowed at any one sighting, so that neither animals nor guests feel crowded. As the Madikwe Game Reserve is home to the big 7 game (lion, buffalo, cheetah, elephant, leopard, black and white rhino and wild dog), there is no lack of animal sightings here, even from the lodge accommodations.

All the five guest suites are situated around one of the hills, radiating outwards so that each has its own view of the waterhole and plains. From the wildebeest and zebra gathering at the waterhole to the lions roaring at night, guests are thoroughly immersed in the sights and sounds

of nature. Yet they are assured of absolute privacy and finely appointed rooms: each suite has its own infinity-edge pool and deck, hand-crafted mahogany furnishings and a four-poster bed. Additional touches such as open-air showers and window salas bring nature ever closer.

The artwork displayed throughout the buildings reiterates the spirit of the beautiful and untamed bush surrounding the lodge. Besides the original artworks found in every suite, Mateya Safari Lodge is also home to one of the world's finest collections of African art, comprising pieces from different cultural traditions. From spectacular oil paintings to life-size bronze sculptures, these works are showcased in the Mateya Gallery, while the Library boasts a collection of rare works of African literature dating back to the turn of the 19th century.

After a day of game-viewing or soaking up some indigenous culture, Mateya brings things to a splendid close with a romantic evening of fine dining in the authentic boma. In the open-air Fire Core, guests dine on the round deck surrounding an open fire, where the chef whips up a sterling African fusion meal. The lodge prides itself on its 8,000-bottle wine cellar featuring South African and French vintages, which can be reserved by guests for a private meal.

At Mateya Safari Lodge, every detail is taken care of to ensure the most comfortable and exclusive safari getaway. The exceptional service and sumptuous accommodations make this a one-of-a-kind experience in northwest South Africa.

ROOMS
5 suites

FOOD
dining room: African fusion • Fire Core boma • private dining

DRINK
wine cellar

FEATURES
African interest library • curio boutique and art gallery • business centre • gym • health spa

NEARBY
Madikwe Game Reserve • Sun City • airstrip

CONTACT
PO Box 439, Molatedi 2838 Northwest Province • telephone: +27.14.778 9200 • facsimile: +27.14.778 9201 • email: info@mateyasafari.com • website: www.mateyasafari.com

morukuru lodge

...a private, luxurious getaway in the heart of the South African bushveldt.

THIS PAGE (FROM TOP): A deft blend of hues ranging from limpid green to earthy browns emphasises the lodge's close affinity with nature; the outdoor pool—perfect for a relaxing afternoon with a book; the lush, comfortable bedrooms.

OPPOSITE (FROM TOP): Enjoy a dinner among family and friends, while soaking in the great outdoors; ultimate indulgence—a bath on the private deck of one's suite.

Along the banks of Morico River in the Northwest Province of South Africa lies Morukuru Lodge, an exclusive bush villa hidden away in the Madikwe Game Reserve. Morukuru means 'Tamboti tree' in Tswana and these trees, along with other native flora, grow fast and plentiful around here and throughout the 75,000-hectare (185,000-acre) reserve. As such, it is perfect for those looking for a private, luxurious getaway in the heart of the South African bushveldt.

The exclusive concept at Morukuru ensures that, first and foremost, guests are in receipt of the unmatched personalised hospitality for which the lodge is renowned. Besides a manager, personal butler and nanny to ensure every need, whim and fancy is met, there is also a personal chef at hand to whip up specific culinary requests, as well as a game ranger and four-wheel-drive game viewing vehicle ready to bring guests on a safari anytime. However, its knowledgeable ranger may recommend the early morning and evening to be the best times to spot prowling lions, leopards and cheetahs, sauntering herds of elephants and buffalos, and over 340 species of birds perched on trees or circling in the sky.

Quiet moments are best spent reclining on a sun lounger at the outdoor wooden deck while sipping on a glass of excellent South African red or white wine selected from Morukuru's impressive wine cellar and reading a book from the lodge's library. It is here, under the shade of the Tamboti trees, where one can indulge in lush views of the bush and wild creatures at rest. However, dipping into the outdoor pool during a sunny afternoon proves just as appealing, especially since it is next to the flowing Morico River. During the evening, the candlelit pool makes a charming dining venue, though on a chilly night, one may choose to have a cosy meal by the warm fireplace in the dining room.

If one is hoping to venture out for a bit of variety, visits to the famous Sun City can be arranged directly from Morukuru. Situated at the heart of an ancient volcano, this mega-resort has plenty of entertainment facilities suitable for the entire family, including two 18-hole golf courses, a casino, a theatre and Valley of the Waves, a water theme park where younger guests—and older ones—can happily spend a companionable afternoon .

The magic of Morukuru lies in the fact that it is a home away from home spent with family and friends, and yet still manages to pamper with its friendly brand of South African luxury and hospitality. Coupled with its access to the finest of nature's beauty, thriving wildlife and close proximity to some of the country's best holiday destinations, this is the place where one can't help but fall head over heels in love with South Africa.

ROOMS
Lodge: 3 rooms •
Owner's house: 2 rooms

FOOD
dining room: international • outdoor private dining

DRINK
wine cellar

FEATURES
outdoor pool • library • baby-sitting services • Internet and satellite access • game drives • guided trails

NEARBY
Sun City

CONTACT
Madikwe Game Reserve 2838 Northwest Province •
telephone: +31.229.299 555 •
facsimile: +31.229.234 139 •
email: info@morukuru.com •
website: www.morukuru.com

tswalu kalahari reserve

...new vistas of possibility in safari travel.

THIS PAGE (FROM TOP): *Tarkuni's dining area, with the pool just beyond; the family suite at Motse, with a large open viewing verandah.*

OPPOSITE (FROM TOP): *Massage and other spa treatments are offered out in the open bush landscape; horseback riding gives a unique perspective of the surroundings; room décor emphasises comfort and simplicity in warm colours.*

The Kalahari's fame has spread far beyond South Africa. Located in the wide open reaches of the Northern Cape, the Kalahari is an expanse of red and white sands that is home to an amazing array of fauna and flora.

In the heart of this spectacular landscape sits Tswalu Kalahari Reserve. Founded in 1995 by Stephen Boler, the reserve was bought over by the Oppenheimers, a diamond-mining family, following Boler's death in 1998. Covering a sweeping 100,000 hectares (247,100 acres), it allows guests the rare chance to view wildlife in their natural habitat.

Tswalu means 'new beginning' in the Tswana language, and Tswalu Kalahari Reserve certainly opens up new vistas of possibility in safari travel. Providing luxurious accommodation while still remaining firmly committed to conservation efforts in this protected area, Tswalu is certainly a model for eco-tourism in our green-conscious times.

Tswalu is ideal for small groups and families. The Motse is a close-knit cluster of eight legaes or suites, and the entire cluster can comfortably accommodate a maximum of 20 people. Six of the legaes are for two guests each, while two legaes were especially designed with families in mind, each accommodating up to four people. Walls are uniquely made from fine, compacted desert sand, and roofs are thatched to blend in with the surroundings. Each legae overlooks the reserve's main watering hole, which at certain times of the day and night, teems with wild animals and birds. For total exclusivity, look to

Tarkuni. Available for a maximum of 12 people, this lodge comprises six beautiful bedrooms, a lounge, dining room, patio and heated outdoor pool. Children need not be left behind as they are also well catered for here. Two bunk beds are included, as are nannies' rooms, a thoughtful touch often overlooked elsewhere. A chef is on hand to prepare meals according to guests' tastes, which are served at their convenience.

A multitude of outdoor activities awaits. Open-sided safari vehicles take guests on game drives, during which they might just find themselves encountering a Kalahari lion or desert black rhino. For those who want a more leisurely approach, or simply to venture where vehicles cannot, horseback rides and bush walks with local guides are available. Discover the many secrets that the Kalahari holds, such as bush medicines and the hunting methods of the San community. Sit down to a refreshing bush meal or take a break in Lekgaba Outlook. As day fades, join fellow guests for regular sundowners on Namakwari's lantern-lit dunes.

ROOMS
Motse: 8 suites • Tarkuni: 6 rooms

FOOD
dining area and boma: African •
Lekgaba Outlook: personal chef

DRINK
wine cellar

FEATURES
outdoor heated pool • children's room
with child minder • library • gift shop •
private game vehicle • telescope •
private plane

NEARBY
abundant wildlife • watering holes •
meerkat colonies • Moffat Mission •
Kuruman Eye fountain • caves •
archaeological sites • Sishen Golf Club

CONTACT
PO Box 1081, Kuruman 8460
Northern Cape •
telephone: +27.11.274 2299 •
facsimile: +27.11.484 2757 •
email: res@tswalu.com •
website: www.tswalu.com

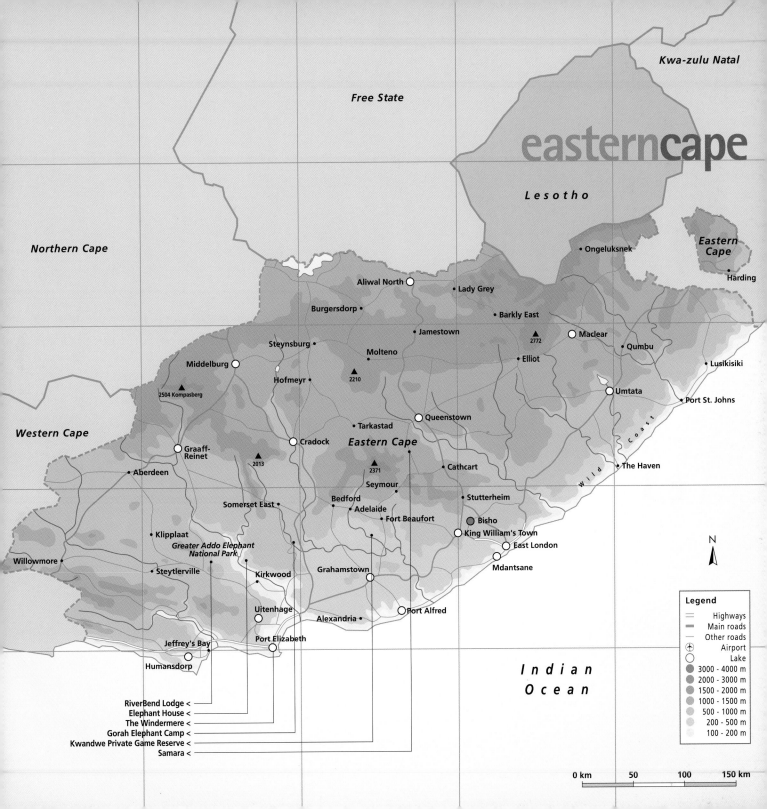

land of heroes and the big 7

The Eastern Cape enjoys an unsurpassed reputation for diversity and the utter enjoyment to be had here. With more than 800 km (500 miles) of unspoilt coastline dotted with historic lighthouses, ideal for dolphin viewing, diving and surfing, the province offers untold opportunities for adventure tourism, the Big 7 (alternatively known elsewhere by the alliterative term of Super 7)—elephant, rhino, lion, buffalo, leopard, whale, great white shark), Africa's most prestigious arts festival, warm and open people, and vistas of exceptional natural beauty.

The world-renowned Garden Route that straddles the Eastern and Western Capes takes in the exclusive holiday playground of the rich and famous at Plettenberg Bay, tiny Xhosa villages and the Addo Elephant National Park's 450-plus elephants and bizarre dung beetle, as it winds its way dramatically through lush fields of pastoral countryside and past endless golden sandy beaches with rocky and remote bays lapped by the invitingly warm Indian Ocean.

Fresh seafood—as is only appropriate to a region with such a splendid coastline, succulent beef, tender lamb, an amazing variety of biltong (dried meats), rich dairy products and fresh fruit are merely a small sampling of the scrumptious, good-value delicacies for which the province is famous. However, the Eastern Cape is probably best known as the birthplace and ancestral home of Nelson Mandela, to whom a museum is devoted in Qunu, and several other struggle heroes who have places named after them. One of South Africa's oldest towns is at Graaff-Reinet, and sports fans can enjoy world-class football, rugby, cricket and boxing events, or join in the wide array of outdoor adventure activities, such as hiking, horse trails, game watching, cliff jumping, abseiling, quad and mountain biking, river and sea fishing, and canoeing.

Even the most jaded traveller cannot help but be fascinated with a destination that has such an intriguing history and vivid contrasts in its vast wilderness; a dramatic coastline, plunging valleys and ski slopes at 'Little Switzerland'; the challenge of catching the perfect wave; and mile upon mile of malaria-free game viewing.

PAGE 152: *A wildebeest stands surrounded by dew-silvered spiderwebs in the morning light.*

THIS PAGE: *A majestic lion at the Addo Elephant National Park.*

OPPOSITE: *Yachting is a popular activity along the Easten Cape's extensive stretches of coastline.*

global arts with a local touch

In June and July every year, the National Arts Festival at Grahamstown—the largest of its kind on the continent—showcases diverse drama, dance, visual arts, music, films, paintings and sculptures from all over the world, but with a strong African flavour. A massed ensemble of talents offer a multi-performance celebration of entertainment and skill, but local accommodation fills up fast and the most popular acts are quickly sold out, so booking well in advance is highly recommended.

One of the most important events on the South African cultural calendar, the festival runs for between eight and 10 days in the small university city of Grahamstown, which has hosted cultural carnivals and rural festivals for more than 160 years. The annual Kirkwood Wildlife Festival, usually also held in June and July, is more family- and local-oriented, with one of the biggest selections of specialist craft stalls in the country. With live music and other entertainment, it is a three-day celebration of the Eastern Cape. This small, friendly cathedral city, however, has more than annual festivals and owes quite a debt to history. Deep in Settler Country, its Georgian and Victorian architecture, dozens of churches and several museums earn Grahamstown high marks from tourists year round.

THIS PAGE (FROM TOP): A musician steps forth into the spotlight at the Grahamstown Arts Festival; the Cathedral of St Michael and St George in Grahamstown.
OPPOSITE: Bustling Port Elizabeth is alive with activity at all hours.

The History Museum reflects the lifestyles of black and white settlers and provides a genealogical service to researchers worldwide; and the Observatory Museum houses one of the few examples of a camera obscura in the southern hemisphere. A journey that spans thousands of years awaits visitors to the Valley of the Ancient Voices, a 20-minute drive from Grahamstown. Ancient rock art, relics and artefacts portray the animals, spirituality and peoples who walked this land many years ago. A 2-km (1.24-mile) hiking trail winds through the valley of incredibly detailed rock art and rich wildlife, where towering cliffs house hundreds of species of birds, reptiles and mammals.

friendly cities embrace nature

Not just well endowed with natural wonders, the Eastern Cape has two other thriving cities with busy nightlife and laid-back lifestyles. Port Elizabeth—called the Friendly City—is the largest city on the coast between Cape Town and Durban. With a year-round holiday atmosphere and more sunshine than any other coastal town in South Africa, it markets sport in, on and under the water and has well-preserved beautiful parks, botanical gardens, nature reserves and numerous coastal hiking trails as well as graceful period homes within a day trip of Tsitsikamma Park. The Sunshine Coast, on a circular self-drive route to the west of Port Elizabeth, passes superb beaches, nature reserves and dense forests. The 1647 Sacramento shipwreck can be seen along the rugged coast, which is a favourite spot for dolphin and whale viewing.

Not crowded and with a pleasant climate, East London is South Africa's only river port city and has sweeping white beaches for swimming, sailing, water-skiing, boardsailing and boating all year round. Perfect as a jumping off point from which to explore the northeastern mountains and the Wild Coast, this city with a slight colonial air has bowling greens, tennis courts and golf clubs with superb views of the Indian Ocean, and fine examples of 19th-century architecture.

elephants and much more

The Addo National Elephant Park is much more than 450 huge beasts. The 164,000-hectare (405,250-acre) park's claim to Big 7 in their natural habitats, together with its archaeological and historical sites, and the world's largest breeding population of Cape gannets and second-largest breeding population of African penguins, all serve to draw thousands of international visitors each year. Yet the park never feels commercialised or spoilt by tourism. The Addo attracts more wildlife enthusiasts than the famous Serengeti National Park in Tanzania, mainly because elephant-viewing at Addo is rated best in the world. Self-drive or guided, by day or night, the dense thicket is true elephant country and you are guaranteed up-close encounters with slow-moving elephants and more adventures.

a walk on the wild side

Lighthouses, whales, shipwrecks and diverse cultures make the Wild Coast a spectacular but safe adventure. No longer serving solely to guide sailors to safety, the four lighthouses along the Eastern Cape coastline form part of a national link, from Cape Town to Durban, developed to welcome tourists. The Great Fish Point lighthouse, 25 km (16 miles) from Port Alfred and 800 m (2,600 ft) off the shoreline, flashes every 10 seconds with the approximate power of 500,000 candles, and can be seen from a distance of 32 nautical miles. With brass and copper cogs and cast-iron mouldings, this beacon of maritime history invites visitors to climb the winding stairs to the tower 80 m (260 ft) above sea level. The three other lighthouses in the Eastern Cape are open between 10 am and 3 pm, Mondays to Fridays. The Wild Coast is littered with the remains of ships and boats, old and new, tragically caught by monster waves or snap storms and dashed onto the rocks, where many sailors have perished. Some have fascinating stories, such as the notorious Grosvenor wreck of 1782, which is believed to have had a considerable amount of riches aboard when wrecked about 43 km (27 miles) from Port St Johns.

THIS PAGE: *A lone jackass penguin leaves a distinct trail of prints behind him in the wet sand.*
OPPOSITE: *The stunning scenery of the Easten Cape's Wild Coast.*

...a spectacular but safe adventure...

The whale-watching season, meanwhile, from June to November draws excited visitors to prime spots around East London, Port Alfred, Jeffrey's Bay, St Francis Bay, the Tsitsikamma National Park and Coffee Bay, where sightings are most common. Perhaps the most well known spot on the Wild Coast is Port St Johns—also good for whale watching—which has become something of a mecca for alternative living where hedonistic young Europeans come to drop out of their hectic lifestyles, but it also has some excellent guest houses and luxury accommodation. The Pondoland region, where Port St Johns lies, is one of the most fertile areas in South Africa—warm, good soil and frost-free. Here are towering cliffs where the Umzimvubu River plunges into the Indian Ocean, and the scenery has served as a backdrop in several major films.

biodiversity hotspot

Tsitsikamma, near the exclusive Plettenberg Bay's time-share resorts and luxury hotels, boasts the world's highest commercial bungee jump at 216 m (709 ft), the highest narrow gauge bridge and, most important, the Tsitsikamma National Park. South Africa's first national marine park has numerous interesting routes, such as the 48-km (30-mile) Otter Trail, the 72-km (45-mile) Tsitsikamma and the luxurious Dolphin trails, with tractors and horses transporting visitors deep into forests. The hanging bridge at Storm's River Mouth is one of South Africa's most visited sites, near a winding road that takes you into the Tsitsikamma National Park. At one end of the Garden Route, the diverse Kouga Route meanders along fields and a surfer's paradise of beaches to the wilderness of Baviaanskloof Mega Reserve's vegetation, 310 bird species, strange reptiles, mammals and fish, and the shy, sly leopard.

The Cape Floral Region, a UNESCO World Heritage Site since 2004, is one of the world's richest areas of plant life and one of 18 biodiversity hotspots in the world. Spanning 90,000 sq km (34,750 sq miles), the Cape Floral Region comprises eight protected areas stretching from the Cape Peninsula to the Eastern Cape, where Baviaanskloof harbours more than 1,000 plant species and a rich and diverse animal population, including leopards, buffalos, kudus, zebras and baboons. This ecologically sensitive area is a prime eco-tourism destination, with numerous nature-based recreational opportunities, including hiking, climbing, camping, wildlife photography, bird-watching and sightseeing. Baviaanskloof's stunning landscapes are unique to the Eastern Cape due to high geological, topographic and climatic diversity. A moderately difficult hiking trail leads to a panoramic view of the Baviaans and Kouga mountain ranges, where you can see one of the oldest surviving prehistoric plant species in the area, a cycad believed to date back more than 3,000 years. The Baviaanskloof Wilderness Area, about 120 km (75 miles) west of Port Elizabeth, comprises 270,000 hectares (667,200 acres) of rugged mountain terrain, including the 203-km (126-mile) Grootrivier Gorge route to Willowmore.

Jeffrey's Bay, with 11 different surf breaks and rolling swells, hosts the annual international Billabong Pro Surf Classic, starring the world's top surfers. There is also fine rock art at St Francis and Cape St Francis, which accommodate anglers and hikers.

a fiery drink in the dry desert

Inland near Jeffrey's Bay, but in what could be another world, lies the Karoo heartland. Many Karoo farms now welcome tourists to sample African nature at its purest—clear night skies, magnificent sunsets, exhilarating horse rides, milking cows, home-cooked rural cuisine and fascinating fossil walks. Becoming increasingly popular as travellers seek alternative destinations, the vast and silent Karoo heartland has a stunning fossil showcase in the Valley of Desolation, and over 9,000 plant species that thrive in very arid conditions. The capital, Graaff-Reinet, has more national monuments than any other

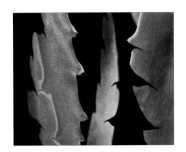

THIS PAGE (FROM TOP): *Detail of the agave cactus—used to make South Africa's answer to tequila; two small monkeys take it in turns to groom each other for lice.*

OPPOSITE: *Bathers in a rock pool at Tsitsikamma National Park*

city in South Africa, but has recently become most famous for producing South Africa's answer to tequila—agave. The succulent cactus that produces this fiery drink is related to the Mexican tequila varieties, and was nearly wiped out by disease some years ago. Some of the Karoo agave plants are 100 years old and the sweet, smooth-tasting 45-proof spirit is now being exported and is widely available throughout the arid Karoo region.

The Mountain Zebra National Park in the Karoo extends over 28,000 hectares (69,200 acres) near Cradock, 280 km (174 miles) north of Port Elizabeth. Dedicated to the protection of the Cape mountain zebra, an endangered species, the park accommodates about 300 mountain zebras and a number of wildebeest, buffalo, springbok, kudu, antelope and black rhino.

struggle country

Not only because it is Nelson Mandela's birthplace is the Eastern Cape known as 'Struggle Country'. At least two more of the most formidable opponents of apartheid have had districts renamed after them here. Although it's the smallest district in the Eastern Cape at just under 8,000 sq km (3,090 sq miles), the peaceful and pastoral Alfred Nzo district exudes charm and history. Quietly developing a global reputation for trout fishing, it is one of the few areas in the Eastern Cape with snow in winter. With spectacular mountain scenery in the southern Drakensberg and a transfrontier park between South Africa and Lesotho planned for the Maluti area, tourism is expected to grow even further. Although roads are poor, accommodation in major towns is gaining a good name for itself, and tourism is taking off as villages open to showcase their cultures and handicraft skills. With high rainfall feeding lush vegetation, thick forests, and towering mountains that are snow-covered in winter, the area is unlikely to remain a tourism backwater much longer. In the northeast of the Eastern Cape, the boundary of the 16,000-sq-km (6,180-sq-mile) OR Tambo district, named after former ANC President Oliver Tambo, stretches from the Indian Ocean in the east to the rolling hills in the west, and to the Mbhashe River in the south and KwaZulu-Natal in the north. In some places, the Wild Coast is untouched— an environmental paradise, with blue lagoons and towering cliffs. At the Jonopo traditional village on the N2 highway in Qunu, visitors can witness Xhosa tribe children's and witch doctor's initiation ceremonies.

early man's ancient art

Since the first dinosaur in South Africa was discovered near Fort Beaufort, many fossils of different dinosaur species have been found throughout the Eastern Cape, one of the oldest land masses in the world, and home to some of the world's oldest sites with traces of modern human beings and cultural activity. Evidence of Stone Age man is seen throughout the province, especially on cliffs along the coast and in the caves of mountainous regions. Many of the much later rock paintings are often called Apocalyptic Rock Art, depicting the arrival of Europeans.

About 1,000 years ago, herders who grew crops and were skilled metal workers appeared in the Eastern Cape. The most southerly of these sites is about 20 km (12.4 miles) south of East London. In the 1760s, Boers appeared and, in 1786, the province's first town, Graaff-Reinet, was established. Splendid examples of Cape

THIS PAGE: Xhosa boys undergoing their manhood initiation rites.
OPPOSITE: The Valley of Desolation offers starkly beautiful views of inland areas of Eastern Cape.

Dutch architecture of the day still stand. The Amathole district, meanwhile, is a land of roaring rivers, fertile floodplains, rolling grasslands, valley bush, pristine estuaries, soft sand beaches, verdant forests and picturesque waterfalls.

Four new Heritage Routes have recently been established and named after Xhosa kings and heroes—Makana, Sandile, Maqoma and Phalo—with a wealth of remnants of forts, mission stations, places of historical significance, and the burial sites of Xhosa kings and struggle heroes. Steeped in a history of legendary Xhosa royalty and tales of early settlers, the Amathole area proudly preserves its prized African art collection at Fort Hare University.

East of Stutterheim is Mgwali Cultural Village, alive with history in the form of colonial forts, battlefields and Xhosa myths and legends. The Eastern Cape comprises many different cultural groups, testament to the diversity of the province. Place names such as Berlin, Stutterheim, Hamburg and Potsdam reveal the Eastern Cape's old German ties that began in 1857 when 2,500 German soldiers were stationed here. The link continues today, with the presence of a German Lutheran church, strong business ties and an annual Weihnachtsmarkt (Christmas market) and Easter market at which traditional fare is sold. And Buffalo City is preparing its bid to host the German national team should it qualify for the 2010 FIFA World Cup.

glorious garden route

With its multitude of trendy seaside resorts, tiny villages and a coast cluttered with secluded beaches and quaint bays, the Garden Route should be an essential and fundamental part of anyone's South African travel itinerary. Prime sections of this scenic route include lakes, mountains, indigenous forests, meandering rivers and sun-kissed beaches ideal for swimming, boating and fishing, with spectacular scenery and a relatively mild climate. Offering inspiration to resident writers and artists, the Garden Route has almost every kind of adventure activity imaginable, including diving, abseiling, fishing and even caving.

THIS PAGE: *The fern-covered floor of an indigenous forest—ferns are one of the oldest species of plant life on the entire planet.*

OPPOSITE: *The Outeniqua Choo Tjoe steam train is one of the attractions of the Garden Route.*

...a coast cluttered with secluded beaches and quaint bays...

samara

...wide plains, endangered species, majestic plateaux and dramatic mountains...

Imagine 28,000 hectares (70,000 acres) of wide plains, endangered species, majestic plateaux and dramatic mountains—and all of it turned into the private game reserve of Samara. Nestled in the remote Great Karoo, this veldt escape boasts a rich wildlife population that is a lasting testament to owners Mark and Sarah Tompkins' near-decade-long efforts to restore the land.

The reserve encompasses four of South Africa's seven biomes—grassland, Nama Karoo (karoo bushland), valley thicket and savannah. The landscape is particularly beautiful in September and October after the spring rains, when much of the vegetation is in flower. It is home to over 60 mammal species, many of them protected, from the cheetah and giraffe, to game animals such as kudu, eland and black wildebeest, to the rare mountain zebra, once-endangered white rhino and elusive, hard-to-spot aardvark.

Guests can enjoy all this and more while staying at Samara's luxurious Karoo Lodge, an original Karoo farmhouse which now contains three suites, or any of the three Karoo Suites housed in nearby cottages. Designed by the South African designer John Zwiegelaar, all suites are decorated in a quietly updated colonial style with zebra skins, antiques and 19th-century lithographs by South African artists. All suites enjoy spectacular views from private porches or the verandah of the Karoo Lodge, and the Karoo suites feature private outdoor showers. The best views are undoubtedly to be had from the honeymoon

THIS PAGE (FROM LEFT): The true spirit of Samara is experienced fully in the spectacular countryside; animal prints and motifs add an exotic edge to this living area.

OPPOSITE (CLOCKWISE FROM TOP): Dine out on the magnificent plateaux; the Karoo Suite is sleekly chic in neutral shades and pastels; after a tough day of tracking cheetah in the bush, an exquisite dining experience awaits guests.

suite, which is located furthest from the Lodge and has uninterrupted clear views on three sides.

Samara provides twice-daily game drives, as well as guided bush walks and visits to sites of historical interest. Run by local bush rangers, these activities allow visitors to escape human presence and experience the untouched beauty of the African landscape. Besides the abundant wildlife, there are also ancient rock paintings and fossils, some of the latter dating back more than 250 million years. And whether guests are out on the plains or back at the Lodge, Samara's Karoo Kitchen delivers a tantalising menu, using only the freshest local ingredients

so as to recreate traditional Karoo culinary flavours complemented by light modern touches.

All told, there are never more than 12 guests at the Samara, though that has now increased by up to eight when the new Camdeboo Manor opened in December 2007. This plush homestead-style accommodation will have four suites, with an infinity-edge pool that descends into a natural waterhole that attracts animals in the early morning and late afternoon. Manor House guests also enjoy the services of a personal ranger, chef and butler.

Opened in late 2005, Samara has quickly distinguished itself among the best of travel destinations around the world, featuring prominently in *Condé Nast Traveller*, UK's 2006 Hot List 60 Best New Hotels in the World, *Tatler*'s 2007 Top 101 Hotels of the Year and *Condé Nast Traveler*, USA's 2007 Hot List Hotels. For a peaceful refuge in the South African wilderness, there's nothing quite like Samara's faultless brand of service and style.

ROOMS
10 suites • Camdeboo Manor: 4 suites

FOOD
The Karoo Kitchen: modern African

DRINK
wine cellar

FEATURES
swimming pool • tennis court • guided bush walks • historical and cultural tours • spa treatments • game-viewing

NEARBY
Port Elizabeth Airport

CONTACT
PO Box 649, Graaff-Reinet 6420 Eastern Cape •
telephone: +27.49.891.0558 •
facsimile: +27.49.892.3751 •
email: reservations@samara.co.za •
website: www.samara.co.za

kwandwe private game reserve

...lush, malaria-free bushveld and amazing vistas of African wildlife.

Kwandwe Private Game Reserve marks the end of the famous Garden Route, but the start of 22,000 hectares (54,400 acres) of lush, malaria-free bushveld and amazing vistas of African wildlife. This reserve, tucked away deep in the very heart of the Eastern Cape, and stretching along 42 km (26 miles) of the Great Fish River, is a biodiversity hotspot and is host to six of South Africa's seven biomes. The mildly undulating terrain is generously scattered with bush clump savanna-thicket, and the north-facing slopes feature Euphorbia, Euclea, Schotia, Carissa and three different species of lush tall Aloe trees in vast abundance.

Kwandwe is also called 'Place of the Blue Crane' in the Xhosa language, and is home to a population of highly endangered birds. The reserve provides a safe sanctuary for various threatened species such as the Knysna woodpecker, Cape grysbok, black wildebeest and crowned eagle making it a tranquil haven for avid bird watchers and wildlife enthusiasts.

Besides boasting some of South Africa's most exotic flora, fauna and the finest of its feathered species, Kwandwe can also lay claim to hosting a remarkable array of Big 5 game. Widely considered to be a conservation victory, this former farmland was restored, replenished with native plants and restocked with thousands of animals—lions, black and white rhino, buffalo, elephant and cheetah can roam freely. In fact, over 7,000 large mammals were released throughout the grounds prior to the opening of the reserve in 2001, allowing visitors to embrace the true safari experience in all its natural splendour.

Visitors have a choice of four lodges, each with their own distinctive styles to enjoy and in which to experience this great wildlife—Great Fish River Lodge boasts a stunning 30 km (19 miles) of privately owned Great Fish River frontage making it a paradise for birdwatchers.

THIS PAGE (FROM TOP): Pool dining at the chic Kwandwe Ecca Lodge; open vistas of the African bush.

OPPOSITE (FROM TOP): The outdoor showers are open yet private; the al fresco dining at Melton Manor is a stunning experience; rooms are the height of comfort.

Ecca Lodge takes on a funk meets futuristic farmhouse design aesthetic, with giant Andy Warhol pop art prints and retro light fittings juxtaposed against sightings of the nocturnal aardwolf and aardvark that are regularly spotted around its grounds.

But if going as a family or in groups of up to six people, Uplands Homestead offers exclusive use of the safari villa where visitors can enjoy their own private ranger, tracker, personal chef and open-top multi-terrain safari vehicle. The privacy of this experience is further enhanced another dimension by the décor, as the entire lodge is set in a beautifully restored 1905 farmhouse featuring three spacious bedrooms with private terraces.

Like Uplands Homestead, Melton Manor is also a sole-use safari villa with private rangers and chefs on hand. Of course, its location is no less stunning with sweeping views of the Great Fish River cliffs. But the highlight has to be its handsome interiors, which combine mid-20th-century furniture with the latest in contemporary South African design. The horseshoe-shaped lodge boasts high ceilings and deep, cool verandas overlooking the large swimming pool, which offer the perfect place to unwind in this contemporary and spacious farmhouse.

ROOMS
Great Fish River Lodge: 9 suites •
Kwandwe Ecca Lodge: 6 suites •
Uplands Homestead • Melton Manor

FOOD
various indoor and outdoor venues:
pan-African

DRINK
full bar and wine list

FEATURES
private outdoor pools • private
verandahs • open safari vehicles

NEARBY
Grahamstown • Port Elizabeth

CONTACT
Conservation Corporation Africa
Private Bag X27, Benmore 2010
Gauteng •
telephone: +27.11.809 4441 •
facsimile: +27.11.809 4400 •
email: information@ccafrica.com •
website: www.ccafrica.com

gorah elephant camp

...an African safari experience nonpareil.

THIS PAGE: *Gorah's luxurious tents offer unprecedented levels of comfort on the African plains.*

OPPOSITE (FROM TOP): *Stately herds of elephants are apt to wander past at various times in a day; private viewing decks are ideal for an afternoon of relaxation; a solitary majestic lion reclines on the grass before the lodge.*

A stately colonial manor house rises out of the morning mists as a golden light emanates from the horizon, silhouetting a herd of elephants passing over the lush swathes of gently undulating grassland. It sounds like a scene out of a movie, the stuff of dreams and legends, about the days when exploration of the African continent was still young. It isn't a dream, however, or a movie—it all happens here at Gorah Elephant Camp.

Combining modern aplomb and age-old traditions of hospitality, Gorah Elephant Camp welcomes guests to the 14,000-hectare (34,600-acre) Big 5 Addo Elephant National Park in the malaria-free Eastern Cape. The name is richly deserved—Addo boasts the highest density of elephants on earth. Together with its wildlife, including the lion, rhino, leopard, antelope and 320 recorded bird species, the park offers an African safari experience nonpareil.

In the midst of all this, Gorah House stands as a bastion of romantic colonial Africa. Originally built in 1856, the building is a National Monument filled with period furnishings evoking the opulence of its era. Wide hallways set with burninshed flagstones, tall, squared-off doorways and generous windows emanate an air that puts visitors instantly at ease.

For purposes of rest and relaxation, Gorah offers visitors a small but well-stocked library, a cosy lounge with a fireplace, and a stunning natural rock outdoor pool. The manor house is situated such that its verandah directly overlooks a well-frequented waterhole, which offers great viewing opportunities for visitors and a constant source of fascination. Sunset is a particularly favourable time to enjoy such scenes, as the last few rays of the afternoon bathe the land in a beatific glow. Sundowners can also be taken further out into the surrounding grounds for a truly contemplative hour of tranquil beauty.

Accommodation at Gorah Elephant Camp comes in the form of 11 elegant and luxurious tented suites, all of which come en suite, with private decks overlooking the grassy plains where the magnificent eponymous pachyderms roam. Modern international gourmet cuisine with African influences is served at regular times in the manor house, on the verandah, or out under the skies, each venue having its own uniquely romantic charm.

Gorah is a mere hour's drive from cosmopolitan Port Elizabeth, so even as guests find themselves transported back to the golden age of safari in the early 20th century, there is always a strong thread binding them to the here and now. It is this finely drawn line between the past and the present, between total indulgence and total freedom of the spirit that persists at Gorah Elephant Camp, that keeps guests coming back year after year.

ROOMS
11 suites

FOOD
indoor and outdoor dining: gourmet international

DRINK
wine list

FEATURES
natural rock outdoor pool • authentic boma • private airstrip • malaria free • game-viewing • densest recorded elephant population on earth • curio shop • waterhole • private decks • library

NEARBY
Port Elizabeth • bird-watching • Zuurberg mountains

CONTACT
PO Box 454, Plettenberg Bay 6600 Western Cape •
telephone: +27.44.501 1111 •
facsimile: +27.44.501 1100 •
email: res@hunterhotels.com •
website: www.hunterhotels.com

the windermere

...a refreshing sense of style and hip hospitality in Port Elizabeth.

THIS PAGE: *Soft, lamp-lit interiors and bright fireplaces add even more warmth to this cosy scene.*

OPPOSITE (CLOCKWISE FROM BOTTOM): *A night spent at The Windermere is a night of comfort and style; outdoor dining is very popular; guests are welcomed by large, colourful flower arrangements; the sleekly white exteriors of the hotel, amidst its lush greenery.*

Staying at The Windermere is arguably the best way to experience the friendly seaside city of Port Elizabeth. This urban boutique hotel is excellently located near an eclectic range of restaurants, safari operators, sporting facilities and entertainment spots; making a thorough exploration of South Africa's fifth largest city little more than a breeze.

At the same time, this exclusively cosy nine-room accommodation nestled in the quiet suburb of Humewood provides that perfect respite, especially for road-weary travellers covering the scenic Garden Route stretch. Its spacious rooms come in a soothing décor palette of muted browns, creams and greys, with sleekly compact sitting areas and huge bathtubs for personal retreats. Complimentary Molton Brown toiletries are provided to bring that level of indulgence up a notch. It is obvious that local *Elle Décor* Designer of the Year, Haldene Martin, has pulled out all the stops to ensure that her custom-made furniture and interiors fully provide guests with this idyllic sense of comfort. In particular, check to see if Room #3 is available—if one is fortunate enough to get this room, a truly breathtaking sea panorama from its private balcony is the reward.

The Windermere staff will be more than delighted to assist guests in arranging sightseeing trips according to each individual preference.

One can opt for safari game drives to Addo Elephant National Park or Shamwari Private Game Reserve, both about an hour's drive away from the hotel. If not, one can follow the Donkin Heritage Trail at the city centre to uncover fascinating facts of South Africa's anti-apartheid history. At the hotel's doorstep, there are more laissez-faire holiday options available, such as dipping into the waters of King's Beach or McArthur Pools to cool off, or going for a round of golf at Humewood Golf Club, one of South Africa's

top links courses. For some razzle-dazzle sophisticated urban entertainment in the evenings, The Windermere provides complimentary shuttle bus services to the magnificent Victorian-styled Boardwalk Casino and Entertainment Complex for round after thrilling round of roulette, adrenalin-charged dice throws, or some good old retail therapy.

Epicureans will be pleased to note that some of the best restaurants in Port Elizabeth are also situated near the hotel, such as 34 Degrees South, Café Brazilia and Mauro's. This city has developed a worthy reputation as a food paradise because of its abundance of fresh seafood, most likely caught that very afternoon. As such, ordering a seafood platter should be a default selection at any of these restaurants, and is almost always guaranteed to satisfy the most finicky diner.

Winding down at The Windermere in the evening is relaxation at its finest. Sip a glass of South African wine at the cocktail deck, where it's possible to get magnificent views of the ocean, said to be some of the finest in the area. The beds, lined with soft percale linen, are a welcome sight for those who long to rest their tired bodies after a thorough day of activity-filled itineraries. Truly, it is only at The Windermere where one will really experience a refreshing sense of style and hip hospitality in Port Elizabeth.

ROOMS
8 rooms • 1 suite

FOOD
Dining Room: international

DRINK
bar • cocktail deck

FEATURES
DVD library • wireless internet • guided tours • ad hoc secretarial services • complimentary shuttle bus to Boardwalk Complex • complimentary gym membership

NEARBY
Humewood Beach • King's Beach • McArthur Pools • Boardwalk Casino & Entertainment Complex • Humewood Golf Course • Addo Elephant House • Port Elizabeth Airport

CONTACT
35 Humewood Road, Humewood Port Elizabeth 6001, Eastern Cape • telephone: +27.41.582 2245 • facsimile: +27.41.582 2246 • email: info@thewindermere.co.za • website: www.thewindermere.co.za •

elephant house

...the embodiment of the spirit and beauty of the Eastern Cape.

THIS PAGE (FROM TOP): *A daybed is surrounded in lush greenery for a relaxing day out in the open; Elephant House's veranda is the heart of the guesthouse, where visitors can sit back and relax; cottages have private terraces.*

OPPOSITE (FROM TOP): *Light shades infuse the rooms with airiness; the courtyard is a welcoming nook in the late afternoon sun; the pool beckons on a hot day.*

This charmingly colonial country lodge of Elephant House is located just beyond the citrus groves of Sunday River Valley, and provides an extensive array of safari and hiking services to gratify any nature lover. As one might expect from the name, visitors to this hotel are, more often than not, avid seekers of just the slightest close encounter of the pachyderm kind. Elephant sightings are fairly common here, but it's also often said that nothing will really prepare for that actual initial thrill of seeing this magnificent land mammal for the very first time.

Hop into an open-top jeep with a knowledgeable ranger from Elephant House Safari Company, and a few minutes' drive away is Addo Elephant National Park, where the largest concentration of elephants in South Africa (over 450 of them) resides with herds of buffalo, black rhinos, zebra and 150 species of birds. For the adventurous, who wish to be even closer to the wildlife, there is also the 'Walk with the Elephants' tour, where visitors are taken through the bush on guided trails with elephants and their experienced minders.

For more challenging expeditions, hikes along the pristine Zuurberg Mountains can be organised where veteran adventure guides will lead visitors through the various caves, waterfalls and rock pools that dot the landscape of the surrounding region. An exhilarating ride in a four-wheel-drive multi-terrain vehicle over the Dunesfield Reserve, one of the southern hemisphere's largest coastal dune field, is also an experience that should not be missed out on, especially since one may even—if lucky—be able to spot the odd occasional surfacing whale and dolphin along the way.

Back at the Elephant House, there are plenty of opportunities to relax and unwind after an action-packed day of activities. This cosy, thatched lodge is adorned with African art, antiques and Persian rugs, exuding an evocative, romantic old-world style that will truly make this a place of comfortable refuge and classic indulgence for visitors. Every room comes with a tranquil private courtyard or verandah for one to curl up with a good book.

ROOMS
9 rooms • 2 cottages

FOOD
Terrace restaurant: international

DRINK
wine list

FEATURES
game drives • private tours • in-house massage • helicopter landing facilities • 2 pools • secretarial services • library • babysitting services • clubroom

NEARBY
Addo Elephant National Park • Addo Polo Club • Kirkwood Golf • Club • Bushman Sand Golf Course • Port Elizabeth

CONTACT
PO Box 82, Addo 6105
Eastern Cape •
telephone: +27.42.233 2462 •
facsimile: +27.42.233 0393 •
email: info@elephanthouse.co.za •
website: www.elephanthouse.co.za

Its two outdoor pools, nestled within lush gardens, are ideal spots for guests to soak up some lazy sunshine and kick back while sipping on the speciality cocktail, a Bombay Sapphire gin and tonic with a dash of Angostura bitters for extra zing.

A truly pampered end to a day of rest and relaxation comes in the form of Tobeka Gana, the Elephant House's highly experienced in-house masseuse, who will be only too pleased to provide a soothing full body massage treatment, removing any residual kinks and tension from the body. Later on in the evenings, dine in true Cape style with a three-course candlelit meal prepared by the chefs using the very best and freshest of local produce.

With the dawn of each new day comes the promise of even more excitement and activity to come, whether it be going on a guided horseback trail at the National Park, taking a panoramic helicopter ride to a secluded beach, or exotic gameviewing at the Schotia Private Game Reserve nearby. The possibilities are endless at Elephant House, an authentic representation and embodiment of the spirit and beauty of the Eastern Cape.

riverbend lodge

Anchored on endless horizons, flanked by the majestic Zuurberg mountains...

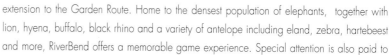

Revitalise the soul and spirit and discover the tranquil, natural beauty at RiverBend Lodge. Anchored on endless horizons, flanked by the majestic Zuurberg mountains and situated within the 14,000-hectare (34,600-acre) private concession of the Addo Elephant National Park, this is Africa at its best.

A mere 45 minutes from Port Elizabeth, this area enjoys a mild climate and is a natural extension to the Garden Route. Home to the densest population of elephants, together with lion, hyena, buffalo, black rhino and a variety of antelope including eland, zebra, hartebeest and more, RiverBend offers a memorable game experience. Special attention is also paid to smaller and more unusual game such as the endangered flightless-dung beetle, the shy Cape fox, more than 300 bird species and many others. Most well known, however, are the gentle Addo elephants, quite unlike their relatives in the Kruger and other parts of Africa. Exclusive to RiverBend is the opportunity of tracking the baby twin elephants of the herd—the first time in recorded history of such a surviving pair.

Dining at RiverBend is a celebration of simplicity and style. Meals can be enjoyed in the privacy of one's suite or in the elegant dining room. Informal lunches are served on the verandah overlooking the watering hole or as a bush picnic. Executive chef Christopher Witham prepares exceptional meals, served in the finest Colonial tradition and accompanied by carefully selected wines.

THIS PAGE (FROM RIGHT): RiverBend Lodge is located in the Greater Addo Elephant National Park; enjoy a glass of champagne while watching the sun set.

OPPOSITE (FROM TOP): An understated country elegance prevails here at RiverBend and is a delightful contrast to the park's ruggedness; enjoy gourmet meals prepared by RiverBend's private chef.

ROOMS
8 suites • Long Hope Villa: 3 rooms

FOOD
various venues and private chef: New World fusion and Mediterranean

DRINK
lounge • bar

FEATURES
pool • watering hole • Vitality Studio • game-drive vehicles

NEARBY
River Bend Private Conservancy and Wildlife Rehabilitation Centre • River Bend Citrus Farm • Grahamstown • Garden Route

CONTACT
PO Box 249, Addo 6105 Eastern Cape •
telephone: +27.42.233 0161 •
facsimile: +27.42 233 0162 •
email: reservations@riverbend.za.com •
website: www.riverbend.za.com

RiverBend offers a choice in luxury accommodation; the 8-suite Lodge or the newly launched Long Hope Villa—an exclusive use safari villa. Lodge suites offer spacious en-suite accommodation with verandahs that open onto the bushveld. There is also a Vitality Health Studio offering pampering treatments after game drives. The Long Hope Villa, a beautifully renovated farmhouse dating back to the early 1900s, comprises 3 en-suite bedrooms with walk-in wardrobes, open-plan lounge, dining and bar area that opens up onto the verandah. There is a also a well stocked library and an interactive kitchen. Guests can can enjoy total privacy in the garden and pool or take a stroll to the Sunset Deck to unwind, sip cocktails and watch the sun set over the plains. The villa comes with a personal guide, butler and chef.

Children of all ages are welcome at both properties and dedicated children's activities, family game drives as well as a play room are available. Interleading rooms at the Lodge are available for families, while at the villa families can enjoy exclusive use of the property.

A wide range of activities is available at RiverBend and include tailor-made game drives hosted by experienced guides, bush walks, picnics in the Zuurberg Mountains, and visits to the RiverBend Wildlife Rehabilitation Centre. Additional activities arranged on request include historical tours, Elephant-back safaris, horse-riding safaris, scenic flights and more.

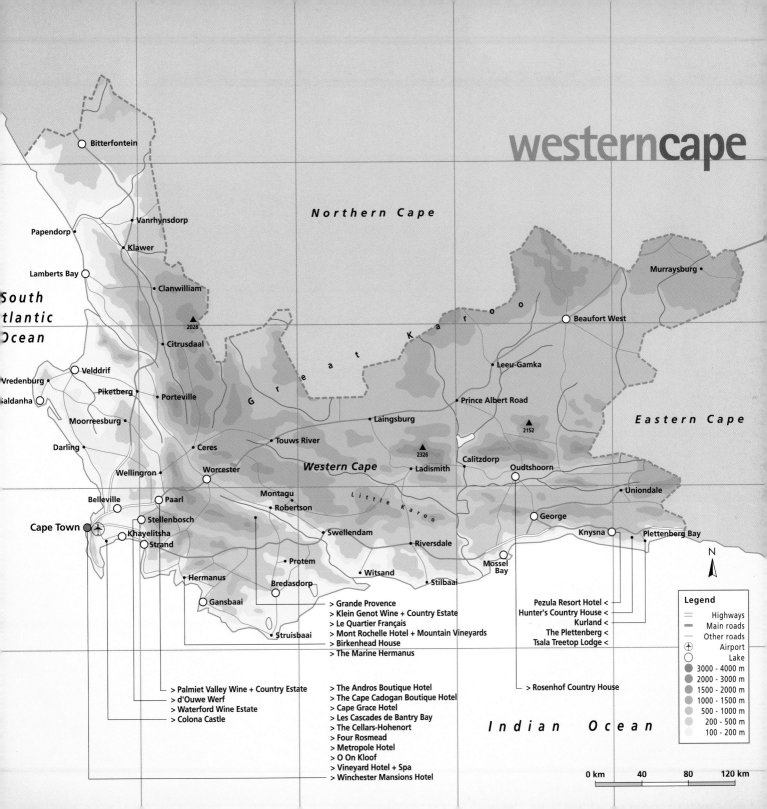

westerncape

Northern Cape

Eastern Cape

Western Cape

Great Karoo

Little Karoo

South Atlantic Ocean

Indian Ocean

Bitterfontein

Vanrhynsdorp

Papendorp

Klawer

Lamberts Bay

Clanwilliam

2028

Citrusdaal

Velddrif

Vredenburg

Piketberg

Porteville

Saldanha

Moorreesburg

Darling

Ceres

Touws River

Wellingron

Worcester

Belleville

Paarl

Montagu

Robertson

Cape Town

Stellenbosch

Khayelitsha

Strand

Swellendam

Hermanus

Protem

Bredasdorp

Gansbaai

Witsand

Struisbaai

Murraysburg

Beaufort West

Leeu-Gamka

Prince Albert Road

2152

Laingsburg

2326

Ladismith

Calitzdorp

Oudtshoorn

Uniondale

George

Knysna

Plettenberg Bay

Mossel Bay

Riversdale

Stilbaai

Pezula Resort Hotel <
Hunter's Country House <
Kurland <
The Plettenberg <
Tsala Treetop Lodge <

> Grande Provence
> Klein Genot Wine + Country Estate
> Le Quartier Français
> Mont Rochelle Hotel + Mountain Vineyards
> Birkenhead House
> The Marine Hermanus

> Palmiet Valley Wine + Country Estate
> d'Ouwe Werf
> Waterford Wine Estate
> Colona Castle

> The Andros Boutique Hotel
> The Cape Cadogan Boutique Hotel
> Cape Grace Hotel
> Les Cascades de Bantry Bay
> The Cellars-Hohenort
> Four Rosmead
> Metropole Hotel
> O On Kloof
> Vineyard Hotel + Spa
> Winchester Mansions Hotel

> Rosenhof Country House

Legend

— Highways
— Main roads
— Other roads
⊕ Airport
○ Lake
● 3000 - 4000 m
● 2000 - 3000 m
● 1500 - 2000 m
● 1000 - 1500 m
● 500 - 1000 m
● 200 - 500 m
● 100 - 200 m

0 km   40   80   120 km

N

spectacular starting point for provincial wonders

Cape Town—the Tavern of the Seas—is the most well-known of the Western Cape's draws, but this city of contrasting fortunes and diverse cultures is just the entry point to a province of beauty, historical significance and adventure opportunities. The designer stores and fine dining restaurants at the Victoria and Alfred (V&A) Waterfront, a sleazy dockside haunt a few years ago, are packed.

Just 30 minutes' drive from the city's luxury hotel district is wine country, where cellar visits and wine tastings are held in mountain settings. Traversing hairpin passes and quiet country lanes, one discovers fine European cuisine and local delicacies. The Garden Route stretches from Swellendam to the ostrich farming haven of Oudtshoorn, and east to exclusive Plettenberg Bay and beyond into the Eastern Cape.

An hour from Cape Town is Hermanus, near the southernmost tip of Africa and home to the Southern Right Whale. This is said to be the best land-based spot in the world where one can get close to these magnificent mammals. Other towns, such as Arniston and Struisbaai are peaceful havens that have preserved their country ways.

The west coast is different again. Its windy coastline with chilly seas and a rugged beauty bursts into amazing colour every September, as thousands of species of flowers bloom in the spring. But apart from in these four distinct regions, travellers can find so many more treasures and never be short of fine food, friendly locals and entertainment.

tavern of the seas

Visitors need at least a week for interesting day-trips around Cape Town, even without shopping, eating and sightseeing at the Waterfront. You can hear legends and sad tales about Robben Island from former political prisoners who were incarcerated there, 9 km (5.6 miles) off the shore of Table Bay. They recount their harrowing experiences during an enlightening tour of the former prison and island.

PAGE 178: *A row of colourful beach huts at Muizenberg.*

THIS PAGE: *Boats along the lively Victoria & Alfred Waterfront.*

OPPOSITE: *A stunning aerial view of the Cape of Good Hope, the southwesternmost tip of Africa.*

Visible from 200 km (124 miles) out to sea, the flat-topped Table Mountain is the spiritual, cultural and suburban heart and soul of Cape Town. The vast 350-million-year-old sandstone block is 1,086 m (3,562 ft) high and stretches some 3 km (1.9 miles). An aerial cable-way that was built in 1929, but restored more recently, allows visitors to glide up and down in seconds, missing the mountain's sharp rocks and crevices by some rather thrillingly narrow margins. Established paths also allow visitors to hike up or down, the weather at any time of year can change abruptly and without warning. Thick cloud can suddenly envelop the mountain and cold snaps descend from all directions.

The 528-hectare (1,300-acre) Kirstenbosch National Botanical Gardens is world-renowned for its beautiful and diverse flora, indigenous South African plants and impressive setting on the eastern slopes of Table Mountain. With a visitors' centre, gardening-themed retail outlets, a coffee shop and restaurants, the gardens provide a thoroughly relaxing way to spend an afternoon, especially on Sundays from December to March, when sunset concerts are held on the lawns. Craft markets located opposite Kirstenbosch open on the last Sunday of most months.

THIS PAGE: The heart and soul of Cape Town, Table Mountain is lit up splendidly in the evenings.

OPPOSITE (FROM TOP): Cape Town spread out at the foot of Table Mountain, in a wash of light; a clutch of pincushion protea flowers, one of the many types of flora that characterise much of the Western Cape's botany.

drake's fairest cape of them all

Some of the Cape peninsula's best swimming resorts are in False Bay and perhaps the most picturesque is Boulders Beach at Simon's Town. Most popular of all is the world's biggest land-based habitat of the jackass, or African, penguin, which can be seen up close from marked paths in the reserve. 'The Fairest Cape of Them All', as Sir Francis Drake called it, includes False Bay and 7,680 protected hectares (19,000 acres) of the most southerly parts of the Cape Peninsula.

Sliced into dramatically plunging cliffs cloaking the 529-m (1,740-ft) Chapman's Peak is perhaps the world's most spectacular scenic drive. Brilliantly coloured layers of red, orange and yellow sit together with dark lines of manganese at this destination favoured by Capetonians for a weekend afternoon drive. At one end of Chapman's Peak Drive, Hout Bay has been transformed from a sleepy village just a decade or so ago to an exclusive suburban retreat, but retains its quaint working harbour to the delight of many visitors. Wet and wild in the winter, Hout Bay has a mountainous setting and popular wharf with numerous markets and restaurants serving freshly caught seafood.

festive atmosphere showcases diverse cultures

There is probably no better way to understand a destination than to take part in its local festivals or cultural events, of which Cape Town and the Western Cape have plenty. Since its inception after the first democratic elections in 1994, which heralded freedom of sexual orientation in South Africa, the annual Mother City Queer Project Festival has become one of the biggest gay and lesbian events in the world. Flamboyant costumes and a party playground with themed stages and dance arenas create a celebration of sexual diversity. Every December, Africa's biggest gay gathering helps put Cape Town squarely on the international map of gay culture. Culminating in a weekend of wild festivities, it draws over 80,000 people, and helps kick-start the summer season.

The New Year is celebrated in earnest, mostly by the mixed race community in a bright, colourful, noisy and musical fashion with the Cape Minstrel Carnival, or Tweede Nuwejaar. Cape Town's biggest carnival, popularly called the Coon Carnival, and its extravagant parades dominate the city for several days. With its roots in the 18th century, when slaves celebrated their only day off by practicing skills learnt from minstrel entertainers on visiting American ocean liners, the street parade starts in the Muslim area of District Six and has many local delicacies on sale along the route.

Until the region became a year-round destination, May used to mark the start of what used to be marketed by tourism authorities as the Secret Season, when visitor numbers and most prices start to fall. It is also when South Africa's biggest culinary event puts on a gastronomic extravaganza. The quality of service, standard of food and all-round ambience of the province's top eating places are put under the spotlight at the Cape Gourmet Festival and some great bargains and promotions are available during the food and beverage industry's start of the relatively quiet winter season.

THIS PAGE: Flamboyant costumes and a party atmosphere flood the streets of Cape Town during its annual gay festival/parade.

OPPOSITE: The brightly coloured houses of the Bo-Kaap region.

The annual Cape Town International Jazz Festival, meanwhile, held at the city's impressive International Convention Centre in late March, has featured star-studded line-ups in its eight years since being launched by local artists, with domestic and international acts often performing to sell-out crowds.

The Two Oceans Marathon, run according to the rules of the International Federation of Athletics Federations, attracts over 20,000 participants and many more spectators to its 56 km (35 miles) of open road and tough mountain sections. It passes the spectacular summits of Chapman's Peak, and some of the city's most salubrious suburbs are closed off as locals swarm to catch a glimpse of the runners.

colourful peoples of a historic province

Direct descendants of political exiles sent from the East Indies as slaves by Dutch settlers more than 300 years ago, the colourful and friendly Cape Malays of the Western Cape have strong traditions and close, sharing communities. Cobbled streets and brightly painted Georgian-style houses are characteristic of the historic Bo-Kaap inner-city area of Cape Town, where Cape Malays first settled. But today, the majority of them live on the Cape Flats to where they were forcibly moved in the 1960s, and rural areas of the Western Cape where they traditionally work on farms. Malay culture may be best sampled through food, most famously the sweet and spicy mutton curry.

With such a huge coastline, fishing folk have, naturally, left their mark. In coastal villages such as Yzerfontein, Hout Bay, Kalk Bay, Struisbaai and Arniston, fishermen learnt their commercial angling skills from their fathers, and their fathers before them. With brightly painted boats, they leave early and return in the afternoon with snoek, yellowtail, mackerel and cob to sell at markets or from the boots of their cars parked at junctions of busy roads. Friendly and down to earth, they are always ready to swap

cheeky banter with strangers. Provincial fishing village life is simple, with hard work for small rewards, but few ever complain as it provides them with freedom and solitude.

The black townships today are, relatively, flourishing; residents take pride in their homes, jobs and communities. However, townships are still unsafe for strangers, so the best way to visit one is to join an organised tour group that takes in local shebeens (bars), some of which serve traditional treats such as samp and beans, wood-fried meat and morogo (wild spinach). If nothing else, townships are vibey places with positive people who don't dwell on bad fortune. Kwaito—South Africa's answer to House music—is the preferred music of the young, and African Jazz is heard everywhere. Life here thrives on its sense of community and belonging, which is reflected in its favourite word 'ubuntu', or togetherness.

musical tribute to many cultures

The Western Cape is a hotbed of musical creativity. Countless radio stations and nightclubs have bred generations of musicians who perform at city centres and suburban venues open to all. Melancholic township swing and sweet African Jazz has survived many fads, but endures today at a number of live-music spots regularly featuring top local and foreign talent. One suburban café is entirely devoted to drumming and, in April, the town of Oudtshoorn hosts the Klein Karoo Nasionale Kunstefees, a serious celebration of Afrikaans music and culture. Live contemporary jazz features throughout the Western Cape's towns, resorts and cities.

Each year, there are more than 100 classical music concerts by the Cape Town Philharmonic Orchestra at the Cape Town City Hall and other venues, while the Cape Winelands area has the very best in student classical music. There is also the very popular Aqua Opera in February at the Waterfront, and the Spring Opera Festival in September. However, the most memorable musical experience for many visitors to South Africa is at St George's Mall in downtown Cape Town—an unofficial festival of live

THIS PAGE: A lone dancer stands under the bright spotlights at a South African dance festival.

OPPOSITE: Hout Bay is among the few fishing ports in the Western Cape that have kept strongly to their traditional ways of life.

local music held on most days and at which African tribal dancers ululate and act out traditional rituals—war cries, the clattering of beadwork, and folkloric lyrics—or perform the famous Gumboot Dance's boot-slapping and stomping, which originated in the gold mines upcountry. In a great free show—although tips are very much appreciated—African song and dance troupes of all ages perform with xylophones, drums, flutes and voices, reciting African lullabies, those melodies sung by ancestors and passed down through the generations.

architecture expresses international influence

From the contemporary penthouses of Cape Town's fashionable beach suburbs, to the Victorian homes and Cape Dutch mission stations and farmsteads, the Western Cape has a truly eclectic mix of architecture, with gables, thatched roofs and sandstone still evident. British influence is obvious in the many Victorian buildings, with bay windows, pitched roofs, pretty gardens, solid pillars, thick columns, and precise attention to detail. St George's Cathedral in Cape Town is a classic example of Victorian design, while just 10 minutes' walk away, the Bo-Kaap suburb features the Cape Georgian style, also seen at Genadendal, where South Africa's oldest mission station is perfectly preserved about 130 km (81 miles) from Cape Town. Construction of older properties throughout the province was influenced by a number of styles, and in recent years there has been a concerted effort to restore such buildings, even as huge blocks of designer apartments and luxury hotels have mushroomed city-wide, and home prices have risen dramatically. Township dwellers have created what they call 'shack chic', using materials that would otherwise be discarded. Homes are constructed of corrugated metal sheets and decorated using such materials as wallpaper made from tin cans or bottle tops.

The Castle of Good Hope—the oldest surviving stone building in South Africa—located in the Cape Town city centre is a museum open to the public and still the administrative military headquarters of the Western Cape. It also has one of the best restaurants to enjoy traditional Cape food. Completed in 1679, the pentagon-shaped castle formed the hub of community life and bureaucracy, housing a bakery, a church, offices, prison cells and living quarters. Much of it has been restored in recent years. Along the coast at False Bay, there is a proliferation of simple, luxurious modern Canadian-style timber homes, such as on the mountainside at Glencairn near Simon's Town, together with those built from sandstone excavated from the mountain slopes. This suburb has become the focus of property buyers. Overseas artists, writers and business people have bought plots and, without destroying its unique charm and character, have made the once-sleepy village into a spectacular haven overlooking the best land-based whale-watching spot in Cape Town.

THIS PAGE: Two girls stop by a gallery to take in paintings by artist Vladimir Tretchikoff while a member of staff looks on.

OPPOSITE: The black townships have developed a unique style of architecture—'shack chic'.

rugged west coast a blooming paradise

The West Coast incorporates the quiet but attractive seaside towns of Langebaan, Saldanha, Vredenburg, Lambert's Bay and beyond, with its bleak, harsh beauty that explodes into life in late August or September as the internationally famous flower season starts. Although the wild seas and sharp rocks have claimed many ships and lives, the West Coast region also showcases millions of beautiful wild flowers. One flower route starts in the Cape Floral Kingdom—the smallest but

richest of the world's six plant kingdoms—in the West Coast Biosphere Reserve, in 2000 proclaimed by UNESCO to be an area of exceptional importance, with the mighty Atlantic Ocean never far away. There are many bird-watching sites, too, and the opportunity for shark diving, scuba diving and big-game fishing.

The focal point of the West Coast National Park, just inland from the secluded harbour of Saldanha Bay, is the bright azure waters of the very windy Langebaan Lagoon, a top international spot for windsurfing competitions and a challenging test ground for European manufacturers' watersports equipment.

routes to wine, food and beauty

Wine lovers or not, the Cape Winelands is on most visitors' itineraries. Steeped in colonial culture and ancient history, the rolling vineyards, preserved Cape Dutch homesteads and quaint villages in several distinct regions of the Winelands are among South Africa's best. Stellenbosch, Franschhoek, Wellington and Paarl are on the leading wine routes, but other estates such as those in the Constantia Valley are also set in beautiful surroundings with stunning mountain backdrops and they produce award-winning wines and other fresh farm produce. The wine farms of Stellenbosch are the closest to Cape Town and, in 1971, were the first to establish a Wine Route in South Africa. A 45-minute drive from Cape Town to the famous university town of Stellenbosch and its oak-lined Dorp Street, with museums, galleries, student cafes and restaurants, is where most visitors start a day or two of wine tasting, cellar tours and appreciating the scenic beauty. Many estates now have restaurants with top chefs and eclectic cuisine.

The Franschhoek Valley—first settled over 300 years ago by the French Huguenots—has many charming old guesthouses, street cafés and award-winning restaurants with a distinctly French accent. The picturesque main street's antique stores, art galleries, bakeries and chocolate shop are the centrepiece to the many festivals held

THIS PAGE: Diving enthusiasts will find much to love in the eco-rich waters of the Western Cape.

OPPOSITE: Keen bird watchers can delight in such scenes as a flock of flamingos taking flight along the coastline just off the Cape.

There are many bird-watching sites, too...

in Franschhoek, including Bastille Day on 14 July, and a number of annual olive, cheese and wine celebrations. Slightly further afield, Paarl and Wellington are similarly historic and surrounded by endless mountains and vineyards.

southerly sights of the garden route

From whale watching at Witsands (June to November) to past Plettenberg Bay, the dry geological basin of the interior and fynbos-rich Heidelberg, and the eastern farm and rock art region is known as the Garden Route and Klein Karoo.

Endless blue skies, white beaches, vast lakes, long empty roads, rolling surf, mountain scenery and hospitality make it a year-round destination. The best beaches include those at Stilbaais and around Mossel Bay, with game viewing (including shark cage diving). Then there are the great lakes at Wilderness and Sedgefield.

THIS PAGE: Wheat fields stretch all the way to the mountains inland of the Cape—true farm country.

OPPOSITE (FROM TOP): Fine dining is one of the many draws of the region that brings visitors back year after year to Cape Town; ostrich farms proliferate all over Oudtshoorn in the Klein Karoo and are a popular attraction.

The exclusive golf resorts and game viewing make sedate George—the Gateway to the Garden Route—at the foot of the Outeniqua Mountains a retirees' paradise; and more energetic pursuits such as quad-biking abound at neighbouring Mossel Bay and Riversdale. There's Oudtshoorn—the Capital of the Klein Karoo—located in a semi-arid valley and noted for its ostrich farms and mammoth omelettes. One important geological feature here is the Cango Caves near Oudtshoorn, a cramped labyrinth of deep caverns and chambers made of limestone and open to the public. The Caves are among the top ten most-visited South African attractions, and the area was in the heart of the ostrich-feather industry in the late 1800s and early 1900s. Today, commercial activities involve the marketing of ostrich products, such as meat, eggs and feathers. While ostrich racing is a hilarious activity for most spectators, it is a serious sport of kings for many locals.

One of the most popular tours along the Garden Route is a trip on the Outeniqua Choo Tjoe, a historical train pulled by a steam engine. The three-hour ride, which starts in George, then passes through Wilderness and ends after crossing a breathtaking lagoon in Knysna, includes stupendous views of fern-topped mountains, wide rivers with sparkling water, murky swamps, blue lagoons, endless beaches and the ocean.

North of the Garden Route's dramatic coastline, snow-capped mountains and the colonial Winelands make the Western Cape perhaps the most diverse of South Africa's nine provinces and a very popular draw for large numbers of eco-tourists, adventurers, international celebrities, film-makers, families and sports enthusiasts. The miles upon miles of sweeping sandy beaches dotted with rocky fishing villages and plush holiday homes are a haven for whales and sharks in season.

Inland, golden vistas of wheat fields, ostrich farms, various orchards and Cape Dutch mansions are a common sight. Bustling Cape Town boasts five of the top 10 most visited tourist attractions in the whole of South Africa and can boast fine examples of most of South Africa's architectural styles. High-end spas, international dining, a vibrant nightlife, friendly people and top hotels attract moneyed Europeans and thrill-seekers to the Cape's many activities and locations.

adrenalin-pumping province

Although all the extreme adventures of other provinces are easy to arrange in the Western Cape, none match Thunder City for sheer adrenalin-pumping activity. It has the world's largest and most diverse private jet squadron and the only civilian operator of supersonic flights in former military jets. After being strapped in, with an oxygen mask on, the engines burst into life, the brakes are released and you are soon at 13,700 m (45,000 ft) and Mach 1 airspeed as the horizon becomes a pronounced curve. Descending, you hurtle along the coastline at 150 m (490 ft) and 600 knots before gently landing with a huge grin and jelly legs. A sports and adventure lovers' paradise, Cape Town's nearby rivers, beaches, gusting wind and excellent climate are perfect for yachting, windsurfing and all such activities. However, there are also paintballing, go-kart racing and firearm shooting ranges.

healthy, healing treatments

Just 100 km (62 miles) from Cape Town, Caledon's original hot springs were first enjoyed by the ancient Khoi-Khoi and San residents here. The Caledon Spa Treatment Centre is just one of many places that pampers, from rustic retreats and holistic healing centres to luxurious spots with splendid views of water or land in a variety of settings. Treatments include massage, wraps, aromatherapy, scrubs and hydrotherapy. Some treatments are unique to the Western Cape and many were developed to cater for the growing number of people who go there for elective cosmetic surgery and need to recuperate in peaceful surroundings. In actual fact, safari surgery, as it is called, with recuperation and rejuvenation packages, is widely marketed abroad. Most common, however, are dental, ophthalmic, orthopaedic and infertility treatment, hair transplants and various cosmetic procedures, which are available at half the price or less compared to what they would cost in Western countries.

THIS PAGE: Hit airspeeds of up to Mach 1 in an exhilarating ride in a Thunder City supersonic jet.

OPPOSITE: Horse riding is only one of the many activities available to adventure seekers in the Cape.

A sports and adventure lovers' paradise...

kurland

...splendid Mediterranean weather all through the year...

THIS PAGE (FROM TOP): Enjoy elegant
country living here at Kurland;
rooms are furnished with such
thoughtful touches as a recliner
allowing you to wait in comfort
as your hot bath slowly fills up;
the spa's plunge pool provides
a cool finish to any treatment.

OPPOSITE (FROM TOP): Kurland's open
air library verandah is an ideal
spot to retire with a good book;
the lush, verdant hotel grounds;
guests can take in the dolphin
viewing to be had off the coast.

Built upon the Kurland Estate—700
hectares (1,730 acres) of luxuriant
greenery between the coastal towns of
Plettenberg Bay and Nature's Valley, on
South Africa's Cape Garden Route—this
Tatler award-winning five-star boutique
hotel is easily one of the region's finest.
Guests enjoy splendid Mediterranean
weather all throughout the year, in full
view of the surrounding Tsitsikamma
nature reserve and mountain range.

Followers of polo in South Africa already know the hotel's name, as the Estate plays host
to the Kurland International Polo Test match each year. Kurland also enjoys especial renown for
its historic rose gardens and exclusive breeds, cultivated by David Austin and a team of
dedicated floral staff. All throughout the property, these flowers are displayed to full and
fragrant effect, imbuing guest rooms and living areas with summery colour.

Featuring 12 exclusive suites, each a fully furnished unique creation with its own
personality and carefully thought-out décor, the Kurland Hotel provides an ideal location for
relaxed family holidays. All suites feature as standard what other hotels only consider for their
best. Every modern amenity, from satellite television to heated flooring, awaits guests in ready
service. Large bedrooms are the undisputed highlight of every suite, replete with over-sized
beds, fine linens, and uncommonly spacious en-suite bathrooms.

Standing by the main homestead and overlooking an outdoor pool are the Elegant Suites
and Luxury Paddock Suites. Along with their sister Luxury Rose Garden Suites, the Paddock
Suites feature the added luxury of tranquil private courtyards with water features. Those in
search of an especially peaceful vacation will be attracted to the two Superior Paddock Suites,
located at a distance from the others. These lavishly appointed suites open out onto private
pool terraces with a superb view of Kurland's majestic natural vistas.

Large families will appreciate the lofts tucked away above each Luxury and Superior Suite.
These separate rooms accessed by stairways are furnished expressly to provide children with
their own 'Kurland experience'. Each sleeps four and provides play areas, toys, and adjoining

ROOMS
12 suites

FOOD
Dining Room: classic South African •
Chef's Table • The Courtyard •
The Verandah

DRINK
The Sitting Room • The Verandah •
The Library • The Blue Room

FEATURES
full service spa • sauna • gym •
outdoor pool • satellite television •
childcare • library

NEARBY
elephant parks • Monkeyland Primate
Reserve • whale and dolphin viewing •
beach • polo • bungee jumping •
Treetop Canopy Tours • Featherbed
Nature Reserve • steam train rides •
scuba diving • mountain biking

CONTACT
PO Box 209, The Crags
Plettenberg Bay 6602, Western Cape •
telephone: +27.44.534 8082 •
facsimile: +27.44.534 8699 •
email: reservations@kurland.co.za •
website: www.kurland.co.za

bathrooms. The needs of young guests are fully accommodated throughout the hotel, offering them a more independent holiday in a warm and friendly environment. Of note is the Children's Dining Conservatory, where they can enjoy a dining experience often reserved for adults. Most activities may also be tailored for children, and experienced nannies are on hand to help.

Consistently found on top restaurant rankings such as those from Diners Club International, the cuisine served here is a heady mix of the very best South Africa has to offer. Guests are free to enjoy meals accompanied by celebrated Cape wines in almost any location. Between quiet lunches around the pool, romantic dinners in the Mediterranean ambience of the hotel courtyard, and evening drinks amidst the perfume of roses in the garden, fine dining rightly marks every guest's memory of a visit to Kurland.

Kurland offers the rare and fortunate problem of having too many opportunities for one visit. Whether one chooses to relax in the sun or venture out, the ideal itinerary is left unwritten. And so every year, the hotel's guest list sees many familiar names as friends and families return to create ever more blissful memories on the Garden Route.

the plettenberg

...breathtaking views of the sea, mountains and miles of golden beaches.

THIS PAGE: *The infinity-edge pool at The Plettenberg overlooks the stunning Western Cape coastline.*

OPPOSITE (FROM TOP): *Pastel colours reflecting the marine theme are used to create a soothing mood; Sand at The Plettenberg serves fine international cuisine with an emphasis on fresh seafood.*

Heated infinity-edge pools seem to flow into the sea, dolphins frolic in the bay and sandy sun-bleached beaches beckon. The Plettenberg is everything one might expect from a hotel set in a playground for the rich and famous, and there are three reasons to come here, or so they say: The view, the view and the view. Built on a rocky headland in Plettenberg Bay, The Plettenberg has breathtaking views of the sea, mountains and miles of golden beaches.

There are 38 superbly furnished rooms and suites with varying sea views here, including the luxurious Blue Wing. All are tastefully decorated in fresh nautical blues and soothing creams, and most suites have French doors and step-out balconies. All suites also come complete with underfloor heating and suite-controlled air-conditioning.

If one is after exceptional luxury and total seclusion, book right into Beach House, the new look-out villa with its own outdoor pool and three en suite bedrooms, a large sitting room with a fireplace, a dining room and a service kitchen. And since room service is available 24 hours a day, oysters and champagne at midnight are just a mere phone call away.

Beach House is decorated with simplicity and elegance, and has beautiful bleached wooden floors which add a warm touch of natural rusticity. The main bedroom leads out onto a sundeck and private pool, with spectacular views of the bay and mountains.

The interior is full of items that look as if they had been bathed in brilliant sunshine and caressed by the sea for generations—lime-washed and weathered furniture, a soothing colour palette, sturdy wooden tables, driftwood mirrors and woven baskets by the dozen.

The Carchele Spa at The Plettenberg specialises in marine-inspired treatments and features a steam room, wet room and steam shower scented with cinnamon, aromatic cedarwood and vanilla. And do check out the Vichy shower, which comes with six individually controlled pressure jets. Guests here have been heard to comment on the atmosphere of tranquillity and serenity which pervades the spa.

One of the best things about staying at The Plettenberg is the dining experience, which can only be described as truly exceptional. The hotel's signature restaurant is Sand at The Plettenberg, which looks out across Formosa Bay, taking in the striking coastal views. The restaurant is relaxed in feel and contemporary in style, and serves a wide menu of international cuisine with an emphasis on fresh seafood and local delicacies.

Chef Christiaan Campbell uses only the freshest local produce. There are summer vegetables, herbs and asparagus from nearby farms, prawns, crayfish, oysters and line fish straight from the sea, and succulent lamb. For those with a sweet tooth, the gratin of passionfruit mousse, trio of sorbets and chocolate tart are well nigh irresistible.

For a romantic dinner for two, try The Plettenberg's state-of-the-art wine cellar, where arrangements can be made for a private meal, surrounded by bottles of the best South African wines as featured in the establishment's award-winning wine list. Sandbar at The Plettenberg is a stunning mix of glass, white leather and marble, natural oak, concealed lighting and photographic art panels. Laid back yet glamorous, relaxed yet sophisticated, it is definitely the place to be seen sipping cocktails.

Nature-lovers will be pleased to know that all year round, dolphins play in the bay, ride the waves and delight onlookers. During whale season from July to October, guests can catch sight of these majestic

creatures from the hotel terrace or their own private balconies. One can also head out to sea on a marine eco-safari for sights such as grinning seals lying flipper-up in the water and pods of frolicking dolphins. Plettenberg Bay and its immediate surrounds are a natural paradise, offering vast expanses of unspoilt Cape flora, delicate eco-systems, wetlands and lagoons. There is a wonderful network of hikes and trails for walkers and ramblers, and one should factor in at least a morning's visit to Robberg Nature Reserve.

For avid golfers, choose from two superb green courses near The Plettenberg, one of which was designed by the legendary golf pro Gary Player. Adrenalin junkies can choose from a wide range of thrilling activities available around here. These include open-cockpit gliding, mountain biking, surfing, and bungee jumping off the nearby Bloukrans Bridge, believed to be one of the world's highest jumps at 216 m (708 ft).

From Plettenberg Bay it is but a short distance to the charming and laid-back seaside town of Knysna, which is set on the banks of an extensive lagoon that opens out to the sea through the soaring sandstone cliffs known as The Heads. These, among others, are just a few of the spectacular sights that await visitors who come to The Plettenberg.

PRAWN AND CALAMARI BROCHETTE
Serves 4

Prawn and calamari skewers
8 tiger prawns (shelled and de-veined)
8 baby squid tubes (blanched and refreshed in ice water)
4 rosemary skewers
chorizo filling

Tomato water reduction
50 g (1¾ oz / ⅜ cup) sliced onions
2 garlic cloves
5 ripe tomatoes
½ red pepper
30 g (1 oz / ¼ cup) sun dried tomatoes
thyme
basil
12½ g (⅜ oz / 1 tbsp) castor sugar
25 ml (⅘ fl oz / 1⅔ tbsp) white wine vinegar
12½ ml water

Balsamic deglaze
100 ml (3½ fl oz / ⅜ cup) balsamic vinegar
100 ml (3½ fl oz / ⅜ cup) port

Chorizo oil and filling
¼ onion, finely diced
2 chorizo sausages, diced
2 garlic cloves, crushed
10 ml (¾ oz / 2 tsp) black peppercorns
thyme
extra virgin olive oil to cover
5 bay leaves

Capsicum and courgette ribbon mélange
1 red pepper (roasted and skinned)
4 medium sized courgettes
olive oil for sautéeing
seasoning

Prawn and calamari skewers Stuff squid tubes with chorizo meat filling and skewer onto the rosemary sprig, alternating with the prawns. Heat a non-stick pan to maximum heat and use some of the chorizo oil in the pan. Seal skewers on both sides and finish off under a grill. Deglaze skewers with the tomato water reduction.
Tomato water reduction Place all the ingredients in a large pot and bring to the boil. Remove from the heat and cover with plastic. Leave for 12 hours. Strain and reserve liquid. Place in a pot and reduce liquid to syrup consistency.
Balsamic deglaze Reduce until syrupy.
Chourizo oil and filling Gently sauté onion, add garlic and remaining ingredients except olive oil. Sauté to release optimum flavour. Top up with olive oil and heat throughout. Remove from the heat. Decant and leave to infuse for 5 hours. Strain oil from filling and reserve both.
Capsicum and courgette ribbon mélange Julienne the red pepper lengthwise and keep at room temperature. Drag a peeler lengthwise down courgettes to form courgette ribbons. Lightly sauté courgettes in oil and season to taste. Remove from heat and add red pepper julienne.
To serve Place courgettes and pepper mélange at the center of the plate and place prawn skewer on top. Drizzle a bit of the chorizo oil on top of the skewer. Garnish plate with balsamic deglaze and remaining tomato essence. Finish off with sprig of cress or similar green.

ROOMS
37 rooms • Beach House: 2 rooms

FOOD
Sand at The Plettenberg: seafood

DRINK
Sandbar • wine cellar

FEATURES
heated pools • Carchele Spa

NEARBY
Tsitsikamma National Park • Stanley Island • golf courses • Robberg Nature Reserve • scuba-diving • Outeniqua Choo Tjoe • Monkeyland sanctuary • Knysna Elephant Park • Knysna

CONTACT
40 Church Street, Plettenberg Bay Western Cape 6600 •
telephone: +27.44.533 2030 •
facsimile: +27.44.533 2074 •
email: plettenberg@relaischateaux.com •
website: www.plettenberg.com

tsala treetop lodge

...boutique accommodation set amidst the canopy of an age-old indigenous forest...

THIS PAGE: *The entrance to Tsala's main lodge, with exposed stone and timber elements, welcomes guests with stylish hospitality.*

OPPOSITE (CLOCKWISE FROM TOP): *Relax before a warm, crackling fire in the private sitting/living area; nature is all around—sit back, and enjoy the bird's-eye view; modernity and luxury are by no means sacrificed here at Tsala's; suites have infinity-edge pools.*

Picture boutique accommodation set amidst the canopy of an age-old indigenous forest and filled with every creature comfort. For anyone who has ever dreamed of green living—with a twist—the time for dreams is past. Tsala Treetop Lodge rises through and above the verdure of the lush South African forest to capture the imaginations of all who hear of it and the hearts of all who visit it.

The exposed stone masonry of the main lodge and underlit water features greet guests as they arrive, giving way to suites of timber and glass, interconnected by elevated wooden walkways. There are 10 lavish suites, each completely private and with unobstructed views of the forest canopy and the valleys and hills beyond. In terms of modern amenities, these rooms are certainly no rustic treehouses. Each generously proportioned en-suite comes with a lounge, and is furnished with little luxuries such as a mini-bar, fireplace, underfloor heating, private decks with seemingly magically supported infinity-edge pools and an outdoor shower. For the technophile in today's age of connectivity, there is no need to worry about falling out of touch—satellite television and DVD players come as standard, with a wide library of films and documentaries to choose from. Internet facilities are also available in the main lodge, as is a reading library.

When it comes to fine dining, Tsala's can by no means be considered inadequate. Tsala's Restaurant serves elegantly plated dishes of local and international flavour—and don't let the fussy presentation distract from the food itself, highly acclaimed and perfectly complemented

by an extensive list of the best South African vintages. The restaurant features light, modern interiors accented with African motifs such as a warrior's shield displayed on a wall, or chair fabrics spotted with leopard prints. For more intimate occasions, meals can be served in individual suites, and it's at these private dinners that the lodge's service truly distinguishes itself.

If all the delights of Tsala Treetop Lodge are not enough, a mere 10-minute drive away is Plettenberg Bay, one of South Africa's premier seaside destinations, with its golden beaches and clean surf. Those who wish to experience the local wildlife may do so at Monkeyland, the world's first and only multi-species free-roaming primate sanctuary. Birds of Eden is a similarly spectacular giant aviary spanning a natural forest gorge, while Elephant Sanctuary is just that—a safe haven for these majestic, endangered animals. The romanticised view of safari drives over miles of open bushveld while taking in sights of magnificent game comes true at Rhino Base Camp, who conduct tours through their specialised guides.

At the close of a long day, however, there is nothing better to look forward to than returning to the perennial warm welcome here at Tsala Treetop Lodge, glowing in the last rays of the setting sun. The very pinnacle of luxury and hospitality in the African bush, a stay at Tsala is undoubtedly a one-of-a-kind experience that will leave fond memories of an unforgettable nature.

ROOMS
10 suites

FOOD
Tsala's Restaurant: international • private dining

DRINK
wine cellar

FEATURES
business services • library • private dining decks • individual infinity-edge pools • DVD players • in-room music • individual fireplaces • outdoor activities

NEARBY
The Garden Route • Plettenberg Bay • Monkeyland • Rhino Base Camp • Birds of Eden • Elephant Sanctuary • Treetop Canopy Tours • golf courses • polo • adventure sports • whale-watching • Qolweni Cultural Village

CONTACT
PO Box 454, Plettenberg Bay 6600 Western Cape •
telephone: +27.44.501 1111 •
facsimile: +27.44.501 1100 •
email: res@hunterhotels.com •
website: www.hunterhotels.com

hunter's country house

...atmosphere of quiet luxury from a bygone era...

THIS PAGE (FROM TOP): *Enjoy dinner under the stars in fine weather; the exclusive Forest Suite has its own pool and thatched gazebo; the Crystal Dining Room is an elegant alternative for meals.*

OPPOSITE (CLOCKWISE FROM TOP): *High tea at Hunter's Country House; dine al fresco at Summer House; the Garden Suite is decorated in shades of cream and taupe.*

Hunter Hotels has garnered significant attention over the years over its reputation for unmatched service in extraordinarily beautiful surroundings. Its flagship property, Hunter's Country House, was established in November 1989, and has since been joined by its equally lauded sister properties Tsala Treetop Lodge, Gorah Elephant Camp and Marataba Safari Company. Now, this grand dame of the scenic Garden Route exudes charm and gracious elegance as it nears its second decade of welcoming guests to the best of the Western Cape.

The hotel is set in sprawling, magnificent gardens reminiscent of an English country estate, with indigenous forests and the Tsitsikamma Mountains beyond. Besides its proximity to Plettenberg Bay, Hunter's Country House is also close to the vibrant town of Knysna, so guests are never short of opportunities to dip into the full range of activities available in the city. Those who seek a restful holiday, however, can do no better than to stay within the grounds.

An old-world ambience permeates the thatched manor house, with its antique-furnished lounges, candlelit dining rooms and sun-drenched conservatory. The atmosphere of quiet luxury from a bygone era carries on into the accommodations, comprising 21 individually decorated suites to match every taste and preference. All of them come en suite, with little touches to make

each guest's stay truly memorable, such as a fireplace, private garden patio and temperature control. While all suites are at the height of South African hospitality, the pinnacle of stylish and comfortable accommodation comes in the Forest Suite, which has a spacious lounge, separate dining area and butler's kitchen, as well as a private pool and thatched gazebo.

Unlike many other exclusive hotels of its calibre, Hunter's Country House welcomes children, and is indeed known for its all-inclusive family policy that ensures young guests are fully catered for. With its well-staffed Cub's Corner that includes a jungle gym, paddling pool and games room, parents need no longer worry about how little ones will keep occupied.

When it comes to dining, the focus is on fresh, wholesome international cuisine with African influences and complemented by the finest wines from the extensive cellar. Meals are served either in the open-air Summer House or the elegant Crystal Dining Room. After a surfeit of gustatory bliss, a little wellness therapy never goes amiss, and various aromatherapy, massage and reflexology treatments are available on request within guests' private suites.

Hunter's Country House enjoys temperate climate—the scenery undergoes little change, which makes for a charming familiarity in the gorgeous surroundings year after year. Guests can also count on the same warm welcome whenever they return—as they always do.

ROOMS
21 suites

FOOD
Summer House, Crystal Dining Room, various outdoor venues: gourmet international with African influences

DRINK
wine cellar

FEATURES
Cub's Corner • in-suite wellness treatments • conservatory • boardroom • business facilities • curio shop • wedding chapel

NEARBY
Plettenberg Bay • Knysna • Outeniqua Moutains • Tsitsikamma Mountains • 5 golf courses

CONTACT
PO Box 454, Plettenberg Bay 6600 Western Cape •
telephone: +27.44.501 1111 •
facsimile: +27.44.501 1100 •
email: res@hunterhotels.com •
website: www.hunterhotels.com

pezula resort hotel + spa

...the very thick of natural beauty—bushes and trees teeming with flowers, birds and insects...

THIS PAGE: *A spectacular evening view of the main building here at Pezula Resort Hotel & Spa.*
OPPOSITE (FROM TOP): *Bright fuchsia flowers on the hotel grounds; from the air, Pezula's 18-hole golf course is a verdant oasis.*

High above the town of Knysna, on the famed Garden Route, is a headland that offers sweeping views of the Indian Ocean and Knysna Lagoon below. This region is home to majestic mountain passes and forests, clad in an aromatic mantle of fynbos unique to the Cape area.

On this cliff top, in the middle of an unspoiled 400-hectare (1,000-acre) private estate, nestles the Pezula Resort Hotel & Spa. Called Africa's first true luxury resort, it is enclosed on all sides by the grandeur of the Western Cape's cliffs, the tranquillity of the Sinclair Nature Reserve, and the dramatic Eastern Head of Knysna. Visitors live in the very thick of natural beauty—bushes and trees teeming with flowers, birds and insects always within reach.

To get an idea of how the hotel aspect works in conjunction with this magnificent environment, it is helpful to know that the estate has been recognized as the Most Environmentally Aware Development in the World, as well as the Best Luxury Development in

the World. Since its opening in 2005, the Resort Hotel & Spa has been an extension of all the values held by Pezula founder and Chairman, Keith Stewart. Falling in love with the location on first sight, he named it after the African word meaning 'high up with the gods', going on to restore the indigenous vegetation. It would be hard to find another place with the blend of natural splendour, idyllic seclusion and excellent service found here.

Pezula upholds exceptional standards of luxury. Each of the hotel's 78 suites is designed to showcase views of the ocean and golf course with a private balcony or patio. Contemporary African interior designs are complemented with real log fireplaces, walk-in wardrobes, and fresh flower arrangements. While not lounging around in appreciation of the superb Egyptian cotton bedding, one might relax with a book in front of the hearth, or enjoy a programme on the large 72-cm (28-inch) flat-screen television. The cosy Studio Suites are 58 sq m (624 sq ft) each, with panoramic views from both ground-floor and upstairs suites. Suites can be joined to accommodate families and parties of three or more. The larger Villa Suites are 68 sq m (732 sq ft) with a foldaway bed for one child.

Kufara and Mufaro are the names of Pezula's incredible Presidential Suites. They include the exclusive services of a butler, and

are lavish in every way. Spacious throughout—bedrooms, lounges, and reception areas—they are ideal for entertaining guests or just living in style. The dining areas are served by well-equipped kitchenettes, and real fireplaces warm both the living areas and bedrooms. Mufaro has private patios off the bedroom and lounge, while Kufara has two balconies.

For accommodations off the beaten track, Pezula's castle suites are the answer. Situated on a secluded stretch of beach, they are built into a coastal cliff-face and are served by a dedicated team of butlers, housekeepers and chefs. The Main Castle has three luxury suites, while the Honeymoon Castle is perfect for newlywed couples.

The gourmet menu, too, reflects the hotel's attention to detail. Only the freshest organically grown produce is used and meals are specially prepared to bring out their full, natural flavour. A wide selection of fine Cape wines as well as international labels are also available.

THIS PAGE: *Relax in the tranquillity of the Sinclair Nature Reserve.*

OPPOSITE (FROM TOP): *The resort is surrounded by lush greenery; take a dip in Pezula's spa pool after indulging in a treatment; a colour palette of warm tones and luxurious furnishing ensure guests have a memorable stay.*

South Africa's glorious climate delights visitors, and the Garden Route is no exception. Summers are warm with plenty of sunshine, and winters are mild and pleasant, allowing guests to enjoy Pezula's outdoor facilities. Golfers can tee off at the hotel's 18-hole championship golf course, while nature-lovers can observe birds and other wildlife in the resort with its indigenous forests and fynbos landscapes. At certain times of the year, majestic Southern Right Whales come to the waters of the Cape to calve, and can also be seen from Pezula's cliffs.

For the sporty guest, there are cricket and tennis academies, as well as horse riding, canoeing, hiking and mountain biking. Nearly everyone, of course, will want to visit the magnificent sheltered beach at nearby Noetzie. There, one can soak up the African sun on soft, golden sand or simply go for a relaxed stroll, taking in the stunning coastal scenery. With its combination of soul-stirring natural beauty, pampered privacy and gentle efficiency, Pezula is destined to become one of the world's legendary retreats, if it isn't already.

ROOMS
78 suites • Main Castle: 3 suites • Honeymoon Castle: 1 suite • 5 Private Residences: 2 double suites each

FOOD
Zachary's: gourmet • 24-hour room service

DRINK
champagne and whisky bar • cigar lounge

FEATURES
world-class spa • fitness centre • heated indoor and outdoor pools • sauna • 18-hole championship golf course • chauffeured limousine • private jet • helicopter • executive boardrooms • wireless Internet access

NEARBY
watersports facilities • horse riding • Tsitsikamma National Park • tennis • Noetzie • Outeniqua mountains • Sinclair Nature Reserve • Cango Caves • Robberg Nature Reserve • Knysna forest • Karoo

CONTACT
Lagoonview Drive
Knysna 6570, Western Cape • telephone +27.44.302 3333 • facsimile: +27.44.302 3303 • email: reservations@pezula.com • website: www.pezularesorthotel.com

rosenhof country house

...rest and relaxation in tranquil surroundings.

THIS PAGE (FROM RIGHT): The dining room exudes warmth, serving up hearty country cuisine with a fine Cordon Bleu influence; the lounge is filled with large, overstuffed chairs, inviting one to sink into their plush depths.

OPPOSITE (CLOCKWISE FROM TOP): The breakfast room and terrace looks out onto the gardens; the hotel's welcoming exterior; suites have private outdoor pools and patio facilities.

A sprawling white homestead surrounded by the sweet-smelling rose bushes that gave the place its name lies quietly on the outskirts of Oudtshoorn, just off the Garden Route. Lovingly restored to its original mid-19th century glory, the building now houses Rosenhof Country House, an exclusive guesthouse that extends its hospitality to visitors seeking a little rest and relaxation in tranquil surroundings.

While the extensive gardens are beautifully kept and redolent with both fragrant and decorative botanicals alike, it's the hotel interiors that remain in the memory long after the end of a stay. The original yellowwood beams and ceilings have been deliberately left exposed—nothing quite like the warm patina of aged wood—and the antique furniture, carefully polished and maintained in top condition, completes the authentic feel.

The 12 bedrooms open out onto the central rose garden, where a tall bronze fountain sends a sparkling stream of water into a marble pool. At night, the scent of roses carries into the rooms and perfumes the air. Each room comes with individual temperature control and other modern amenities such as satellite television. The two executive suites boast even higher levels of luxury, with private outdoor pools of their own, and are located slightly further away from the main house for privacy. These suites are almost mini-cottages in themselves, with separate lounge and patio areas, and command impressive views of the Swartberg Mountain. Mini bars and tea trays are provided as standard in all rooms, for guests' convenience.

For something a little more substantial, however, Rosenhof Country House's dining room serves traditional country cuisine with a fine French finish. A specially selected wine menu sets off the menu to perfection, and the cheeerful staff will be more than

pleased to recommend the chef's choice for the evening, with a complementary glass of fine wine to go with. The breakfast room, alternately used as a day lounge, is light and airy, overlooking the extensive manicured gardens—guests may also choose to take their morning coffee out on the open terrace.

A trellised walkway from the main house leads to the pretty, tiled outdoor pool and a number of well-placed sun loungers and garden seating, where guests may enjoy a laid back afternoon read with a good book, cooling off with a refreshing dip in the pool when it gets too hot. The guesthouse also offers a fully equipped yet surprisingly compact gym for those looking to shake off the tendency to kick back completely that most have at Rosenhof Country House.

For all its self-containment, there may be some who wish to get out beyond the guesthouse; to this end, Oudtshoorn presents a surprisingly wide range of options. Chances to observe the rich ecology of the region come in the form of the Wildlife Ranch and Ostrich Farm, while the geologically inclined will favour the Cango Caves, and sports enthusiasts are well looked after at Oudtshoorn Adventure Centre. A truly spectacular experience, however, is the champagne breakfast followed by hot air balloon ride, which the hotel concierge can assist in arranging.

Rosenhof Country House comes strongly recommended by past guests, and it's easy to see why—its ambience, service and facilities leave nothing to be desired, and guests leave only reluctantly, with memories of a thoroughly enjoyable stay in a beautiful old homestead touched by the scent of roses.

ROOMS
12 rooms • 2 suites

FOOD
dining room: country with French influences • breakfast room

DRINK
pub

FEATURES
beauty treatments • massages • gym • outdoor pool • landscaped gardens • satellite TV

NEARBY
Cango Wildlife Ranch • Cango Ostrich Show Farm • Cango Caves • meerkat-watching • camel-riding • hot air ballooning • Oudtshoorn Adventure Centre • Swartberg Mountain • Swartberg Adventures • Abuakwa Arts & Crafts • Arbeidsgenot Museum

CONTACT
264 Baron Von Rheede Street Oudtshoorn 6625, Western Cape • telephone: +27.44.272 2232 • facsimile: +27.44.272 3021 • email: rosenhof@xsinet.co.za • website: www.rosenhof.co.za

birkenhead house

...everything and more one would expect of a private hotel...

From the glass of champagne that welcomes guests at check-in to the gourmet cuisine served with effortless flair at every meal, a stay at Birkenhead House is everything and more one would expect of a private hotel experience. Located in Hermanus about an hour and a half from Cape Town, the property makes the most of its dramatic position overlooking Walker Bay, with terraces, an infinity-edge pool and every suite's floor-to-ceiling windows designed to lap up the view.

The opulent 11 guest suites are centred on a sheltered courtyard with a split-level outdoor pool. No two suites are alike—from African to Asian motifs, each space is individually decorated with antiques from around the world, artfully juxtaposed with contemporary pieces. Eclectic accents make all the difference, whether it is a Persian rug or lacquer wardrobe, claw-foot bath or Zen-inspired sunken tub. Yet the property remains true to its homey holiday-home origins, with soothing stone walls, travertine floors and sumptuous couches that sprawl in front of the fireplace. At night, what better lullaby than the crashing of the waves to lull one off to sleep?

Guests who choose not to venture outdoors will find that their suites can also double up as prime locations for whale-watching during the season from May to November, with easy sightings of Southern Right Whales coming to calve in the sheltered waters below Birkenhead's clifftop location. Their distinctive blowhole exhalations of water vapour—two long V-shaped streams—are truly a sight to behold. Hermanus is well known for some of the best land-based whale-watching in the world, not to mention frequent cruise sightings of great white sharks, Cape fur seals, bottlenose dolphins, African penguins and other sea creatures.

THIS PAGE: The split-level outdoor pool at Birkenhead House is a sight to behold in the evening.

OPPOSITE (CLOCKWISE FROM TOP): The panoramic view over the coast; a stunning sunken marble bath; warm lighting and soft couches lend a hospitable atmosphere; the sumptuous bedrooms offer unsurpassed comfort to guests.

Birkenhead House also overlooks a number of spectacular beaches and, landward, the majestic fynbos-covered Overberg mountains. Guests can avail themselves of a plethora of marine or land-based activities at any time during their stay, ranging from easy to challenging, that will give them a taste of the splendour of this rugged setting and diverse botanic ecosystem.

Back at the House, other memorable tastes await, in the form of the lavish meals prepared by Birkenhead's award-winning international chefs. Fresh seafood and game are the centrepiece of their delicately concocted menus, a dining experience all the more unforgettable when dinner is served beside the pool with a panoramic view of the bay.

With the harmony of space, light, water and nature, Birkenhead House brings its own brand of breezy comfort to the world of luxury accommodation. Named one of the Top 101 Hotels of the Year by *Tatler* UK in 2006, this is a gem of a coastal hideaway.

ROOMS
11 suites

FOOD
dining room: international

DRINK
wine list

FEATURES
3 pools • whale-watching • library • treatment rooms

NEARBY
Dyer Island Cruises • Grootbos Private Nature Reserve • 2 golf courses • sea activities • quad biking • Hermanus city centre • shark diving • wine tours

CONTACT
7th Avenue, Voelklip
Hermanus 7200, Western Cape •
telephone: +27.15.793 0150 •
facsimile: +27.15.793 2879 •
email: reservations@
    theroyalportfolio.com •
website: www.royalmalewane.com

the marine hermanus

The Marine Hermanus overlooks Walker Bay...

THIS PAGE: The Marine Hermanus is magnificently located with a stunning view of the coastline.

OPPOSITE (FROM TOP): A deft blend of comfort and luxury is found throughout the hotel interiors; catch the sunset over a cocktail; the Marine suite offers a higher level of elegance and privacy.

The Marine Hermanus is arguably the finest spot from which to engage in whale-watching, an activity which can be by turns exciting and calming. Set on the sea front at Hermanus, The Marine overlooks Walker Bay, the preferred haunt of humpbacks and Southern Right Whales who come here from July to December to mate and calve.

For those who love to watch these gentle giants at play, The Marine is as close as it gets to having whales in one's back garden. Take early morning strolls along the cliffs to see them frolic in the waters, or watch them close up from the hotel telescope. At The Marine, guests can even whale-watch from their beds—the ocean views here stretch all the way to Antarctica.

The five-star Marine has 42 individually-decorated bedrooms and suites, each one as luxurious and sophisticated as the one before. Fresh creams and sea blues reflect the myriad hues of the Indian Ocean. There are also the hotel's beautifully-landscaped gardens—

gardening happens to be one of the passions of owner Liz McGrath—a romantic inner courtyard and even more glorious views that look out onto the Overberg mountains, renowned for their unique natural vegetation known locally as fynbos.

Along with its sister properties The Cellars-Hohenort and The Plettenberg, The Marine is a member of the exclusive Relais & Châteaux group, which means guests can expect an array of delightful luxuries such as large beds dressed in the finest linen, huge deep-soaking baths, fluffy towels, fresh flowers, a heated pool and of course, excellent service.

Indulge the tastebuds at Seafood at the Marine with a menu that makes the most of the fresh fish and seafood available from the surrouding waters of the Indian Ocean. There is also the elegant The Pavilion restaurant, which serves contemporary South African cuisine and some of the world's finest wines from the nearby Cape Winelands. In fact, two of South Africa's premier vineyards are right on The Marine's doorstep—Bouchard Finlayson and Hamilton Russell—and guests can arrange for a fascinating day-trip to both vineyards. Sun Lounge is a sophisticated cocktail bar and a lounge is available for both hotel residents and local visitors to relax and enjoy the view. Adjoining The Sun Lounge is The Sea Food Express One Plate Cafe offering a light seafood menu. Enjoy the sights and flavours of Walker bay from the Cafe whilst sipping on a glass of wine. The menu features a selection of regional wines which are offered by the glass.

Along with sessions of whale-watching, a relaxing session at the Carchele Health and Beauty Spa is also recommended. This world-class marine therapy salon follows the French tradition that require their centres to be located within a few metres of the ocean to benefit from the minerals in the air and seawater. Guests can select from a variety of therapies using seaweed and plant extracts, leaving the spa refreshed by the treatments, not to mention feeling years younger. There's no end, it seems, to the benefits of a visit to the spa.

Guests can while away the day with champagne by the heated pool, or take a romantic walk down memory lane to visit the Old Harbour, which features a number of World War I artillery. Nearby, Danger Point is also a local historical draw, and the lighthouse here marks the point where the ill-fated HMS Birkenhead went down. At the southern end of the bay is De Kelders, the site of caves once occupied by 'strandlopers' or 'beach walkers', who were the original inhabitants of this coastline. Archaeologists have spent years here to try and learn more about the strandlopers' hunter-gatherer lifestyle. The region also offers a glimpse of nature at its most impressive. Hermanus offers miles of sandy white beaches and hikes along cliff-hugging paths, while the nearby Fernkloof Nature Reserve has over 40 km (25 miles) of walks through the beautiful Overberg mountains.

Every day during the whale season, the local whale crier—easily identified from afar by his sporting of a jolly giant Bavarian hat—hails the arrival of each new whale by blowing loudly on a kelp horn. During the whale-watching festival in October, the town is abuzz with holiday-makers, whale-lovers, families and travellers galore.

The Marine was built in 1902 by Walter McFarlane, who moved here from the nearby agricultural village of Elgin in the 1880s. The hotel started with a modest 21 rooms and underwent many changes over the years, until it fell into the loving hands of David Rawdon in the early 1980s. He renovated and ran The Marine for a total of 13 successful years before selling it on to Liz McGrath, who steered the hotel into the new millennium and secured its position as one of the world's finest guesthouses and a Western Cape treasure.

THIS PAGE: *The Sun Lounge & Bar is aptly dressed in golden hues, giving the room a cheerful air.*

OPPOSITE (CLOCKWISE FROM TOP): *The hotel is well known for the fresh menu of Seafood at The Marine; the outdoor pool and terrace is a cool option on a hot afternoon; a succulent grilled crayfish dish is a highly popular hotel speciality.*

GRILLED CRAYFISH WITH PEPPADEW BUTTER, SAUTÉED BABY POTATOES AND ROASTED ASPARAGUS

Serves 6

6 whole crayfish tails
2 L (4 pt 3⅜ fl oz / 8½ cups) seawater
30 ml (1 fl oz / ⅛ cup) olive oil
salt and freshly-ground black pepper to taste
500 g (1 lb 1⅝ oz) baby potatoes
50 g (1¾ oz / ¼ cup) butter
handful of fresh parsley, chopped
48 spears green asparagus
olive oil for roasting

Peppadew butter

80 g (2⅞ oz / ⅜ cup) peppadews, finely chopped
200 g (7 oz/ ⅞ cup) butter, softened
salt and freshly-ground black pepper to taste

Crayfish Blanch the crayfish for 5 minutes in the boiling seawater. You can substitute with salted water if seawater is not available. Butterfly the crayfish and clean the heads thoroughly. Rub the flesh with olive oil and place under the grill for 1 to 2 minutes. Season the crayfish thoroughly with the salt and freshly-ground pepper before transferring to an oven preheated at 180° C (356° F), and roast for 5 minutes.

Peppadew butter Mix the peppadews into the butter. Add salt and freshly-ground black pepper. Roll the peppadew butter firmly in cling film. Leave to set in the refrigerator for at least 20 minutes.

Sautéed baby potatoes Cook the baby potatoes in boiling salted water for about 10 minutes. Remove from heat and drain. Sauté the potatoes in 50 g (1¾ oz/ ¼ cup) butter until they are golden-brown and tender. Sprinkle the potatoes generously with the chopped fresh parsley just before serving.

Roasted asparagus Blanch the asparagus spears in boiling salted water for 1 minute, then refresh in ice water. Sprinkle the asparagus with olive oil and roast them in the oven at 180° C (356° F) for 2 minutes.

To serve Arrange the sautéed baby potatoes in the centre of each plate and top with 8 asparagus spears in a fan. Rest the crayfish on top of the potatoes and asparagus. Dot the crayfish and potatoes generously with peppadew butter.

Wine Beaumont Chardonnay 2000

ROOMS

14 suites • 28 rooms

FOOD

The Pavilion: South African • Seafood at the Marine: fresh seafood • Seafood Express Plate One Cafe: light menu

DRINK

'floating wine cellar' at The Pavilion • The Orangery • Sun Lounge & Bar

FEATURES

reading room • marine helipad • Carchele Health and Beauty Spa • heated pool • conference room

NEARBY

Fernkloof Nature Reserve • De Kelders • air charters • Bouchard Finlayson and Hamilton Russell vineyards • Old Harbour • Danger Point • golf courses

CONTACT

PO Box 9, Marine Drive
Hermanus 7200, Western Cape •
telephone: +27.28.313 1000 •
facsimile: +27.28.313 0160 •
email: hermanus@relaischateaux.com •
website: www.marine-hermanus.com

grande provence

...truly a gorgeous visual feast.

THIS PAGE (FROM TOP): *The outdoor pool provides guests with cool respite from hot summer days; The Jonkershuis is available for private events and functions.*

OPPOSITE (CLOCKWISE FROM TOP): *Little seating arrangements are found scattered throughout the estate; rooms come in a light, modern palette of charcoal and white; the welcoming and cosy lounge.*

Cradled in the magnificent wine-producing Franschhoek Valley in the Western Cape is a stunning combination of boutique hotel, vineyard, art gallery and fine dining establishment—Grande Provence. Sister property to Huka Lodge, New Zealand and Dolphin Island, Fiji, Grande Provence is part of the exclusive trio known as The Huka Retreats. Visitors will be struck by the exceptional natural beauty of the surroundings and the simple elegance of the whitewashed Cape Dutch Estate Manor House and The Owner's Cottage. With 30 hectares (74 acres) of vineyard spread across the lush valley floor, set against the rugged mountain vista and beyond that the clear azure of South African skies, Grande Provence is truly a gorgeous visual feast.

Accommodating guests at this 'landscaped Eden' are the four rooms and one suite at The Owner's Cottage. Interiors of contemporary luxury blended with period grandeur in a subtle, stylish design aesthetic feature throughout in a palette of charcoal grey and white linen—both understated and timeless. Also within the building is the conservatory, offering a quiet nook for those who crave a little solitude, and the lounge, perfect for that post-dinner hour accompanied by a glass of the Estate's finest vintage. An outdoor pool gives guests the space for rest and relaxation, and the spa pool's elevated location offers a unique opportunity to view the magnificence of the surrounding landscape.

One particularly delectable highlight of a stay here is the opportunity to sample the Estate wines in situ. Their eponymous premier range features world-famous varieties—Sauvignon Blanc, Chardonnay, Cabernet Sauvignon and Shiraz—infused with the distinctive flavour of the soil of this temperate, crisp climate. Harvested

with passion and enthusiasm, the wines reflect perfectly the spirit of Grande Provence, full-bodied and unforgettable. Walking tours of the estate can be easily arranged, with a tasting session to round off a delightful and informative afternoon.

As a complement to Grande Provence's award-winning range of wines, The Restaurant serves regional cuisine with global influences—a confluence of ingredients and technique that is a fine example of modern gastronomy at its peak. Industrial chic dictates the interiors of The Restaurant, with steel joinery, galvanised metals and large skylights being distinguishing elements of this design approach. Rich table linen and soft white leather upholstery soften the look, and the soft chink of polished silver on china and shining glassware make for a refined dining experience like no other. Quite in a class of its own, however, is The Jonkershuis at Grande Provence, a private function area reserved for special dinners, small weddings, and similar select events that require the use of its dedicated rooms and kitchen.

A special treat is reserved for art lovers—besides the beautiful pieces of modern art displayed throughout the strikingly designed accommodations, there is also a specialist collection of contemporary South African art available to view and purchase at The Gallery. There is a new exhibition of South Africa's most talented artists every six to eight weeks, and not to be missed, as an essential part of the grace and charm of Grande Provence.

ROOMS
4 rooms • 1 suite

FOOD
The Restaurant: regional with global influences • The Jonkershuis: private dining

DRINK
estate wines

FEATURES
outdoor pool • spa pool • lounge • conservatory • The Jonkershuis event facilities • The Gallery • winery

NEARBY
Franschhoek village • Paarl • Stellenbosch • Cape Town

CONTACT
PO Box 102, Franschhoek 7690 Western Cape • telephone: +27.21.876 8600 • facsimile: +27.21.876 8601 • email: enquiries@ grandeprovence.co.za • website: www.grandeprovence.co.za

klein genot wine + country estate

...a vineyard, a spa and spectacular scenery all at one's very doorstep.

THIS PAGE (CLOCKWISE FROM BOTTOM): *An evening stroll around the lake is an ideal activity before dinner; the outdoor pool is popular on warm, lazy summer afternoons.*

OPPOSITE (CLOCKWISE FROM TOP): *The tiniest details in each room are aimed towards guests' comfort; the spa offers a wide range of pampering wellness treatments; each unique suite bespeaks the warm hospitality of Klein Genot.*

Wellness and wineries don't necessarily sound like they go together at first, and it's a rare thing to come across a place like Klein Genot Wine & Country Estate, where this combination does go together, and very well at that. In this Cape Dutch farmhouse, constructed according to the principles of feng shui in a tranquil corner of Franschhoek Valley, visitors are promised a rejuvenating stay with a vineyard, a spa and spectacular scenery all at one's very doorstep.

Klein Genot, which appropriately means 'little indulgence' in Afrikaans, is the perfect place to take life a couple of gears slower and relax among a few luxuries of one's choice. Laze in a hammock on a clear sunny day to take in the panoramic views of nature's wonderful landscapes. Stroll along the tranquil lake beside the graceful, gliding black swans, or go for a leisurely evening row. Reach out and pluck juicy, sun-ripened fruit right from the balcony of your room if the fancy should happen to strike, or enjoy a thoroughly healthy yet satisfying meal of organic food fresh from Klein Genot's own vegetable and herb garden. For the wine connoisseurs, Klein Genot proudly rolled out its maiden harvest of 2005, aiming to make young, modern wines. There is a 20-hectare (50-acre) red varietal vineyard for guests to tour around that produces all the estate wines. The vineyard currently features an eminently drinkable batch of spicy Shiraz, fruity Merlot, delightfully complex Cabernet Sauvignon and a superb Bordeaux blend of Cabernet Franc and Cabernet Sauvignon.

Indoors promises just as much enjoyment, with The Klein Genot Wellness Spa which provides over 40 different types of spa treatments. The Signature Massage, which combines core elements of Swedish massage, lymphatic drainage, reflexology and deep tissue

manipulation, is a popular choice, ideal for those hoping to get fully into the spirit of rest and relaxation. Alternatively, the African Experience treatment, involving rooiboois exfoliation with an African wrap, may be just the thing to restore one's radiant glow.

There is plenty to do out of Klein Genot. Guests can visit acclaimed wineries nearby such as Graham Beck and Rupert & Rothschild Vignerons. Food lovers will not be left out, for some of South Africa's top restaurants are nearby, such as Bouillabaisse and Haute Cabrière Cellar Restaurant. With all the food and wine, one can burn the calories off with a walk through the Huguenot Museum to find out about the French heritage of this area, or through some shopping for local crafts and jewellery along Main Street. For substantial fresh air and exercise, there's always the option of renting a bicycle, trout-fishing or hiking at Dewdale Fly Fishery.

Of course, guests can always stay in, making the most of the plush accommodations. Each of Klein Genot's six sumptuous suites is decorated with original artwork and hand-quilted French linen, promising a tasteful, comfortable experience. With an oversized tub and complimentary Aloe Ferox toiletries, soaking in a hot bath may well prove to be far more tempting than a night out. Whatever the case, Klein Genot promises all the wonders of the Cape Winelands, with every single creature comfort available to provide an unforgettable travel experience.

ROOMS
6 suites

FOOD
dining room: international

DRINK
estate wines

FEATURES
spa • outdoor pool • winery • vineyard • lake

NEARBY
Cape Town • Franschhoek village

CONTACT
Green Valley Road
Franschhoek 7690, Western Cape •
telephone: +27.21.876 2738 •
facsimile: +27.21.876 4624 •
email: info@kleingenot.com •
website: www.kleingenot.com

le quartier français

...it is impossible to leave without memories to last a lifetime.

THIS PAGE: The Tasting Room has garnered numerous accolades from various sources and is an ongoing highlight of the hotel.

OPPOSITE (FROM TOP): Bright flowers and wall hangings add cheer; The Four Quarters Suites are an unmatched exercise in luxury, with a private pool and lounge.

Wine lovers the world over know the Cape Winelands to be a premier tasting route replete with fertile vineyards and extraordinary cuisine, and blessed with perfect summer sun. Nowhere on the route is this more true than in Franschhoek, where the village stands undisputed in the eyes of critics as home to some of the country's finest restaurants. So it is very fortunate for visitors to the French Huguenot valley that the brightest star in South Africa's gourmet capital, The Tasting Room, is also part of one of the most exciting and luxurious hotels in the country.

Le Quartier Français (the French Quarter) is a five-star auberge that has won international acclaim for its commitment to service and attention to 'small unexpected luxuries'. Every guest at Le Quartier Français is made to feel at home by a team of dedicated professionals for whom no request is ever out of the question. The Relais & Châteaux establishment was named Best Small Hotel in the World in 2005 by the UK's *Tatler* magazine, and has made top hotel lists in *Travel and Leisure*, *Condé Nast Traveler* USA (best for location in 2008), and *The Daily Telegraph* UK.

Indeed, the only list of accolades as long as the hotel's comes from its own restaurant. Under the direction of Executive Chef Margot Janse, The Tasting Room has earned a name for itself as one of the best fine dining restaurants in the world, alongside such greats as Alain Ducasse in Paris, Thomas Keller's Per Se in New York, and El Bulli in Barcelona. For three years since 2005, *Restaurant Magazine* has recognised it as one of the World's 50 Best Restaurants, and as the Best Restaurant in the Middle East & Africa for two years. Guests of Le Quartier Français can expect to experience superlative cutting-edge cuisine in the form of The Tasting Room's menus that constantly evolve to make best use of fresh, seasonal ingredients. Thus inspired, they can attend exclusive cookery classes conducted by Ms Janse and her team.

The hotel's culinary pedigree even extends to the relaxed bistro, iCi, and its sister restaurant Bread & Wine at the nearby Môreson Wine Farm. The relaxed sophisticated bar and café-styled iCi invites people to linger over cappuccinos, strawberry daiquiris and delicious food from a wood-burning oven. For character-filled food, look no further than Bread & Wine Vineyard Restaurant and Farm Grocer on Môreson Wine Farm. Serving award-winning homemade charcuterie, a selection of breads and other seasonal dishes, this restaurant is a firm favourite with all. Nothing quite compares to the utter bliss of spending an afternoon in the lemon orchards indulging in hearty food and passion-infused Môreson wine.

One sees the hotel's way of keeping things simple yet exceptional throughout its accommodations. All strive to deliver home comforts with a full complement of amenities, and extra touches that make all the difference. The 15 Auberge Luxury Rooms are tucked away in secluded privacy amidst greenery. Arranged around a central courtyard garden highlighted by a sparkling pool, they offer old-world elegance and a view to remember. Like all rooms, they feature separate shower and bath areas, fireplaces, large beds with luxurious linens, underfloor heating throughout, DVD players, safes, and complimentary wireless Internet access.

The owners' original home has been converted into two luxury Pool and House suites, each with a private pool and garden. Generous living and sitting areas within and without offer an incomparable vacation atmosphere. Lounge on deck chairs by the pool, or read the morning papers over breakfast in bed, or out on the patio. With extra loft rooms above, the Auberge Suites are ideal for families with children.

THIS PAGE: *All rooms feature such exclusive amenities as wood-burning fireplaces, sumptuous furnishings and fine bedlinen.*

OPPOSITE (FROM TOP): *An exquisite creation from The Tasting Room; modern bathrooms are given a touch of warmth with natural materials such as marble tiles; the outdoor pool sparkles in the sunshine, perfect for relaxation.*

The Four Quarters Suites at Le Quartier Français feature spacious living rooms that connect by way of large panel doors to sumptuous deluxe bedrooms. With two plasma televisions per suite, separate dressing rooms, full complimentary bars in the lounge areas, iPod docking stations, and a butler service, they are the epitome of luxury living. Encircling a courtyard with private lounge space and a pool by which complimentary lunches are served, each of the four suites provides everything for an enchanting, romantic getaway.

The Cottage is a villa-like two-bedroom suite situated across the road. Upon arrival, guests receive complimentary Pinehurst wines, and breakfast comes with the news each morning. The Cottage comes fully equipped with a kitchen and dining area, two lounges with fireplaces, and a guest bathroom. All rooms open out to a delightful walled garden and private pool.

The pampering doesn't end there either. A Treatment Room offers an Aroma-Skincare therapy system that soothes and promotes an increased sense of well-being and vigour. Rounding up the trio of indulgent pleasures are the Screening Room, where guests can enjoy classic and modern films with a glass of champagne, and Touches and Tastes, a very special gift boutique. Declared 'the best hotel shop anywhere' by *Tatler* UK, Touches and Tastes carries an intriguing range of premium items so guests can bring a part of the valley home with them.

With unforgettable food, luxury accommodation, and friendly service, Le Quartier Français offers the quintessential Cape Winelands holiday. Bring a loved one, or a few close friends, and it is impossible to leave without memories to last a lifetime.

ROOMS
15 rooms • 6 suites • 1 cottage

FOOD
The Tasting Room: international fine dining • iCi: casual dining • Bread & Wine: rustic country lunches

DRINK
iCi: cocktails, wine list and coffee

FEATURES
outdoor solar-heated pools • gift shop • screening room • free transfers within Franschhoek • wireless Internet access • cooking courses with Margot Janse • treatment room • bread-baking courses at Bread & Wine • romantic bath menus

NEARBY
golf • tennis • hiking trails • biking excursions • horse riding • wine tours • horseback wine tasting • chocolate tastings • scenic helicopter tours • paragliding • crocodile farm • butterfly sanctuary

CONTACT
PO Box 237, 16 Huguenot Road Franschhoek 7690, Western Cape • telephone: +27.21.876 2151 • facsimile: +27.21.876 3105 • email: res@lqf.co.za • website: www.lequartier.co.za •

mont rochelle hotel + mountain vineyards

...the consummate Cape Winelands experience.

Not far from Cape Town lies the town of Franschhoek. Home to a premier wine-producing valley and outstanding restaurants, this 'French Corner' is increasingly referred to as the republic's food and wine capital.

It is here that the highly regarded La Couronne Hotel stood until the February of 2006. Rebuilt and brought together with its sister winery in October of that year, the La Couronne has been reborn as the Mont Rochelle Hotel and Mountain Vineyards—an even finer example of hospitality and comfort on the Western Cape.

Enjoying superior views of Franschhoek's landscape of valleys and vines from its elevated situation, Mont Rochelle offers the consummate Cape Winelands experience. From the moment one first walks up the path to the appropriately named Garden Wing, there is little else but to be charmed by the union of nature and luxury.

Over three wings, the boutique hotel of only 22 rooms impresses with classic architecture and décor. Nowhere can this be better appreciated than out on the terrace of the Manor House, which bridges the Garden and Vineyard wings. At the same time, facilities such as a gymnasium and wellness facility see to every need.

Each of the 16 bedrooms and six exclusive suites exudes its own unique charm and character by virtue of being individually designed and decorated. Whether one chooses a Contemporary, Classic, or Colonial African interior, each en suite room features all imaginable amenities from televisions and climate control, to in-room refreshment facilities.

Rooms at Mont Rochelle are named after grape varietals of the Franschhoek Valley. The standard Shiraz Rooms and deluxe Merlot Rooms feature Romeo & Juliet balconies, perfect for observing a day's end over some wine. The Cabernet Rooms offer an unforgettable breakfast opportunity as guests can enjoy room service on their own private terraces, which come with loungers and a dining table, as the morning sun breaks over the surrounding mountains.

Luxury lovers seeking more spacious alternatives will appreciate that all suites have attached living areas. Bedrooms in the plush junior Pinotage Suites also feature en suite dressing rooms in addition to bathrooms. The single Reserve Suite exudes exclusivity with a private, walled Zen garden that boasts a jacuzzi and an outdoor dining area.

The very ultimate in presidential suites comes in the form of the two Cap Classique Suites. Ideal for extended stays, these offer the comforts of home with separate living and dining areas, jacuzzi-equipped bathrooms, and tasteful furnishings. The highlight of a Cap Classique Suite is its private terrace and pool, from which one has incomparable views of the land.

Epicures will find no end of delights at Mange Tout, the Manor House's fine dining restaurant with elegant Provençal-inspired decor. If al fresco dining is desired, The Country Kitchen over at the winery caters for all tastes. Gourmet picnic baskets are also available for guests to create their own dining experiences under the willows.

Light sandwiches and salads are also available throughout the day at the Colonial Cigar Bar, and at the hotel's outdoor pool. No visit is complete until one has spent an afternoon

basking in the sun with a cocktail from the pool bar, with every mile of lovely Franschhoek and the mountains above visible beyond the cool waters.

With its long list of possible excursions, not to mention the full complement of on-premise wine tasting tours and activities, there's never a slow moment until you decide it's time for one. At which point, the scenery and clement weather will serve as accompaniments to the freshly uncorked bottle of wine that is never far from hand in the valley. If one is ever found in the vicinity of picturesque Franschhoek, wondering how things could possibly be better, a visit to Mont Rochelle will provide many answers.

ROOMS
16 rooms • 6 suites

FOOD
Mange Tout: fine Provençal dining •
The Country Kitchen: al fresco •
Colonial Cigar Bar: snack menu

DRINK
winery • Colonial Cigar Bar • Pool Bar

FEATURES
cellar tours • gymnasium • Internet access • massages • outdoor pool • sauna • vineyard tours • wine sales • wine tasting

NEARBY
golf • hiking • horse riding • hang-gliding • fly fishing • hiking • mountain biking • museums • shopping • Franschhoek wineries

CONTACT
PO Box 448, Franschhoek 7690 Western Cape •
telephone: +27.21.876 2770 •
facsimile: +27.21.876 3788 •
email: info@montrochelle.co.za •
website: www.montrochelle.co.za

palmiet valley wine + country estate

...a sanctuary of restfulness and genteel hospitality.

Nestled deep in the heart of the Cape Winelands, surrounded by the tranquil beauty of austere mountains and mirror-like lakes, Palmiet Valley Wine & Country Estate awaits—a sanctuary of restfulness and genteel hospitality.

The typical white gabled walls of classic Cape Dutch architecture bring a quiet elegance to the sprawling homestead, while grounds carpeted with a profusion of jacaranda and lavender segue into lush vineyards that stretch to the foot of the distant mountain. Interiors are a palette of rich chrysanthemum yellows and burnt oranges, setting off the dark carved woods, stuffed chairs and warm leather. The nine en-suite rooms and two cottages are more of the same, with charmingly old-fashioned furnishings and fittings, such as polished brass taps and marble-topped dressers. Individually decorated, each room or cottage boasts a unique accessory or two, giving it a character of its own—stand-out pieces include an antique safe, a 1920s travelling suitcase and a period copper kettle. Despite these nostalgic touches, modern comforts are still made available, such as CD players, temperature control, and high-quality bedlinen.

In keeping with the unconstrained, open-skied environs, guests usually keep fairly relaxed itineraries. Afternoons are usually taken up in long walks, lazily tracing paths through the country while the guesthouse glows in the post-meridian sun like a homecoming beacon in the distance. Alternatively, a day spent by the pool followed by a rooftop massage is also a popular option. The thatched attic lounge, with its leather sofas, selection of estate wines, roaring fire, and well-filled bookshelf is something for the evenings, or colder weather. In the evenings, options vary between the 18th-century dining room, set with fine linen and china, or al fresco under the star-studded South African sky, all accompanied by the finest estate wines.

THIS PAGE: The white homestead is a beautiful example of the Cape Dutch local style of architecture.

OPPOSITE (CLOCKWISE FROM TOP): Enjoy a hearty spread at breakfast—Palmiet Valley Wine & Country Estate chefs go all out for guests; the quaint, old-fashioned 18th-century dining room at the hotel; the lush vineyards stretch all the way to the foot of the mountain; each room is uniquely furnished.

Guests at Palmiet Valley Wine & Country Estate are more often than not perfectly happy to remain within the comfortable confines of the homestead—however, there are plenty of activities to choose from when so desired. Apart from the extensive Estate itself, there are various other vineyards close by to visit and engage in a thorough session of wine-tasting. The surrounding towns of Franschhoek and Stellenbosch in particular are renowned for the quality of their wines. Golf courses are scattered through the region for those who fancy a day well-spent in 18 holes of verdant bliss. For the adventurous, various choices are available at different levels, ranging from leisurely walks to mountain biking and abseiling. For some urban excitement, Cape Town, V&A Waterfront, and the various Cape attractions and beaches are within half an hour's drive.

Palmiet Valley Country & Wine Estate is especially popular for weddings, and it's easy to see why, with the lush landscape around and pristine white homestead itself a confection of pure newlywed romance. That said, however, the inviting estate extends its welcome to all who pass its doors, and it's only all too common to experience a reluctance to leave at the end of a stay, and a persistent urge to return soon to its familiar warmth.

ROOMS
9 rooms • 2 cottages

FOOD
indoor dining room: daily international menu • al fresco dining

DRINK
estate wines

FEATURES
massage treatments • outdoor pool • wine tasting • lounge library

NEARBY
golf courses • vineyards • nature trails • Franschhoek • Stellenbosch • mountain bike trails • abseiling • hot air ballooning • Cape Town • V&A Waterfront • beaches

CONTACT
PO Box 9085, Klein Drakenstein Paarl 7628, Western Cape • telephone: +27.21.862 7741 • facsimile: +27.21.862 6891 • email: info@palmiet.co.za • website: www.palmiet.co.za

d'ouwe werf

...established in 1802, d'Ouwe Werf is the oldest inn in South Africa.

Massive urban renewals of late have breathed a new lease of life into the sleepy town of Stellenbosch in the Cape Winelands. Once merely a restful old university town, Stellenbosch is now the heart of the burgeoning South African wine industry. Its old buildings still sit along beautiful oak-lined streets, but various new art galleries, boutiques and bistros have recently sprung up, giving the town a modern panache it never thought it would have.

D'Ouwe Werf Country Inn is the best way to get a feel for Stellenbosch's marriage of old and new. Established in 1802, d'Ouwe Werf is the oldest inn in South Africa. The inn stands on the hallowed grounds of the town's first church, which dates back to 1686, and the remains of the church can still be seen beneath the floorboards of the inn's kitchen. Indeed, d'Ouwe Werf's own history is not without drama. It was razed to the ground several times by fires in the 18th and 19th centuries, and rebuilt each time. Today, a charred door and some window frames in the Voorkamer (front room) are the only survivors from the hotel's chequered past.

Though the inn's foundations are ancient, there is certainly nothing primitive about the present building facilities, which are rich and sumptuous. No two rooms are alike—d'Ouwe Werf freely furnishes each room in either Georgian, Victorian or traditional Cape style. The hotel's 32 rooms are spread over five buildings, each looking out onto either the lush, verdant garden and courtyard or Church Street. Divided into Superior, Luxury and Classic rooms, many are decorated with exquisite antiques that hint at the hotel's poignant history.

Traditional South African fare—bobotie, smoorsnoek, Biltong pâté and Cape brandy pudding, to name a few dishes—is served up at the 1802 Restaurant, a Stellenbosch culinary institution in its own right. Hearty eaters will find South African dishes satisfying, while diners who prefer lighter meals can tuck into Continental alternatives. The extensive Stellenbosch wine-of-origin list makes it possible for d'Ouwe Werf Restaurant to be one of the best places where one can enjoy some of the finest wine this area has to offer.

A fine way to while away the daylight hours is to curl up beside the antique stove fire in the high-vaulted Voorkamer with a good book, or browse local newspapers in de Kromme Elleboog, the informal lounge. For outdoor enjoyment, savour a slice of cheesecake, said to be the best in town, in the vine-covered coffee garden.

Days here are easily filled with wine-tasting tours, shopping and walking. The welcoming glow of d'Ouwe Werf awaits tired guests at the end of each day, its central location in Stellenbosch easily accessible from anywhere on the Wine Route.

ROOMS
32

FOOD
1802 Restaurant: traditional South African, Continental and international • coffee garden: light meals

DRINK
1802 Restaurant • coffee garden

FEATURES
pool • garden • Voorkamer • beauty salon • lounge • meeting room • facsimile • wireless high-speed Internet connection • conference facilities

NEARBY
Cape Town • museums • art galleries • golf courses • vineyards and wine cellar

CONTACT
30 Church Street, Stellenbosch 7600 Western Cape •
telephone: +27.21.887 4608 •
facsimile: +27.21.887 4626 •
email: ouwewerf@iafrica.com •
website: www.ouwewerf.com

waterford wine estate

...a jewel of the Cape Winelands, with an international reputation that far precedes it...

THIS PAGE: *The main entrance of Waterford Wine Estate and the Helderberg in the background.*

OPPOSITE (FROM TOP): *Comfortable furniture and quirky décor sets the tone for relaxed enjoyment; the living room is cosily rustic; a variety of tables and seating make wine tasting all the more flexible, informal and personal.*

Amidst the soaring peaks of the Helderberg range in Stellenbosch lies a jewel of the Cape Winelands, with an international reputation that far precedes it—Waterford Wine Estate. A joint effort of the Ord and Arnold families and a product of their combined expertise in business, hospitality and winemaking, Waterford is not just an average vineyard.

Rows of bright green, grape-laden vines stretch for miles on the estate. Crystalline streams trickle down from the mountains to the homestead, whose rugged timber beams and stonework have sheltered visitors and brought to them Waterford way of life for over a decade. The philosophy here celebrates food, wine and life in the company of friends, and nowhere is this more apparent than when guests meet—as they often do—members of the Ord or Arnold family on the estate.

Waterford aspires to create the iconic red wine of the Stellenbosch region, drawing on eight excellent varietals for a consistent, drinkable blend that represents the very best of South African vineyards. Already the accolades are pouring in, as Waterford has received several regional and international wine awards over the years for their various vintages.

The varieties planted in the vineyard include Cabernet Sauvignon, Shiraz, Merlot, Cabernet Franc, Mouvedre, Barbera, Petit Verdot and Malbec. Future plantings will include Tempranillo and Grenache, while existing vineyards that are between 12 and 14 years old include the well known Cabernet Sauvignon, Chardonnay and Sauvignon Blanc varietals. Wines are marketed all over the world, but there's nothing quite like dropping by Waterford Wine Estate for an in-situ wine tasting with friends, family and other loved ones.

Wine connoisseurs can enjoy all the different varieties Waterford has to offer from Mondays to Saturdays, while weekdays are open to wine and chocolate tastings as well. Visitors often spend the whole day at tastings and leave with one or two bottles (or more!) of excellent estate wine to take home and enjoy at their leisure.

Rows of little tables set with flowers and covered with bright cloths line the terraces of the homestead, overlooking great views of the surrounding country and the majestic Helderberg range rising up in the distance. The cosy living room, dressed in earthen and cream shades, also provides a comfortable seating area while the carved stone fireplace, crowned by two magnificent sets of spiralling antelope antlers, introduces warmth on chill days with a cheerful wood fire. Nearby, a large tranquil lake is the perfect spot for a late afternoon stroll and gives a picturesque vantage point of the homestead and the grounds.

The pleasant year-round weather of the region makes for a thoroughly enjoyable visit no matter when one chooses to come to Waterford. In any case, it's said that the company makes the experience, and among friends, with the welcoming smiles of the Waterford Wine Estate staff, there is no better place to experience the superb range of South African wines.

PRODUCTS
wide variety of red and white South African wines

FEATURES
wine tastings • wine and chocolate tastings • terrace seating • international distribution

NEARBY
Helderberg Mountains

CONTACT
Blaauwklippen Road
Stellenbosch 7600, Western Cape •
telephone: +27.21.880 0496 •
facsimile: +27.21.880 1007 •
email: info@waterfordestate.co.za •
website: www.waterfordestate.co.za

colona castle

...Colona Castle graces the mountainside above a tranquil lake district...

Guests feel like royalty as they walk into Colona Castle. The entrance hall is a majestic turret, with French doors leading onto a balcony that reveals panoramic lake, sea and mountain views. A five-star Mediterranean-style retreat, Colona Castle graces the mountainside above a tranquil lake district on the False Bay coastline, offering travellers an enchanting base from which to explore the Cape and Cape Town.

The turreted and crenellated Colona Castle was built in 1929 by a Scottish physician, Dr Munro Grier, who fell for the scenic charms of the Cape. In 1996, Nicole and Michael Brand bought the property and turned it into the stylish, elegant hotel it is today. Keeping the original foundations and character, they enlarged the entrance tower and refurbished the interiors.

Colona Castle is Tuscan-inspired and filled with the Brands' collection of antiques and objets d'art—life-sized Buddha statues, upholstered recliners, lavishly ornate mirrors and ornately carved fireplaces. By day, the interiors are suffused with a soft, golden glow. By night, the exteriors twinkle with the thousands of tiny lights coming in from Cape Town. In summer, cool breezes waft in from the ocean, while open hearth fires warm the lounges in winter.

The five luxury suites, two superior bedrooms and a family suite are individually decorated according to geographical themes. The Moroccan bedroom has an evocative, exotic North African appeal, while the classic European-inspired English suite opens onto a large private terrace where guests can enjoy breakfasts overlooking False Bay.

THIS PAGE (FROM TOP): The Chinese suite contains suitably Oriental accents, imparting an exotic air; the Mediterranean-style exterior with its cheerful buttercup walls.

OPPOSITE (CLOCKWISE FROM TOP): Enjoy refined dining at Colona Castle; spectacular panoramas of Table Mountain from the open terrace; the three-storey entrance tower, which the owners furnished with antique pieces and objets d'art.

Dinners at Colona Castle are a grand affair. With its superb position and bold proportions, the dining hall is a special place to eat, and the resident chef's creatively presented cuisine makes use of the Cape's finest and freshest ingredients.

Because Colona Castle is on the warmer False Bay coastline, it is mild in winter and cool in summer. Whales and varying types of marine life populate the Bay, depending on the season. The attractions of Cape Town and its environs are a short drive away, as are the Winelands. Visit a penguin colony at nearby Boulders, or head out to the dramatic Table Mountain National Park on the very edge of the Cape of Good Hope, the Western Southernmost Point of Africa.

ROOMS
2 rooms • 6 suites

FOOD
dining hall: international

DRINK
poolside bar

FEATURES
historical residence • antique collection • art collection

NEARBY
Cape Point • Boulders Beach • Kalk Bay Harbour • St James Beach • Muizenberg Beach • Boyes Drive • PostHuis and Rhodes Cottage Museums • Silvermine Nature Reserve • Cape Winelands • V&A Waterfront • Table Mountain

CONTACT
Verwood Street, Lakeside Cape Town 7945, Western Cape • telephone: +27.21.788 8235 • facsimile: +27.21.788 6577 • email: colona@link.co.za • website: www.colonacastle.co.za

the andros boutique hotel

...a true reflection of the beauty and heritage of Cape Town.

THIS PAGE (FROM TOP): A dazzling night view of the hotel building; the outdoor pool, set in the lush gardens, is the perfect place to kick back on a hot afternoon.

OPPOSITE (CLOCKWISE FROM TOP): Dine at the Andros is the hotel's fine dining restaurant that serves up French-inspired country cuisine; plaids and botanical motifs are used to create an atmosphere of elegant countryside living; enjoy a drink or two at the bar.

Step into the grounds of The Andros Boutique Hotel, and it's almost as if one has stepped back in time. Whether one arrives by day or night, the immaculate white walls of this early 20th-century manor house are an arresting sight, glowing in the sunlight or illuminated at night by the numerous lights surrounding the building. The architecture is classic Cape Dutch, and every single feature of the property, right down to the extensive park-like gardens, has been lovingly preserved to offer guests a full and nuanced enjoyment of its rich Cape heritage.

As appropriate for a hotel of this distinction, there are only 13 highly exclusive rooms, each uniquely furnished in a modern take on the sort of sumptuous country elegance characterised by polished walnut, sober plaids and delicate botanical prints. Over and above its standard share of luxuries, The Suite has a separate living area, and its popularity with honeymooners stems from its private entrance and pool.

The lush gardens make an exploration of the grounds a pleasure, and there is plenty of open lawn to stretch out on—or one can enjoy the surroundings from the shade of the well-pruned trees. The pool and fully equipped gym provide more rousing forms of exercise, while the on-site beauty salon, Bliss, offers two treatment rooms with experienced and qualified beauticians on hand.

True to form, The Andros Boutique Hotel's restaurant is also a boutique, exclusive affair. Dine at the Andros describes itself as an 'intimate 34-seater restaurant' that serves up romance and elegance along with its gourmet creations, a description

certainly filled by Chef Nicolene Barrow's exquisite menu. The interiors feature polished marble floors and South African art, set off to great effect by well-placed candles. The selection of dishes, put together with only the freshest local produce, are best described as country cuisine with subtle French influences, and changes to reflect the seasons. The menu is also brilliantly paired with a hand-picked wine list.

While the hotel's location, tucked away in Claremont, one of the southern Cape Town suburbs, may be a bonus for those seeking an idyllic holiday nestled in solitude and natural beauty, those who want a little more excitement certainly need not look elsewhere. With Kirstenbosch and the Constantia Winelands close by, offering vineyard tours, and V&A Waterfront a short drive away, there is plenty of opportunity for guests to embark on a fulfilling day-trip, which the concierge will be only too pleased to assist with in the planning and booking of.

It almost seems unnecessary to enumerate the hotel's multiple charms and qualities—one need only walk into its light, airy reception and witness first hand the excellent service rendered to guests to be convinced of having made the right choice. Enjoy pre-dinner drinks at the restaurant's champagne room as the sun sets over The Andros Boutique Hotel, a true reflection of the beauty and heritage of Cape Town.

ROOMS
12 rooms • 1 suite

FOOD
Dine at the Andros: country with French influence

DRINK
champagne room

FEATURES
beauty salon • outdoor pool • gym • landscaped gardens • meeting and conference facilities

NEARBY
Kirstenbosch • Constantia Winelands • V&A Waterfront • beach • city centre • golf course

CONTACT
Corner of Phyllis & Newlands Road Claremont 7708, Cape Town Western Cape • telephone: +27.21.797 9777 • facsimile: +27.21.797 0300 • email: info@andros.co.za • website: www.andros.co.za

the cape cadogan boutique hotel

...the very definition of a boutique experience.

Nestled in a beautiful residential area in the revitalised Gardens area of Cape Town, The Cape Cadogan Boutique Hotel is a refreshing oasis of sophisticated charm set against the backdrop of the unmistakable silhouette of Table Mountain. The hotel comprises an elegant 19th-century building that is also a national monument, the Owners Villa and several self-catering luxury apartments. Family-owned and managed, it offers all the comforts and warmth of a stay in a private home, just a short walk away from fashionable Kloof Street.

While the Georgian and Victorian exterior bespeaks its historic status, the main building offers bohemian chic within, marrying contemporary and antique furniture to dramatic effect. Inspired by the opulent flamboyance of Oscar Wilde, the hotel décor is accented with lavish fabrics, wrought-iron chandeliers and sepia prints in silver ornamented frames. The 12 guestrooms vary in size, but all are light and airy. The larger rooms boast spacious open-plan bathrooms and room number 8 is highly sought after, with a balcony that looks out to Table Mountain.

The Cape Cadogan opened in 2004 and picked up a *Condé Nast Traveller*, UK mention as one of the world's hottest, most promising new hotels for the year. Buoyed by this success, the Cape Cadogan apartments were opened shortly thereafter,

THIS PAGE (FROM TOP): The welcoming and graceful façade of the hotel; an invitingly padded sun lounger proves irresistible on a hot day.

OPPOSITE (FROM TOP): A tempting dish of chocolates—a welcome gift; clean lines and lustrous marble define this chic guest bathroom; rooms are modern, with hints of luxury in the finishing touches.

linked to the hotel by a cobbled private walkway. These five apartments have been refurbished and modernised for guests who prefer a more home-like stay; the largest apartment, the Redcliffe, has an outdoor entertainment area and pool patio as well.

The most exclusive accommodation at The Cape Cadogan is the Owners Villa, recently opened to select guests and friends of the Owner. Located in a stand-alone building with its own plunge pool, the villa has been designed along the lines of a presidential suite, ensuring the utmost privacy. Rich textures matched with simple lines create an atmosphere of stylish modernity in every room, from the lounge area that opens onto an outdoor deck to the sumptuous bedroom suite upstairs.

Regardless of their choice of rooms, guests can be assured of an impeccable standard of service. It is not uncommon for guests to be welcomed back from a day's sightseeing with a complimentary glass of wine or sherry in the lounge. Hotel staff are extremely knowledgeable of the dining and entertainment options on Kloof Street, and can also make arrangements for guests with some of these establishments.

With some of the city's most fascinating sightseeing, dining and people-watching hotspots just a short drive away or even within walking distance, The Cape Cadogan is well-situated for a leisurely exploration of Cape Town, without the hustle and bustle of being planted in the middle of a tourist district. Discreet yet welcoming, a stay here certainly illustrates the very definition of a boutique experience.

ROOMS
12 guest rooms • 5 apartments • villa

FOOD
breakfast room: Continental • in-room dining • third-party catering

DRINK
hotel lounge • wine list

FEATURES
garden • satellite television • laundry service • library • computer facilities • plunge pool

NEARBY
Camps Bay • Table Mountain Cable Car Station • V&A Waterfront • Boulders Beach • Cape Point Nature Reserve • Stellenbosch Centre • Franschoek Town Centre

CONTACT
5 Upper Union Street, Tamboerskloof, Cape Town 8001, Western Cape • telephone: +27.11.484 9911 • facsimile: +27.11.484 9916 • email: reservations@ capecadogan.com • website: www.capecadogan.com

cape grace

...a special appreciation of Cape Town that cannot be acquired anywhere else.

Capturing the essence of a five-star boutique hotel in one of the world's most fashionable cities is Cape Grace, situated on Cape Town's mesmerising waterfront. Its stately, classically inspired façade looks out over the water from the privacy of its own quay on the famed Victoria & Alfred Waterfront, beautiful both day and night. Within, the hotel's warm and elegant furnishings offer discerning travellers nothing less than the very finest in comfort and grace. In every room, guests enjoy double-glazed French doors that showcase unrivalled views of either the international yacht marina, majestic Table Mountain or the Waterfront's vibrant harbour.

Opened in 1996 by Charles Brand and family, Cape Grace has earned a reputation for warmth and intimacy akin to what one expects in the home of an old friend. Expect attentive service from some of the most warm and genuine staff in the world, and be sure to take

THIS PAGE: Cape Grace offers an unmatched view of the harbour.

OPPOSITE: The hotel's outdoor pool is a popular retreat on hot days.

advantage of the hotel's many complimentary services. The day starts with a full breakfast at the restaurant or in one's own room, while pastries, coffee, and tea are served in the library from dawn. Luxury transport to nearby locations is provided, and a typical day ends with complimentary port and sherry in the library every evening.

All of the property's 121 guestrooms and suites feature a wealth of elegant furnishings, services, and thoughtful amenities designed to make every stay an extraordinary one. Fresh flowers placed near comfortable chairs and sofas further brighten the naturally illuminated bedrooms and living areas, creating the perfect conditions for guests to enjoy an hour or two with their personal book and newspaper selections from the library. Every room is also equipped with a fully stocked mini bar, exquisite Charlotte Rhys bath and body products, satellite television channels, Internet access, safe, and ironing facilities.

The hotel's 80 Luxury Rooms cover the first three floors and offer excellent views of the marina, harbour, and Table Mountain. Their relaxed layouts accommodate double or twin beds, an intimate reading area, and access to connecting rooms upon request. Superior Rooms are more spacious and each of the 10 comes with step-out balconies from which the Waterfront's sights can be better enjoyed. They are ideal for families and have foldaway sofas for children to sleep in.

Above it all are eight Rooftop Luxury Rooms and 10 Rooftop Terrace Rooms that, as their names imply, take five-star living to the next level. These rooms let guests stroll out to private patios for uncompromised views of their beautiful surroundings. Starting the day with a newspaper and full breakfast spread on the Cape Grace's roof is a luxury with few equals. Both rooms are similarly sized and feature reading areas complete with a selection of books, while the Terrace Rooms enjoy more balcony space.

The ultimate Cape Town getaway, however, begins with one of the hotel's lavishly appointed suites. They are individually designed, with large living and dining areas for extended stays, honeymoons, and first-class

comfort. Hi-fi sound systems and DVD players, to name just a few modern amenities, are standard in all suites.

Two 1-Bedroom Suites overlook Signal Hill and Table Mountain, providing the perfect settings for private balcony dining experiences. Guests may also want to take their complimentary gourmet picnic baskets out to have a closer look at Cape Town's natural wonders. Six 2-Bedroom Suites feature guestrooms with en suite bathrooms, linked by kitchens, lounges and dining areas. Three 3-Bedroom Suites feature balconies over the marina and Waterfront, large enough for all occupants to dine together all night.

For those who seek nothing less than the most unforgettable experience, or a romantic holiday to cherish, the Cape Grace's two Penthouse Suites answer the call. As soon as guests arrive, an unpacking service is on hand to assist in settling in. One may start off by admiring the view from the top floor terrace, or taking a dip in its private outdoor jacuzzi. A little later on, meals can be specifically planned with the hotel's Executive Chef, or, in the evenings, one may indulge in a glass of complimentary cognac. The possibilities are endless in a room where delicate canapés are served every evening and a spacious walk-in closet awaits the rewards of daily shopping.

Whether guests find themselves at Cape Grace as newlyweds, or on business—here invariably mixed with pleasure—the hotel is prepared to cater to their every need. Conferencing and communication facilities are top of the line, and the Library offers a quiet reading spot with light refreshments. The award-winning restaurant, onewaterfront, reduces the entire Cape experience down onto a finely plated work of high gastronomy. Fresh seafood and gourmet creations inspired by the coast mingle effortlessly with local art and indigenous

THIS PAGE: The library is a cosy nook where guests can spend a quiet afternoon reading a book.

OPPOSITE (FROM TOP): The penthouse jacuzzi—the ultimate in luxury; enjoy a cool cocktail or a good glass of neat whisky at Bascule; rooms are filled with thoughtful touches such as fresh flowers.

floral arrangements. Between meals, consider Café Bascule, a coffee house and popular meeting place by day and a glamorous whisky and wine bar by night. With over 400 whiskies available, it forms one of the largest collections in the Southern Hemisphere.

And when the time comes for pure relaxation, lounge and watch the marina down by the 15-m (50-ft) heated pool, or submit to the joys of The Spa in full view of Table Mountain and the city. A range of therapies is available, from massages to luxury manicures/pedicures. The Spa is the perfect place to rejuvenate the body and mind after a long blissful day in the city.

Promising sheer elegance, luxury, and top facilities, Cape Grace offers some of the most delightful vacations on the coast. Its exclusive situation on the waterfront impresses upon visitors a special appreciation of Cape Town that cannot be acquired anywhere else. The pages of the hotel's guestbook are thick with fond recollections of romantic evenings spent enjoying the harbour's incredible views. Most significant, however, is the tone in which these entries are written—they sound almost like conversations with old friends.

ROOMS
108 rooms • 13 suites

FOOD
onewaterfront restaurant: modern South African • Bascule: café

DRINK
Bascule Whisky Bar and Wine Cellar

FEATURES
24-hour Internet access • boardroom • hot spa • wine tastings • luxury private transfers • secure parking • access to nearby health club • meeting room • online honeymoon registry • disabled facilities • communication centre

NEARBY
Camps Bay • Cape Point • Castle of Good Hope • aquarium • gardens • Greenmarket Square • museums • St Georges Cathedral • winelands • whale watching • V&A Waterfront

CONTACT
PO Box 51387, Waterfront Cape Town 8002, Western Cape • telephone: +27.21.410 7100 • facsimile: +27.21.419 7622 • email: info@capegrace.com • website: www.capegrace.com

les cascades de bantry bay

...the manifold glories of Cape Town are laid out at one's feet.

An oceanside road winds uphill through one of Cape Town's most exclusive suburbs, leading to Les Cascades de Bantry Bay, where the stunning backdrop of the Atlantic Ocean imbues every moment with heady splendour. Tucked away high up on the slopes of a mountain, Les Cascades serenity comes from its seamless inter-weaving with the natural elements surrounding it. The invigorating ocean air gives the setting an unmistakable degree of freshness and comfort, while the sparkling azure of the water goes straight to all the senses. An eye-catching creation at any time of the day, it is in the early evening that Le Cascades truly outshines itself, bathed in the vivid gold and vermillion glow of a South African sunset.

Les Cascades is Cape Town at its idyllic best while still offering its guests a bird's-eye view of the bustling city. The modern and cultural influences of Cape Town are distinctly highlighted throughout the hotel, with sleek furnishings and art incorporating African and Asian elements. The 10 rooms offered by Les Cascades use these elements to create a homely atmosphere of understated luxury. The earthy colours, liberal use of alder wood, and soft leather armchairs blend with the contemporary artistic design to create a space which is unpretentiously chic yet exudes warmth and hospitality. The large bay windows and private balconies overlooking the ocean illuminate these airy rooms, further creating the illusion of surprising, spacious depths. For an afternoon siesta, the latticed shutters bathe the rooms in a soothing auroral glow.

THIS PAGE (CLOCKWISE FROM TOP): **The** **shimmering infinity-edge pool; original pieces of South African artwork and sculpture comprise the décor of the outside lounge; Les Cascades shows a distinctly Balinese influence in its design.**

OPPOSITE (FROM TOP): **A breathtaking view of the Atlantic at sunset; each room has its own balcony; a corner to sit back and relax.**

ROOMS
10 rooms

FOOD
dining room: international • poolside lunches and afternoon teas • Main Lodge: full English or Continenal breakfast

DRINK
lounge

FEATURES
balé • 3 pools • sun decks • wireless Internet connection

NEARBY
V&A Waterfront • Table Mountain • Clifton beaches

CONTACT
48 de Wet Road, Bantry Bay Cape Town 8005, Western Cape • telephone: +27.21.434 5209 • facsimile: +27.21.439 4206 • email: info@cascadescollection.co.za • website: www.lescascades.co.za

Eating at Les Cascades is an extraordinary experience. The French-influenced cuisine is pure gastronomical delight, and meals here are touted as the best to be had in all of Cape Town. The restaurant, with its exposed-stone walls and polished crystal, combines rustic settings with cutting-edge dining. Guests can also rendezvous on the deck in the Main Lodge to savour the evening air. The thoughtful and unobtrusive service makes dining an intimate affair, interrupted only by dish after dish of exquisite creations from the kitchen and the refilling of one's glass with only the very finest South African vintage.

During the summer months, guests have the luxury of lounging in the three large outdoor pools, or enjoying the afternoon rays on the sun decks, with a panoptic view of the diamond-bright ocean. Cape Town's main attractions are also only a short drive away, and Clifton's popular beaches are a leisurely walk away. Most guests however, find it difficult to tear themselves away from Les Cascades radiant atmosphere and blissful setting. After all, here, the manifold glories of Cape Town are laid out at one's feet.

the cellars-hohenort

...the tradition of fine living, epitomised by the stately Hohenort manor house...

Two great traditions have been elegantly combined at The Cellars-Hohenort, a historic hotel nestled in the heart of Constantia Valley, Cape Town. One is the tradition of fine wine, continued in the magnificently restored 18th-century Klaasenbosch cellars. The other is the tradition of fine living, epitomised by the stately Hohenort manor house once owned by the illustrious Spilhaus family, which still continues to welcome visitors into its gracious embrace.

The Cellars-Hohenort is situated next door to the famous Kirstenbosch Botanical Gardens, one of the city's top tourist attractions, and the hotel itself looks out across exceptional views of the 9 acres of landscaped gardens and verdant vineyards.

There are 53 luxury rooms and suites, as well as Madiba Villa, named for Nelson Mandela, who is nicknamed Madiba. Tucked in a quiet corner of The Cellars-Hohenort's gardens, the Madiba Villa is a double-storey Cape-style home, offering complete privacy and tranquillity along with 24-hour room service. The Madiba Villa has a large sitting and dining room with a fireplace, bar and service kitchen, and two double en suite bedrooms. The Villa is fully air-conditioned, and has a private courtyard with its own exclusive outdoor pool.

THIS PAGE: The verdant surrounds complement the stark white of the Cape Dutch homestead.

OPPOSITE (FROM TOP): Potted plants are arranged along the walls, giving the room a cheerful air; The Martini lounge is the ideal place for a post-dinner drink.

Guests should also take some time to stroll through the lush gardens at Cellars-Hohenort. Lovingly tended by Jean Almon, the gardens were voted to be among one of the top 30 hotel gardens in the world by *Garden Design*. Liz has applied to the National Monuments Board of South Africa to have the gardens gazetted as a National Monument. The estate dates all the way back to 1693, and among the most impressive features here are the eight magnificent camphor trees that are 200 years old. They were planted in the time of Simon van der Stel, one of the first Europeans to set foot in the Cape, who had tiny camphor slips shipped in on a vessel sailing from the East.

The Cellars-Hohenort has a lovely indigenous garden, planted in 1997 by members of Kirstenbosch, that features a selection of plants from every region in South Africa. There is also a landscaped Edwardian garden showcasing a variety of traditional English flowers, as well as a rose garden sporting a myriad of colours and blooms. The rose garden was planted in 1997, but before the seedlings were put in the ground, a hurricane tore through the property, ripping off their labels, hence the varied, rather random mix that lines the vineyard perimeter.

In the Constantia Valley, one will find seven of the finest vineyards in South Africa, so it is no surprise that Cellars-Hohenort has an

award-winning wine list. The hotel's small vineyard itself is planted with four different varieties of table grapes. 2007 will see the launch of the first vintage of Vin de Hohenort, the hotel dessert wine.

The Greenhouse restaurant, open for lunch and dinner, serves superb South African and international cuisine. The restaurant offers garden and mountain views from its sun-drenched terrace. The Cape Malay Restaurant is a unique dining encounter. One of the few venues where tourists and Capetonians can enjoy traditional local fare. The comprehensive menu has a good selection of dishes from the subtly smooth to the pungent and aromatic. Waterblommetjie soup, snoek soup, pumpkin bredie, bobotie, denningvleis and other local delicacies feature strongly.

The Martini is not just another hotel bar but a place where guests and visitors to the hotel can enjoy afternoon tea and possibly an early afternoon martini in a chic, contemporary space. At night the bar transforms into a sophisticated place to be seen, where guests can sample the signature drink, the martini, of which there are 153 on the menu, making this one of the worlds longest martini lists. Besides martinis, there are numerous other cocktails on the menu, champagne by the glass and of course all the fabulous wines of the Cape with emphasis on the wines of the Constantia Valley.

Life at The Cellars-Hohenort moves at a languid pace. At the in-house Carchele Spa, therapists are on hand to ease away various stresses and strains, and there are two outdoor pools for lazing about in when the weather is fine, as well as a tennis court and a Gary Player-designed golf putting green.

THIS PAGE (FROM RIGHT): Clean lines and sleek materials define this modern, uncluttered interior; a contemporary take on the traditional four-poster bed is the focus of this guest suite.

OPPOSITE (CLOCKWISE FROM TOP): The neatly-organised herb gardens; guests can enjoy breakfast in the Greenhouse Conservatory; the delicious signature chocolate dessert at The Cellars-Hohenort.

CHOCOLATE PLATE 'LIZ MCGRATH'
Serves 8

Gâteau
250 g (8⅞ oz / 1⅞ cups) dark Callabaut or other good, dark Belgian chocolate
250 g (8⅞ oz / 1⅞ cups) unsalted butter
5 eggs
3 egg yolks
100 g (3½ oz / ½ cup) castor sugar
150 g (5⅝ oz / 1¼ cups) cake flour

Ice cream
250 ml (8½ fl oz / 1 cup) milk
300 ml (10⅛ fl oz / 1¼ cups) double cream
100 ml (3⅜ fl oz / ⅜ cup) glucose
225 g (8 oz / 1 cup) castor sugar
225 g (8 oz / 1 cup) white chocolate
4 egg yolks
melted chocolate for decorating
icing sugar for dusting

Gâteau Melt the chocolate in a bain-marie. In a pan, melt the butter over low heat and stir it into the chocolate. In a bowl, mix the eggs, egg yolks and castor sugar together until well-incorporated. Add the warm, but not hot, chocolate and butter mixture to the egg mixture, then fold in the flour. Spoon the mixture into 8 buttered moulds and refrigerate for a few hours until chilled. Bake in a preheated oven at 200° C

(392° F) for 10 minutes just before serving.

Ice cream Bring the milk, cream and glucose to a boil. Add half the sugar, stir well, then remove from the heat and stir in the white chocolate until melted. Mix the remaining sugar and the egg yolks together and incorporate it into the ice cream mixture. Strain, churn in an ice cream maker according to manufacturer's instructions and freeze.

To serve Decorate a plate with melted chocolate, then turn out the warm gâteau. Add a ball of white chocolate ice cream on the side. Dust with icing sugar.

Wine A sweet red dessert wine

ROOMS
33 rooms • 19 suites • Madiba private villa

FOOD
The Greenhouse: organic contemporary French and British • The Cape Malay: traditional Cape Malay

DRINK
The Martini • wine list

FEATURES
Carchele Spa • boutique • 2 heated pools • tennis court • golf green • hair salon • conference room

NEARBY
Cape Point • Cape Town • golf • Winelands • Camps Bay • Kirstenbosch Botanical Gardens • Hout Bay • Robben Island • Table Mountain

CONTACT
93 Brommersvlei Road, Constantia Cape Town 7800, Western Cape • telephone: +27.21.794 2137 • facsimile: +27.21 794 2149 • email: cellars@relaischateaux.com • website: www.cellars-hohenort.com

four rosmead

...a harmonious blend of traditional and contemporary chic...

What once used to be a three-bedroom home is now a spacious eight-bedroom boutique hotel sitting atop the slopes of Table Mountain. Owned by former investment banker David Shorrock, who finally realised his dreams of owning his own guesthouse, Four Rosmead is now an exclusive retreat that enjoys 360° views of the mountain, Lion's Head, Table Bay and the bustling city of Cape Town.

One need only step into its stylish interiors to find a harmonious blend of traditional and contemporary chic with a design aesthetic that emphasises clean lines and earthy colours. Of course, a distinctive local flavour is ever present with original, authentic South African artwork displayed prominently throughout. An angular wood and steel loggia which extends out above the garden terrace overlooks Four Rosmead's Mediterranean landscaped garden and pool deck. It's no wonder then, that this classified monument, built in 1903, is considered Cape contemporary classic for its elegant and charming interiors.

In the day, the eight bespoke en-suite bedrooms are constantly awash in sunlight and, coupled with indulgent amenities such as the latest high-tech gadgetry and high-quality linens, might very well induce guests to stay indoors. Another tempting option is to check out the in-house Holistic Pamper Spa for some of the many relaxing massages and wellness treatments available on its extensive menu. If not, Four Rosmead's proximity to Cape Town's myriad attractions is an opportunity simply too alluring to pass up.

This boutique guesthouse is within easy walking distance of the city as well as vibrant Kloof Street, which is well known for its flourishing restaurant and café culture. It is also close to Green Market Square, which became a farmers' market in 1710 and is now the city's best-known flea market and an important cultural landmark in its own right. Green Market Square is home to a large community of buskers, including dancers, singers and musicians as well as some of Cape Town's more colourful characters. The square is also bordered by a fascinating little selection of restaurants and cafés with outdoor tables for alfresco afternoon coffees in between shopping forays—the perfect opportunity to indulge in a spot of people-watching.

ROOMS
8

FOOD
breakfast room: Continental or full English breakfast • lunch and dinner on request

DRINK
honesty bars

FEATURES
landscaped garden • outdoor pool • iPod docking stations • DVD player • high-speed wireless Internet • Holistic Pamper Spa

NEARBY
Kloof Street • V&A Waterfront • Green Market Square • Table Mountain cable car • Robben Island • Clifton and Camps Bay beaches • Kirstenbosch gardens • Company Gardens

CONTACT
4 Rosmead Avenue, Oranjezicht Cape Town 8001, Western Cape • telephone: +27.21.480 3810 • facsimile: +27.21.423 0044 • email: info@fourrosmead.com • website: www.fourrosmead.com

Day tours to Cape Point and the Winelands can easily be arranged, and for the slightly more adventurous, the guesthouse can also help to plan and book a wide range of adventure activities, including shark diving, through specialised guides. At the end of an activity-filled day spent out in the field, visitors can look forward to a warm reception back at Four Rosmead, and stylishly appointed room to retire to for the night.

Its extensive breakfast menu offers both Continental and full English breakfasts as well as vegetarian friendly options and lunch and dinner is available on request. Guests can experience a truly dazzling sunset over Lion's Head while enjoying an aperitif on the patio, which overlooks the hotel's aromatic herb gardens and the shimmering salt-water pool.

Be it enjoying the creature comforts and amenities of this guesthouse or taking in sights of the vibrant Kloof Street, it is this rare combination of style, authenticity and personal service that makes Four Rosmead such a shining representative of the spirit and beauty of Cape Town.

metropole hotel

Inspired glamour meets historic dignity at the Metropole Hotel...

Inspired glamour meets historic dignity at the Metropole Hotel, a four-storey Victorian townhouse in the heart of Cape Town. While its remodelled interiors are an edgy showcase of daring urban design, this boutique hotel still sparkles with old-world charm nonetheless, offering a trendy yet comfortable home base for exploring the city centre.

The highlight of the lobby is the antique cast-iron elevator, the oldest functioning one in the city. Guestrooms are on the two floors above the restaurant and bar area, clear above the level of street noise, and are extremely spacious, as the hotel has stayed true to the original floor plans despite its makeover. Decorated in soothing hues like taupe and white, the luxuriously appointed rooms are fitted with all the particular conveniences for the hip global traveller, from Internet connections to satellite television and even special universal electricity outlets. Most rooms have a Juliet balcony, ideal for scoping out busy Long Street below—people-watching is certainly not a neglected activity with the city centre so close by.

The Metropole's proximity to Long Street is reason enough to plan a stay here, as the party in the streets and off it, in the hotel, regularly goes on well after midnight. The hotel's extravagantly kitsch M Bar is one of the hottest spots on the local nightlife scene, drawing fashionable South Africans as well as in-the-know visitors. Where the stuffed heads of game animals once adorned the interiors, now hang tongue-in-cheek wire-bent figurines rendered in

THIS PAGE (FROM TOP): Rooms display a strong, modern sense of style; the M Café offers a light casual dining menu in a chic interior.

OPPOSITE (FROM TOP): Veranda has an enviable view of Long Street; Metropole Hotel shines at night; M Bar, with its distinctive flavour and that crimson Versace sofa.

ROOMS
29 guestrooms

FOOD
Veranda: modern South African •
M Café: casual meals

DRINK
M Bar

FEATURES
business centre • boardroom

NEARBY
Cape Town city centre

CONTACT
38 Long Street, Cape Town 8001
Western Cape •
telephone: +27.21.424 7247 •
facsimile: +27.21.424 7248 •
email: info@metropolehotel.co.za •
website: www.metropolehotel.co.za

stark white or playful primary colours. Opulence is the watchword here, with vividly deep red fabrics dominating the surfaces and emphasised by dramatic lighting, not to mention the centrepiece Versace sofa that flamboyantly dominates the space.

A tamer but no less impressive setting is the Veranda restaurant, with huge glass windows that flood the room with daylight and allow an uninterrupted view of Long Street. The restaurant décor is all clean lines and white upholstery with black accents—elegant simplicity at its best. The menu is an unpretentious spread of modern South African: comfort food with a twist, meaning that guests can expect hearty fare served with a dash of eclectic flair.

The confident personality of the Metropole, combined with its prime location within walking distance to the historic areas and lively De Waterkant area, make it the obvious choice for discriminating travellers who want an alternative to the predictable guidebook experience. A stay here will pamper the body, quicken the soul and energise the spirit.

o on kloof

...furnished like any space found in a glossy interior design magazine...

THIS PAGE (CLOCKWISE FROM BOTTOM): *The hotel lounge is the perfect place for relaxing after dinner; rooms are modern and stylish; the cosy hotel bar and lounge.*

OPPOSITE (CLOCKWISE FROM TOP): *The new patio is a popular option on warm summer afternoons; a private nook for sunbathing; the welcoming main entrance.*

At first glance, one might easily be forgiven for taking O on Kloof to be nothing more or less than a fabulously designed private mansion, all sleek modern lines and stylish décor. It's not too far off the mark—Olaf Dambrowski, the renowned Cape hotelier and owner of this luxurious boutique hotel, designed it especially for the discerning traveller who wishes to enjoy Cape Town in sumptuous, urbane, yet home-like surroundings.

Upon arrival, guests are greeted with complimentary drinks and canapés, the very first taste of the decadent pampering that O on Kloof lavishes upon all its visitors. Dark woods and a deep, rich colour palette characterise the interiors, with exquisite monogrammed French table linens creating an elegant, snowy contrast. Rooms—of which there are only eight, to heighten the exclusivity—are furnished like any space found in a glossy interior design magazine, and most come with a separate lounge or study so the sleeping area is kept as a pristine sanctuary of rest. This feature is paramount to the comfort of guests, whether their purposes incline towards business or leisure—a good night's sleep, as O on Kloof is fully aware, makes a crucial difference to the day ahead.

Dining options abound on Cape Town, especially in the trendy suburb of Fresnaye on Signal Hill, where O on Kloof is located. For a light, modern dining experience, however, look no further than O's, the hotel restaurant, whose bar is a convenient gathering spot in the evening for guests. O's is open for breakfast, lunch and dinner—guests often choose to have their meals served out on the main deck overlooking the sea. Inside, a wide skylight frames a view of Lion's Head in all its glory.

For the health conscious, O on Kloof thoughtfully provides a range of facilities, ranging from a compact but well-stocked juice bar, a well-equipped gym and a large heated indoor pool where a physiotherapist gives aquarobic lessons each morning. Indeed, it's all these little touches that make a stay at O on Kloof so pleasant and keeps guests returning year after year. From the bilingual staff who help foreign guests adapt to local situations to the impressive DVD library catering for those who fancy a quiet night in, every aspect of the hotel is geared towards guests' enjoyment and succeeds with consummate panache.

Just minutes away from V&A Waterfront, Table Mountain and the city centre, not to mention its proximity to Camps Bay and Clifton's beaches, O on Kloof's location is practically flawless. With the many and varied attractions of Cape Town so close at hand and the promise of a luxurious retreat to bask in upon return, it is well nigh impossible to resist a visit to O on Kloof—one may even find it a challenge trying to leave its chic, comfortable confines.

ROOMS
8 rooms

FOOD
O's: international

DRINK
hotel bar • juice bar

FEATURES
gym • heated indoor pool • DVD library • Internet connection

NEARBY
V&A Waterfront • city centre • Camps Bay • Clifton's beaches

CONTACT
92 Kloof Road, Bantry Bay
Cape Town 8005, Western Cape •
telephone: +27.21.439 2081 •
facsimile: +27.21.439 8832 •
email: olaf@oonkloof.co.za •
website: www.oonkloof.co.za

vineyard hotel + spa

...an ideal choice for visitors to Cape Town.

This establishment in Cape Town's peaceful Newlands suburb offers guests a rewarding intersection of history, nature, convenience, and luxury. Built in 1799 by Lady Anne Barnard, the Vineyard Hotel & Spa's original manor has since been expanded with the addition of new rooms designed by architects Jack Barnett and Revel Fox. The property's 2.5 hectares (6 acres) of immaculately landscaped greenery are situated on the banks of the Liesbeeck River, which flows down to the sea from mountains high above Newlands. Along with majestic views of Table Mountain's forested slopes, the tranquillity of this beautiful enclave cradles the deluxe 175-room hotel in the very lap of nature. So it is with great surprise that one learns the city centre and the Victoria & Alfred Waterfront are only a mere ten minutes' walk away.

THIS PAGE (FROM TOP): *The reception of Angsana Spa features Asian interior themes and furnishings; the light and airy atmosphere is typical through the entire hotel.*

OPPOSITE (FROM TOP): *Enjoy breakfast overlooking the stunning view; the hotel has two heated pools; a quiet, tranquil corner in the hotel, surrounded by greenery.*

Each room at the Vineyard is positioned to enjoy a carefully cultivated view of the location's natural sights, and has a full complement of modern amenities such as free high-speed Internet access, satellite television, mini bars, and wall safes. Courtyard rooms overlook a Japanese-inspired garden with water features and delicate tree ferns. In this shaded area, beautiful birds are a common sight on most mornings as well as evenings. The 68 Courtyard Facing rooms each feature double beds and bathrooms with separate baths and showers. Alternatively, 15 Courtyard Deluxe rooms offer larger ground and second storey options that either open out to, or overlook, exclusive private gardens/patios.

For visitors who relish the thought of rising each morning to the sight of iconic Table Mountain, the Vineyard's Mountain rooms offer the best vantage points. 40 Mountain

Facing rooms provide unobstructed views of the famous landmark and the hotel's picturesque gardens, with the same facilities as Courtyard Facing Rooms. Mountain Deluxe rooms, of which there are 22, are more spacious and have private balconies or patios where one may lounge and take in Table's splendour at one's own pace.

Junior Suites also provide views of Table Mountain, but primarily overlook either the Liesbeeck River or the estate's beautiful gardens. Guests can enjoy their surroundings from private balconies, or in lounge areas enclosed with glass, letting an optimum amount of natural light into each of the 16 suites. The adjoining double bedrooms with en suite bathrooms complete the experience. For those who desire even more luxurious accommodation, there are

nine luxury Suites comprised of beautiful, tastefully appointed living areas that connect to spacious bedrooms. Suites on the ground floor have floor-to-ceiling glass sliding doors that open out spectacularly to their own gardens and terraces.

Perhaps the most luxurious guestrooms, however, are the ones that are not really rooms at all. Removed from the main building, five Garden Cottages accommodate large families, groups of friends, or guests wishing to stay for longer periods of time in absolute comfort. These cottages have two bedrooms and bathrooms, a kitchen, dining room, and living room each.

If the lush parkland grounds, light resort atmosphere, and soothing water features were not enough in the way of relaxation, the Vineyard's Angsana Spa is guaranteed to take all one's troubles away. The Angsana Spa is owned and operated by the world-renowned Banyan Tree group, and takes its name from the exotic tree whose flowers bloom without warning for just one day. The spa's location by the tranquil Liesbeeck River offers the perfect foundation for an afternoon of unique therapies in complete privacy with a loved one.

As a complement to the range of services offered at the Angsana Spa, the hotel also boasts a 20 m (66 ft) heated outdoor pool and a modern Health & Fitness centre. Stylishly composed of glass and steel, the latter is a state-of-the-art facility anchored by a heated

THIS PAGE: *Cheerful hues create an energising air at Angsana Spa.*
OPPOSITE (FROM TOP): *A relaxing spa treatment soothes cares away; Table Mountain plays a major part in the magnificent scenery; plush furnishings and a private patio are some of the luxuries that await guests at Vineyard.*

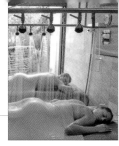

indoor pool and a fully equipped gymnasium. The health centre's café, Splash, has a light menu designed specifically with the health-conscious in mind. For more traditional dining, the Vineyard has two superb restaurants catering to a wide range of tastes. The Square is a brasserie-style restaurant at the center of the hotel that blends nature and modern refinement. Guests are served exquisite dishes and fine wines in full view of the stars beneath a magnificent glass roof. The Square also features a sushi bar, where skilled masters prepare fresh ingredients to infuse meals with a delightful touch of the Orient. Myoga, under the direction of acclaimed restaurateur chef Mike Bassett, serves contemporary global fusion cuisine in a relaxed and intimate setting. The menu mirrors Mr Bassett's very successful Cape Town restaurant, Ginja, which has recently been voted South Africa's Best Restaurant by *House & Leisure* magazine.

Well-known for its warm and efficient service, the Vineyard Hotel & Spa is an ideal choice for visitors to Cape Town. Staff are always on hand to assist with special needs and requests, so time is always spent on the things that matter most. From its charming and private location, holidaymakers enjoy a side of the region rarely seen by other travellers, and leave with an intimate knowledge of pleasure that is often difficult to convey with words.

ROOMS
145 rooms • 25 suites • 5 cottages

FOOD
Splash Café: light healthy meals • The Square: contemporary dining and sushi bar • Myoga: global fusion

DRINK
wine list

FEATURES
free parking • complimentary high speed Internet access • gymnasium • 2 heated pools • 3 gift boutiques • landscaped gardens • 24 hour medical support • Angsana Spa

NEARBY
beaches • city centre • Kirstenbosch Botanical Gardens • Table Mountain • wine routes • 18-hole golf course

CONTACT
PO Box 151, Newlands Cape Town 7725. Western Cape • telephone: +27.21.657 4500 • facsimile: +27.21.657 4501 • email: hotel@vineyard.co.za • website: www.vineyard.co.za

winchester mansions hotel

...an enduring favourite with visitors ever since its establishment in the 1920s.

THIS PAGE (FROM TOP): *The courtyard at Winchester Mansions Hotel; guests can relax by the heated outdoor pool with a cool drink; Harveys at The Mansions serves delightful authentic Cape cuisine.*

OPPOSITE (CLOCKWISE FROM TOP): *The hotel's Sunday Jazz Brunch is an institution—a decadent buffet spread of delicacies and bubbly; the shining white hotel exteriors; rooms are warmly lit, with dark woods and bright fabrics adding welcome touches of elegance.*

The charming personality of Winchester Mansions Hotel is like a whiff of fresh sea air, which is what guests will get plenty of, should they spend a few days in this elegant Cape Dutch-style beach boutique hotel that faces the Atlantic Ocean. This four-star beachfront hotel has remained an enduring favourite with visitors ever since its establishment in the 1920s. The past decade of expansion and refurbishment has continued to keep this grand dame in good stead, winning AA accommodation awards in 2001, 2002, 2004 and 2006 in South Africa and being rated by *Travel + Leisure* (UK) as one of the 65 Affordable Hotels of the World in 2003.

Winchester Mansions Hotel is conveniently located in Sea Point on the famous Platinum Mile, which is one of Cape Town's finest seaside locations, just 10 minutes' drive away from the hub of the city centre and a mere seven minutes away from the highly popular Clifton beaches. Even if guests at Winchester Mansions Hotel do not wish to venture too far from the

hotel premises, there are more than enough engaging activities to keep one's time well occupied in this charming old-world mansion by the sea. Guests will always be assured to find the tried and tested winning combination of homely cosiness and luxurious indulgence here.

On warm summer days, a walk by the ocean is just at one's doorstep, made all the more enjoyable by a spectacular mountain backdrop. In the cooler season, there is an outdoor heated pool for guests to soak in. The ultimate retreat, however, is at The Gingko Health and Wellness Spa located within the hotel. It provides a range of massage and spa treatments such as Deep Tissue Massage and Ocean Therapy Wrap to get one all energised and glowing.

The one thing one should by no means miss while at Winchester Mansions is its legendary Sunday Jazz Brunch, which showcases the best of Cape Town's vibrant jazz scene. Listening to the rhythmic improvisations of a live jazz band over fine bubbly and a sumptuous buffet brunch is an experience to be savoured and cherished, which is why local jazz lovers and tourists flock to this hotel without fail every Sunday morning. This event has become such an institution that the hotel has even released a 'Jazz at the Mansions—Volume One' CD for guests and fans who would like to remember this classic Winchester Cape Town experience.

On other days, its restaurant, Harveys at The Mansions attracts epicureans to the hotel with its delectable classic Cape Cuisine such as A Trio of African Game consisting of grilled ostrich steak, pan-fried crocodile tail and seared springbok loin and African linefish with chilli lime

salsa and coriander mash. On a clear day, Harveys' range of tantalising dishes can be enjoyed in the elegantly colonnaded Courtyard, amidst the swaying palm trees and gushing fountain for that intimately romantic meal.

Undoubtedly, staying at Winchester Mansions Hotel is the best way to appreciate Cape Town—with the sea, the city and a little bit of jazz to make one's stay a memorable and worthwhile one.

ROOMS
76 rooms

FOOD
Harveys at The Mansions: international with classic Cape influences • Jazz at the Mansions: Sunday Jazz Brunch

DRINK
The Harveys Bar

FEATURES
Italian-style courtyard • The Gingko Health & Wellness Spa • heated pool • complimentary transport to the V&A Waterfront • conference and banqueting facilities • secretarial services • family friendly

NEARBY
Clifton Beaches • V&A Waterfront • Cape Town city centre

CONTACT
221 Beach Road, Sea Point Cape Town 8001, Western Cape • telephone: +27.21.434 2351 • facsimile: +27.21.434 0215 • email: sales@winchester.co.za • website: www.winchester.co.za

tourism corporation africa

...one of the most diverse and exclusive luxury property portfolios of its kind...

THIS PAGE (FROM TOP): Spend a night out under the stars at Londolozi; the exclusive Birkenhead House overlooks the magnificent ocean.

OPPOSITE (FROM TOP): Enjoy a view of the mountains here at Aquila; the vineyards of Mont Rochelle; British Airways is one of TCA's exclusive airline partners.

Tourism Corporation Africa is perfectly positioned to meet the needs of a new class of independent global travellers eager to experience both the authentic charm and magnificence of Africa, and the classic allure of Europe. With one of the most diverse and exclusive luxury property portfolios of its kind, composed of prime destinations spanning two continents, the company appeals to their sense of adventure, challenges their imaginations, and above all, lets them do it in style. Tourism Corporation Africa's international reach is achieved via select partnerships with leading boutique hotels, villas, and lodges stretching from vibrant Cape Town to the private Sabi Sands Reserve in Africa, Tuscany's picture-perfect Arno Valley in Italy, and the French countryside, where the charm of the old-world lives on in grand chateaus.

The properties in TCA's portfolio have been recognised as the very best, winning annual awards and scores of accolades from publications as prestigious as *Condé Nast Traveller*, *Tatler*, and *Andrew Harper*. The secret that powers the success of any premium property can be summed up in two words: Service and Luxury. Without exception, every establishment TCA offers pairs personalised, concierge-style attention with the highest standards of quality living.

Because true luxury knows no limitations, this applies not only to cutting-edge urban boutique hotels, idyllic European villas and beach resorts, but also to secluded game lodges in the most inaccessible places imaginable. In that regard, Tourism Corporation Africa more than understand the expectations of discerning global travellers, it aims to surpass them, and surpass them it does. All together, this collection provides them with the most outstanding and memorable travel experiences available anywhere in the world.

Conscious of the fact that how one begins a journey will then go on to set the tone for everything that follows, immense care is taken to ensure that things get off to a comfortable and hassle-free start. To that end, Tourism Corporation Africa have arranged strategic partnerships with best-of-class air travel companies across the Western hemisphere. All trips begin and end in grand style with facilitating partners British Airways, Swiss International Airlines, Lufthansa, and Airlink. Today's affluent, well-informed traveller seeks not to follow beaten paths, but to explore uncommon, exotic grounds. What TCA have to offer will bring about nothing less than a paradigm shift in global luxury travel—a new voyage of discovery— and so it is fitting that it should come from the place where it all began. It's time the world headed back to the source. Africa is out there and waiting.

PROPERTIES

South Africa: Aquila Private Game Reserve, the Karoo • Birkenhead House, Hermanus • Birkenhead Villa, Hermanus • La Residence, Franschhoek • Londolozi, Mpumalanga • Mont Rochelle Hotel & Mountain Vineyards, Franschhoek • Royal Malewane, Limpopo • Savanna Private Game Reserve, Mpumalanga • St Johns Private Estate & The Manor House, Cape Town

Italy: Villa Mangiacane

France: Château Soussac

UK: No 7 Edgerton Gardens

Nassau: The Beachhouse–Paradise Islands (2009)

FEATURES

partnerships with British Airways, Lufthansa, Swiss International Airlines and Airlink

CONTACT

1 St Johns, Higgo Crescent, Higgovale Cape Town 8001, Western Cape • telephone: +27.21.462 0436 • facsimile: +27.21.462 2529 • email: tcorp@iafrica.com • website: www.tourismcorp.co.za

cape town + garden route itinerary

THIS PAGE (FROM TOP): Gather round the evening campfire to swap stories about the day's activities; iCi, the stylish restaurant at the acclaimed Le Quartier Français.

OPPOSITE (FROM TOP): Landscaped gardens at the Vineyard Hotel & Spa provide a perfect spot for leisurely, picturesque walks; dolphin viewing is a must when one is travelling along the coast.

With its warm Mediterranean climate, colourful mix of people and the impressive backdrop of Table Mountain, Cape Town makes an ideal starting point to any South African itinerary. The city is laid back, ringed with white sandy beaches and imbued with colonial and more recent history. A few days in the mother city offers stunning views from the top of Table Mountain, a windswept visit to the Cape of Good Hope—the south-western tip of Africa, a casual stroll around the Victoria & Alfred Waterfront with its boutique shops and quayside restaurants, and the chance to relax on your choice of Clifton's four beaches.

A short drive away are the Cape Winelands of Stellenbosch and Franschhoek, where old settler homesteads offer luxurious accommodation in the heart of working vineyards, surrounded by spectacular mountains. Travelling south to Walker Bay, enjoy the best cliff-based whale watching in the world as these mighty creatures of the deep seek the shelter of calmer waters to calve and mate from June to December.

The Cape's famed 'Garden Route' extends eastwards from Mossel Bay to Port Elizabeth. Spectacular hiking trails, exciting water sports, paragliding, abseiling and mountain biking attract the adventurous at heart while the abundant bird and wildlife, vast beaches, cool forests and magnificent vistas soothe the soul. The waterways around Wilderness and Knysna offer visitors the pleasures of canoeing, sailing, waterskiing and fishing; while the beaches of Plettenberg Bay offer sandy access to the warm waters of the Indian Ocean.

Inland of Port Elizabeth, the Eastern Cape offers a number of safari options. From the large elephant numbers in the Greater Addo Elephant National Park, to the Big 5 game reserves of Kwandwe and Samara, it's time to grab your binoculars and head out into the bush.

Highlights

Cape Town • Table Mountain • Victoria & Alfred Waterfront • Cape Winelands • Knysna • Port Elizabeth • Walker Bay • Plettenberg Bay • Greater Addo Elephant National Park

Suggested itinerary

- Fly into Cape Town in the Western Cape.
- Transfer from the airport for a three night stay at Cape Grace Hotel or the Vineyard Hotel & Spa for a taste of luxury in the heart of a bustling city.
- Picking up your own car, head inland for two nights in the Winelands at either Klein Genot

Wine & Country estate or Le Quartier Français, taking in the full measure of South Africa's fine wines and elegant country living.

- Heading south from the Winelands to the spectacular Walker Bay Coastline, stay for two nights at Grootbos Private Nature Reserve to get up close and personal with nature at its most spectacular.
- Travelling east along the Garden Route to Plettenberg Bay, shore up in style at Tsala Treetop Lodge or Kurland Hotel.
- Head inland to the Elephant House for a short trip back to colonial times and the chance to safari in the Addo National Park.
- Continue your safari at either CC Africa's Kwandwe Private Game Reserve or Samara Private Game Reserve.
- Travel on to Port Elizabeth, drop your car off and catch your return flight homewards or on to other regional destinations.

FACE AFRICA

All of the lodges mentioned above have been selected for their commitment to their staff and outstanding contributions to the environment and local communities. To personalise the above itinerary to suit your ideal South African getaway, please contact Face Africa in the UK on +44.871.218 3595 or send an email to chic@faceafrica.com. To find out more, visit www.faceafrica.com.

kruger + the waterberg itinerary

THIS PAGE: *Romantic outdoor fine dining at a private table at Sabi Sabi Private Game Reserve.*

OPPOSITE (FROM TOP): *A spectacular view from one's own bathroom; Londolozi's safari themed décor is maintained throughout, so its guests are always aware of their proximity to the African bush.*

No visit to South Africa can be considered complete without a safari, complete with spectacular game viewing. The Kruger National Park incorporates a huge protected wilderness area as part of the Great Limpopo Transfrontier Park, and its western edge offers an unfenced boundary with some of Africa's finest private game reserves and lodges. Safari chic is certainly showcased at its very best here, with beautifully appointed luxury tented suites meticulously blended into the wilderness that surrounds the viewer on all sides. The wide range of daily activities available to guests include game drives in open safari vehicles with experienced game rangers, informative bush walks, horseback riding and more. Food is an important element of any safari, and the South Africans do it particularly well, bringing equal aplomb to international cuisine served up in fine dining rooms and traditional African dishes shared by an open fire in authentic bush bomas.

In the heat of the day, one can always relax in the bush spa, before spending the cooler evening hours on the lodge verandah with a cocktail in hand, watching the various species of wildlife gather around a nearby watering hole.

To complement the Big Game safari journeying, the Waterberg area to the north of Pretoria offers a vast tract of mountainous wilderness on the edge of an ancient escarpment. Hiking is particularly favoured here, as a more leisurely alternative to take in areas not accessible by safari vehicles. Old settler farmhouses offer luxurious accommodation, and more relaxed game watching on large private reserves.

Highlights

Kruger National Park • Private game reserves • Health spas • Game viewing • Waterberg mountains • Luxurious farm stays

Suggested itinerary

- Fly into Johannesburg and connect to Nelspruit, capital of Mpumalanga and gateway to the Kruger National Park
- Transfer from the airport to Lukimbi Safari Lodge for four nights on an extended safari stay in a private concession within the Kruger National Park.
- Take a private transfer through the Kruger National Park to the Sabi Sands Private Game Reserve, home to some of the best big cat sightings on the continent.
- Spend four nights at Sabi Sabi Private Game Reserve, Londolozi or CC Africa's Kirkman's Kamp, all of which offer superb service and sumptuous bush accommodations.
- Head north and west to the Waterberg for five nights at Jembisa, a converted family home that comes with its own private game reserve—the Palala River Reserve.
- Return to Johannesburg for your flight homewards or on to other regional destinations.

ꝫ︖ FACE AFRICA

All of the lodges mentioned above have been selected for their commitment to their staff and outstanding contributions to the environment and local communities. To personalise the above itinerary to suit your ideal South African getaway, please contact Face Africa in the UK on +44.871.218 3595 or send an email to chic@faceafrica.com. To find out more, visit www.faceafrica.com.

the kalahari + johannesburg itinerary

For those with the need to get off the beaten track in style, the vast expanse of the Kalahari Wilderness beckons. The 100,000-hectare (250,000-acre) Tswalu Reserve is the largest private game reserve in South Africa and a dedicated conservation area. This Fair Trade and Tourism South Africa accredited lodge has won numerous awards for its efforts towards wildlife conservation and local community development. Enjoy scenic game drives (the majestic black-maned Kalahari Lion is a prominent resident frequently spotted on the reserve), horse riding, bush walks and even a visit to an habituated meerkat colony. These small mammals live in large communities within the Kalahari desert and present an amusing and picturesque spectacle when they emerge en masse in the dawn hours to greet the sunrise—in actuality sunning their bellies to rid themselves of the night chill. In the desert, temperatures tend to fall quickly in the night, and the endless stretches of cloudless African night skies mean that the stars are all part of the essential viewing after the sun goes down.

The Madikwe Game Reserve in the Northwest Province was developed specifically to provide local development opportunities to the surrounding communities and to reintroduce indigenous game to a region troubled by cattle overgrazing. The result is one of the best Big Five reserves in South Africa with more than its fair share of eco-sensitive luxury lodges. Particularly well known for sightings of the critically endangered African wild dog, the reserve offers fantastic game-viewing and bird-watching opportunities.

Why not finish your trip with a couple of days in Johannesburg and pick up the Jozi vibe. The nearby suburb of Rosebank is an upmarket residential enclave with excellent weekend markets, and don't miss the opportunity to visit the newly hip Soweto township, with its lively shebeens and the excellent Apartheid Museum.

Highlights

Kalahari Desert • meerkat population • Endangered African wild dog • Madikwe Game Reserve • Johannesburg • seasonal festivals and parades • Soweto township

Suggested itinerary

- Fly into Cape Town or Johannesburg.
- Connect by private air charter to Tswalu Kalahari Reserve for a four-night stay at the border of the Northern Cape and Northwest Province, where game viewing opportunities come aplenty along with the luxurious suite accommodations.
- Return to Johannesburg for a transfer, and move far up into Northwest Province to the Madikwe Game Reserve for a four-night stay at Etali Safari Lodge or the exclusive Mateya Safari Lodge, both set amidst a panoramic bush landscape.
- Return to Johannesburg and transfer to Tintswalo at Waterfall, a stylish hotel on the outskirts of the city with an arresting equestrian theme and design, for a two-night stay.
- Return to Johannesburg for your flight homewards or on to other regional destinations.

FACE AFRICA

All of the lodges mentioned above have been selected for their commitment to their staff and outstanding contributions to the environment and local communities. To personalise the above itinerary to suit your ideal South African getaway, please contact Face Africa in the UK on +44.871.218 3595 or send an email to chic@faceafrica.com. To find out more, visit www.faceafrica.com.

index

Numbers in *italics* denote pages where both the relevant pictures and text are found. Numbers in **bold** denote the relevant property profiles.

index

picturecredits+acknowledgements

The publisher would like to thank the following for permission to reproduce their photographs:

Adam Jones/Getty Images 155
AFP/Getty Images 23 (bottom), 107 (top), 194, 184
Alain Proust; Cape Photo Library/iAfrika Photos 82, 105
Aquila Private Game Reserve 263 (top)
Babak Fakhamzadeh 24–25 (top)
Bernard van Berg/Getty Images 29
Bill Hatcher/Getty Images 4
Birkenhead House 212–213, 262 (bottom)
Bobby Haas/Getty Images 191
Bread and Butter/Getty Images 111 (top)
British Airways 263 (bottom)
Cape Grace Hotel 15 (bottom), 240–243
Charles Krebs/Getty Images 56
Charles O'Rear/Corbis 18
Chitwa Chitwa Private Game Lodges 58–59
Christopher Thomas/Getty Images 180
Colona Castle 234–235
Connie Coleman/Getty Images 154
Conservation Corporation Africa 2, 17, 68–69, 168–169, 264 (top)
Corbis 132 (top)
Craig Dutton 109 (bottom), 113
Darrell Gulin/Getty Images 108
David Turnley/Corbis 132 (bottom)
d'Ouwe Werf 230–231
Elephant House 174–175
Etali Safari Lodge 136–139, 268 (top), 269 (top)
Fairlawns Boutique Hotel & Spa 36–39
Fordoun 122–123
Four Rosmead 250–251
Gavin Hellier/Getty Images 178
Getty Images 27 (bottom), 30 (bottom)
Gideon Mendel/Corbis 76
Gorah Elephant Camp 170–171
Grande Provence 15 (top), 218–219
Grant Faint/Getty Images 74
Hein von Horsten/Getty Images 81
Heinrich van den Berg/Getty Images 111 (bottom), 160, 164
Hoberman Collection/Corbis 186
Hunter's Country House 204–205
Inyati Game Lodge 60–61
Jake Wyman/Getty Images 83
Jembisa 96–97
John Hogg/EPA/Corbis 187
Jon Hicks/Corbis 133, 165

Jon Hrusa/epa/Corbis 20, 21, 25 (bottom), 27 (top)
Jonathan Blair/Corbis 112
Klein Genot Wine & Country Estate 220–221
Kurland 196–197, 265 (bottom)
KwaZulu-Natal Philharmonic Orchestra 107 (bottom)
Le Quartier Francais 222–225, 264 (bottom)
Les Cascades de Bantry Bay 244–245
Lesheba 88–89
Lion Sands Private Game Reserve 70–71
Londolozi 62–63, 262 (top), 267 (bottom)
Louise Gubb/Corbis Saba 80 (bottom)
Lucas Lenci Photo/Getty Images 48
Lukimbi Safari Lodge 72–72
Madikwe Hills Private Game Reserve 140–141
Makanyane Safari Lodge 142–143
Makweti Safari Lodge 98–99
MalaMala Game Reserve 64–65
Manus van Dyk/Getty Images 51 (top)
Marataba Safari Company 8–9, 90–91
Mark Bloomfield 13 (top)
Martin Harvey/Corbis 52 (bottom), 79, 134, 183 (bottom)
Mateya Safari Lodge 144–145, 268 (bottom)
Melrose Arch Hotel 40–41
Metropole Hotel 252–253
Mhondoro Game Lodge 92–93
Michael Nichols/Getty Images 51 (bottom)
Michele Westmorland/Corbis 158
Mike Hill/Getty Images 100
Mont Rochelle Hotel & Mountain Vineyards 226–227, 263 (centre)
Morukuru Lodge 146–147
Mount Grace Country House & Spa 32–35
Nathan Bilow/Getty Images 16
Nicholas DeVore/Getty Images 30 (top)
Nicholas Haralambous 156 (top)
Nicole Duplaix/Getty Images 13 (bottom)
Nigel J Dennis; Gallo Images/Corbis 28, 131 (bottom)
O On Kloof 254–255
Palmiet Valley Wine & Country Estate 228–229
Pascal Deloche/Godong/Corbis 23 (top)
Pat O'Hara/Getty Images 161 (top)
Per-Anders Pettersson/Getty Images 26, 110
Per-Anders Pettersson/iAfrika Photos 128
Pete Turner/Getty Images 50, 124
Pezula Resort Hotel & Spa 206–209

Philip Perry; Frank Lane Picture Agency/Corbis 78
Photolibrary 54, 102, 126, 152, 161 (bottom)
Pieter Malan/iAfrika Photos 189
Richard Du Toit/Getty Images 31
Riehan Bakkes/Getty Images 135
RiverBend Lodge 176–177
Robert Ross/Getty Images 193 (top)
Roger de la Harpe/Corbis 156 (bottom)
Roger Horrocks/Getty Images 190
Rosenhof Country House 210–211
Royal Malewane 84–85
Sabi Sabi Private Game Reserve 66–67, 266, 267 (top)
Samara 166–167
Sami Sarkis/Getty Images 52 (top)
Sediba Private Game Lodge 94–95
Shaen Adey/Getty Images 127
Shoula/Getty Images 188
Smith Collection/Getty Images 12
South African Tourism 22, 53, 55 (bottom), 57, 103–104, 106, 109 (top), 129–131 (top), 157, 159, 162–163, 182, 185, 192, 193 (bottom)
Steve Bloom/Getty Images 14
Stock4B/Getty Images 183 (top)
Stuart McClymont/Getty Images 195
Ten Bompas 42–43
Teremok 120–121
Terranova/Getty Images 5
Thanda 114–119
The Andros Boutique Hotel 236–237
The Cape Cadogan Boutique Hotel 238–239
The Cellars-Hohenort 246–249
The Grace in Rosebank 44–45
The Marine Hermanus 214–217
The Plettenberg 198–201
The Windermere 172–173
Tintswalo at Waterfall 46–47, 269 (bottom)
Tintswalo Safari Lodge 77, 86–87
Tom Fox/Dallas Morning News/Corbis 80 (top)
Tsala Treetop Lodge 202–203
Tswalu Kalahari Reserve 148–149
Vineyard Hotel & Spa 256–259, 265 (top)
Walter Bibikow/Getty Images 181
Waterford Wine Estate 232–233
Winchester Mansions Hotel 260–261
Winfried Wisniewski/Getty Images 55 (top)

directory

Birkenhead House (page 212)
7th Avenue, Voelklip
Hermanus 7200, Western Cape
telephone: +27.15.793 0150
facsimile: +27.15.793 2879
reservations@theroyalportfolio.com
www.royalmalewane.com

Cape Grace Hotel (page 240)
PO Box 51387, Waterfront
Cape Town 8002, Western Cape
telephone: +27.21.410 7100
facsimile: +27.21.419 7622
info@capegrace.com
www.capegrace.com

Chitwa Chitwa Private Game Lodges (page 58)
PO Box 781854, Sandton
Johannesburg 2146, Gauteng
telephone: +27.11.883 1354
facsimile: +27.11.783 1858
info@chitwa.co.za
www.chitwa.co.za

Colona Castle (page 234)
Verwood Street, Lakeside
Cape Town 7945, Western Cape
telephone: +27.21 788 8235
facsimile: +27.21 788 6577
colona@link.co.za
www.colonacastle.co.za

d'Ouwe Werf (page 230)
30 Church Street
Stellenbosch 7600, Western Cape
telephone: +27.21.887 4608
facsimile: +27.21.887 4626
ouwewerf@iafrica.com
www.ouwewerf.com

Elephant House (page 174)
PO Box 82, Addo 6105
Eastern Cape
telephone: +27.42.233 2462
facsimile: +27.42.233 0393
info@elephanthouse.co.za
www.elephanthouse.co.za

Etali Safari Lodge (page 136)
Tshukudi Area in Madikwe
Game Reserve 8460, Northwest Province
telephone: +27.12.346 0124
facsimile: +27.12.346 0163
info@etalisafari.co.za
www.etalisafari.co.za

Fairlawns Boutique Hotel + Spa (page 36)
PO Box 61, Gallo Manor
Johannesburg 20525, Gauteng
telephone: +27.11.804 2540
facsimile: +27.11.802 7261
reservations@fairlawns.co.za
www.fairlawns.co.za

Fordoun (page 122)
PO Box 17 Nottingham Road
Midlands 3280, KwaZulu-Natal
telephone: +27.33.266 6217
facsimile: +27.33.266 6630
info@fordoun.com
www.fordoun.com

Four Rosmead (page 250)
4 Rosmead Avenue, Oranjezicht
Cape Town 8001, Western Cape
telephone: +27.21.480 3810
facsimile: +27.21.423 0044
info@fourrosmead.com
www.fourrosmead.com

Gorah Elephant Camp (page 170)
PO Box 454, Plettenberg Bay 6600
Western Cape
telephone: +27.44.501 1111
facsimile: +27.44.501 1100
res@hunterhotels.com
www.hunterhotels.com

Grande Provence (page 218)
PO Box 102, Franschhoek 7690
Western Cape
telephone: +27.21.876 8600
facsimile: +27.21.876 8601
enquiries@grandeprovence.co.za
www.grandeprovence.co.za

Hunter's Country House (page 204)
PO Box 454, Plettenberg Bay 6600
Western Cape
telephone: +27.44.501 1111
facsimile: +27.44.501 1100
res@hunterhotels.com
www.hunterhotels.com

Inyati Game Lodge (page 60)
PO Box 38838, Booysens
Johannesburg 2016, Gauteng
telephone: +27.11.880 5907
facsimile: +27.11.788 2406
inyatigl@iafrica.com
www.inyati.co.za

Jembisa (page 96)
PO Box 162
Vaalwater 0530, Limpopo
telephone: +27.14.755 4415
facsimile: +27.14.755 4444
info@jembisa.com
www.jembisa.com

Kirkman's Kamp (page 68)
Conservation Corporation Africa
Private Bag X27
Benmore 2010, Gauteng
telephone: +27.11.809 4441
facsimile: +27.11.809 4400
information@ccafrica.com
www.ccafrica.com

Klein Genot Wine + Country Estate (page 220)
Green Valley Road
Franschhoek 7690, Western Cape
telephone: +27.21.876 2738
facsimile: +27.21.876 4624
info@kleingenot.com
www.kleingenot.com

Kurland (page 196)
PO Box 209, The Crags
Plettenberg Bay 6602, Western Cape
telephone: +27.44.534 8082
facsimile: +27.44.534 8699
reservations@kurland.co.za
www.kurland.co.za

Kwandwe Private Game Reserve (page 168)
Conservation Corporation Africa
Private Bag X27
Benmore 2010, Gauteng
telephone: +27.11.809 4441
facsimile: +27.11.809 4400
information@ccafrica.com
www.ccafrica.com

Le Quartier Francais (page 222)
PO Box 237, 16 Huguenot Road
Franschhoek 7690, Western Cape
telephone: +27.21.876 2151
facsimile: +27.21.876 3105
res@lqf.co.za
www.lequartier.co.za

Les Cascades de Bantry Bay (page 244)
48 de Wet Road, Bantry Bay
Cape Town 8005, Western Cape
telephone: +27.21.434 5209
facsimile: +27.21.439 4206
info@cascadescollection.co.za
www.lescascades.co.za

directory

Lesheba (page 88)
PO Box 795
Louis Trichardt 0920, Limpopo
telephone: +27.15.593 0076
facsimile: +27.86.689 4790
lesheba@mweb.co.za
www.lesheba.co.za

Lion Sands Private Game Reserve (page 70)
Sabi Sand Game Reserve
PO Box 2667
Houghton 2041, Gauteng
telephone: +27.11.484 9911
facsimile: +27.11.484 9916
res@lionsands.com
www.lionsands.com

Londolozi (page 62)
PO Box 41864, Hyde Park
Johannesburg 2024, Gauteng
telephone: +27.11.280 6655
facsimile: +27.11.280 6610
reservations@londolozi.co.za
www.londolozi.com

Lukimbi Safari Lodge (page 72)
PO Box 2617, Northcliff
Johannesburg 2115, Gauteng
telephone: +27.11.431 1120
facsimile: +27.11.431 3597
info@lukimbi.com
www.lukimbi.com

Madikwe Hills Private Game Reserve (page 140)
PO Box 612, Hazyview
Johannesburg 1242, Gauteng
telephone: +27.13.737 6626
facsimile: +27.13.737 6628
reservations@madikwehills.com
www.madikwehills.com

Makanyane Safari Lodge (page 142)
PO Box 9, Derdepoort 2876
Northwest Province
telephone: +27.14 778 9600
facsimile: +27.14 778 9611
enquiries@makanyane.com
www.makanyane.com

Makweti Safari Lodge (page 98)
PO Box 310
Vaalwater 0530, Limpopo
telephone: +27.11.837 6776
facsimile: +27.11.837 4771
makweti@global.co.za
www.makweti.com

MalaMala Game Reserve (page 64)
PO Box 55514
Northlands 2116, Gauteng
telephone: +27.11.442 2267
facsimile: +27.11.442 2318
reservations@malamala.com
www.malamala.com

Marataba Safari Company (page 90)
PO Box 454, Plettenberg Bay 6600
Western Cape
telephone: +27.44.501 1111
facsimile: +27.44.501 1100
res@hunterhotels.com
www.hunterhotels.com

Mateya Safari Lodge (page 144)
PO Box 439, Molatedi 2838
Northwest Province
telephone: +27.14.778 9200
facsimile: +27.14.778 9201
info@mateyasafari.com
www.mateyasafari.com

Melrose Arch Hotel (page 40)
1 Melrose Square
Melrose Arch, Sandton
Johannesburg 2076, Gauteng
telephone: +27.11.214 6666
facsimile: +27.11.214 6600
info@melrosearchhotel.com
www.africanpridehotels.com

Metropole Hotel (page 252)
38 Long Street
Cape Town 8001, Western Cape
telephone: +27.21.424 7247
facsimile: +27.21.424 7248
info@metropolehotel.co.za
www.metropolehotel.co.za

Mhondoro Game Lodge (page 92)
PO Box 938
Vaalwater 0530, Limpopo
telephone: +27.11.958 2914
facsimile: +27.11.958 2913
reservations@sediba.com
www.sediba.com

Mont Rochelle Hotel + Mountain Vineyards (page 226)
PO Box 448, Franschhoek 7690
Western Cape
telephone: +27.21. 876 2770
facsimile: +27.21. 876 3788
info@montrochelle.co.za
www.montrochelle.co.za

Morukuru Lodge (page 146)
Madikwe Game Reserve 2838
Northwest Province
telephone: +31.229.299 555
facsimile: +31.229.234 139
info@morukuru.com
www.morukuru.com

Mount Grace Country House + Spa (page 32)
Private Bag 5004
Magaliesburg 1791, Gauteng
telephone: +27.14.577 5600
facsimile: +27.14.577 1202
mountgrace@mountgrace.co.za
www.mountgrace.co.za

O On Kloof (page 254)
92 Kloof Road, Bantry Bay
Cape Town 8005, Western Cape
telephone: +27.21.439 2081
facsimile: +27.21.439 8832
olaf@oonkloof.co.za
www.oonkloof.co.za

Palmiet Valley Wine + Country Estate (page 228)
PO Box 9085, Klein Drakenstein
Paarl 7628, Western Cape
telephone: +27.21.862 7741
facsimile: +27.21.862 6891
info@palmiet.co.za
www.palmiet.co.za

Pezula Resort Hotel + Spa (page 206)
Lagoonview Drive
Knysna 6570, Western Cape
telephone +27.44.302 3333
facsimile: +27.44.302 3303
reservations@pezula.com
www.pezularesorthotel.com

RiverBend Lodge (page 176)
PO Box 249, Addo 6105
Eastern Cape
telephone: +27.42.233 0161
facsimile: +27.42 233 0162
reservations@riverbend.za.com
www.riverbend.za.com

Rosenhof Country House (page 210)
264 Baron Von Rheede Street
Oudtshoorn 6625, Western Cape
telephone: +27.44.272 2232
facsimile: +27.44.272 3021
rosenhof@xsinet.co.za
www.rosenhof.co.za

directory

Royal Malewane (page 84)
PO Box 1542
Hoedspruit 1380, Limpopo
telephone: +27.15 793 0150
facsimile: +27.15 793 2879
info@royalmalewane.com
www.royalmalewane.com

Sabi Sabi Private Game Reserve (page 66)
PO Box 52665, Saxonwold
Johannesburg 2132, Gauteng
telephone: +27.11.447 7172
facsimile: +27.11.442 0728
res@sabisabi.com
www.sabisabi.com

Samara (page 166)
PO Box 649, Graaff-Reinet 6420
Eastern Cape
telephone: +27.49.891.0558
facsimile: +27.49.892.3751
reservations@samara.co.za
www.samara.co.za

Sediba Private Game Lodge (page 94)
PO Box 938
Vaalwater 0530, Limpopo
telephone: +27.11.958 2914
facsimile: +27.11.958 2913
reservations@sediba.com
www.sediba.com

Ten Bompas (page 42)
10 Bompas Road, Dunkeld West
Johannesburg 8001, Gauteng
telephone: +27.11 325 2442
facsimile: +27.11 341 0281
reservations@mix.co.za
www.tenbompas.com

Teremok Marine (page 120)
49 Marine Drive
Umhlanga Rocks 4320, KwaZulu-Natal
telephone: +27.31.561 5848
facsimile: +27.31.561 5860
marine@teremok.co.za
www.teremok.co.za

Teremok Riverside (page 120)
3–10 Riverside Road
Beverley 2191, Gauteng
telephone: +27.11.467 7791
facsimile: +27.11.467 7137
riverside@teremok.co.za
www.teremok.co.za

Thanda (page 114)
PO Box 652585, Benmore
Johannesburg 2010, Gauteng
telephone: +27.11.469 5082
facsimile: +27.11.469 5086
reservations@thanda.co.za
www.thanda.com

The Andros Boutique Hotel (page 236)
Corner of Phyllis & Newlands Road
Claremont, Cape Town 7708
Western Cape
telephone: +27.21.797 9777
facsimile: +27.21.797 0300
info@andros.co.za
www.andros.co.za

The Cape Cadogan Boutique Hotel (page 238)
5 Upper Union Street, Tamboerskloof
Cape Town 8001, Western Cape
telephone: +27.11.484 9911
facsimile: +27.11.484 9916
reservations@capecadogan.com
www.capecadogan.com

The Cellars-Hohenort (page 246)
93 Brommersvlei Road, Constantia
Cape Town 7800, Western Cape
telephone: +27.21.794 2137
facsimile: +27.21 794 2149
cellars@relaischateaux.com
www.cellars-hohenort.com

The Grace in Rosebank (page 44)
54 Bath Avenue, Rosebank
Johannesburg 2196, Gauteng
telephone: +27.11.280 7200
facsimile: +27.11.280 7474
graceres@thegrace.co.za
www.thegrace.co.za

The Marine Hermanus (page 214)
PO Box 9, Marine Drive
Hermanus 7200, Western Cape
telephone: +27.28 313 1000
facsimile: +27.28 313 0160
hermanus@relaischateaux.com
www.marine-hermanus.com

The Plettenberg (page 198)
40 Church Street, Plettenberg Bay
Western Cape 6600
telephone: +27.44.533 2030
facsimile: +27.44.533 2074
plettenberg@relaischateaux.com
www.plettenberg.com

The Windermere (page 172)
35 Humewood Road, Humewood
Port Elizabeth 6001, Eastern Cape
telephone: +27.41.582 2245
facsimile: +27.41.582 2246
info@thewindermere.co.za
www.thewindermere.co.za

Tintswalo at Waterfall (page 46)
Maxwell Drive, Kyalami
Midrand 8001, Gauteng
telephone: +27.11.464 1070
facsimile: +27.11.464 1315
info@tintswalo.com
www.tintswalo.com

Tintswalo Safari Lodge (page 86)
PO Box 70406, Bryanston
Johannesburg 2021, Gauteng
telephone: +27.11.464 1070
facsimile: +27.11.464 1315
info@tintswalo.co.za
www.tintswalo.com

Tourism Corporation Africa (page 262)
1 St Johns, Higgo Crescent, Higgovale
Cape Town 8001, Western Cape
telephone: +27.21.462 0436
facsimile: +27.21.462 2529
tcorp@iafrica.com
www.tourismcorp.co.za

Tsala Treetop Lodge (page 202)
PO Box 454, Plettenberg Bay 6600
Western Cape
telephone: +27.44.501 1111
facsimile: +27.44.501 1100
res@hunterhotels.com
www.hunterhotels.com

Tswalu Kalahari Reserve (page 148)
PO Box 1081, Kuruman 8460
Northern Cape
telephone: +27.11.274 2299
facsimile: +27.11.484 2757
res@tswalu.com
www.tswalu.com

Vineyard Hotel + Spa (page 256)
PO Box 151, Newlands
Cape Town 7725. Western Cape
telephone: +27.21.657 4500
facsimile: +27.21.657 4501
hotel@vineyard.co.za
www.vineyard.co.za

Waterford Wine Estate (page 232)
Blaauwklippen Road
Stellenbosch 7600, Western Cape
telephone: +27.21.880 0496
facsimile: +27.21.880 1007
info@waterfordestate.co.za
www.waterfordestate.co.za

Winchester Mansions Hotel (page 260)
221 Beach Road, Sea Point
Cape Town 8001, Western Cape
telephone: +27.21.434 2351
facsimile: +27.21.434 0215
sales@winchester.co.za
www.winchester.co.za